GW01048645

Roman Law

ORIGINS AND INFLUENCE

Roman Law

ORIGINS AND INFLUENCE

D.G. CRACKNELL & C.H. WILSON

HLT PUBLICATIONS
200 Greyhound Road, London W14 9RY

First published 1964 by Butterworth & Co (Publishers) Ltd as
'Law Students' Companion, No 4, Roman Law'

© The HLT Group Ltd 1990

All HLT publications enjoy copyright protection and the
copyright belongs to The HLT Group Ltd.

All rights reserved. No part of this publication may be
reproduced or transmitted in any form or by any means,
electronic, mechanical, photocopying, recording or
otherwise, or stored in any retrieval system of any nature
without the written permission of the copyright holder,
application for which should be made to The HLT Group Ltd.

ISBN 1 85352 823 4

Acknowledgements

The authors gratefully acknowledge permission by Oxford
University Press and IPC Magazines Ltd to reproduce
illustrations on page 4 and pages 9, 16, 17, 22 and 27
respectively.

Cover illustration reproduced by kind permission of
Topham Picture Source.

British Library Cataloguing-in-Publication.

A CIP Catalogue record for this book is available from the
British Library.

Printed and bound in Great Britain.

Contents

List of Illustrations

Preface

Since this book first appeared, in England and Wales, at least, the importance of Roman Law as an examination subject has declined sharply: no longer is it a compulsory paper for professional examinations or for law degrees at the vast majority of universities.

Of course, taking a wider view, the significance of the law of Rome is undiminished. It remains the foundation of the law of many other countries and, to varying extents, it is an essential element of any classics course. More even than this, as the late Professor R W Lee once wrote: 'Roman Law is one of the great things which have happened in the world. It is part of a liberal education to know something about it.'

For these reasons we are very pleased to have been able to prepare a fresh edition of this work, retaining the depth of detail required by law students but remembering also the needs of those for whom Roman Law is part of a larger concern – or even a point of passing reference.

To these ends, the Historical Background has been entirely rewritten and illustrations have been introduced; there is also a new chapter, Reception and Continuing Influence. Although the reconstruction of the Twelve Tables and the concise translation of the Institutes of Justinian have not been altered, the Glossary has been revised as necessary and a new index has been included.

In relation to Justinian's Institutes, the word 'concise' is used to denote only that non-essential parts have been omitted and that words have been used economically: as a statement of law, we trust that the presentation is accurate, readable and complete.

D. G. Cracknell
C. H. Wilson

Heads of State

Kings

c753–717 BC	Romulus
c715–673	Numa Pompilius
c672–641	Tulla Hostilius
c640–617	Ancus Martius
c616–579	Lucius Tarquinius
c578–535	Servius Tullius
c534–509	Tarquinius Superbus

Consuls

During the republic (510–27BC) in normal times the heads of state were two consuls, who were elected annually.

Emperors

27BC–AD14	Augustus
AD14–37	Tiberius
37–41	Caligula
41–54	Claudius
54–68	Nero
68	Galba
69	Otho
69	Vitellius
69–79	Vespasian
79–81	Titus
81–96	Domitian
96–98	Nerva
98–117	Trajan
117–138	Hadrian
138–161	Antoninus Pius
161–180	Marcus Aurelius Antoninus
180–193	Marcus Aurelius Commodus Antoninus
193	Pertinax
	Didius Julianus
193–211	Septimius Severus
211–217	Caracalla
211–212	Geta
217–218	Macrinus
218–222	Elagabalus
222–235	Alexander Severus
235–238	Maximinus
238	Gordianus I
	Gordianus II
	Pupienus Maximus
	Balbinus
238–244	Gordianus III
244–249	Philippus
249–251	Decius

AD251–254	Hostilianus
	Trebonianus Gallus
253	Aemilianus
253–260	Valerian
260–268	Gallienus
268–270	Claudius II
270–275	Aurelian
275–276	Tacitus
276	Florianus
276–282	Probus
282–283	Carus
283–284	Carinus
	Numerianus
284–305	Diocletian
286–305	Maximian
305–306	Constantius I
305–311	Galerius
306–337	Constantine I
306–312	Maxentius
306–310	Maximian
306–307	Severus
307–313	Maximin
307–323	Licinius
337–340	Constantine II
337–350	Constans
337–361	Constantius II
361–363	Julian
363–364	Jovian
364–375	Valentinian
364–378	Valens
367–383	Gratian
383–388	Maximus
375–392	Valentinian
392–395	Theodosius I

Division of the empire:

	West		East
395–423	Honorius	395–408	Arcadius
423–425	Theodosius II	408–450	Theodosius II
425–455	Valentinian III	450–453	Pulcheria
455	Petronius Maximus	450–457	Marcian
455–456	Avitus	457–474	Leo I
457–461	Majorian	474	Leo II
461–467	Libius Severus	474–491	Zeno
467–472	Anthemius	491–518	Anastasius I
472	Olybrius	518–527	Justin I
473–474	Glycerius	527–565	Justinian
474–475	Julius Nepos		
475–476	Romulus Augustulus		

1 Historical Background

Beginnings

The tradition of Rome's founding was made canonical by the works, still surviving, of Virgil, Ovid and Livy at the end of the pre-Christian era. The tradition may have taken shape two centuries before that, and the Greek elements in it may be traced two centuries earlier still. After Troy's defeat by the Greeks in the Trojan war, the Trojan prince Aeneas led a band of survivors to the west coast of Italy and established a settlement at Lavinium. After his death, his son Ascanius founded Alba Longa (Castelgondolfo), where his descendants ruled as king for 400 years, until Romulus founded Rome and became its first king. The date of the foundation was in the first century BC established as 753BC.

The part played by Aeneas, and Romulus (whose name simply means 'the Roman one'), may well be non-historical; but archaeological research suggests a core of truth in the traditional legend. There were early settlements at Lavinium and on the Alban hills (Monte Cavo), though these do not seem to be earlier than the settlement on the Palatine Hill at Rome (traditionally the site of Romulus' settlement), which is probably from the tenth century BC. The site is one of a number in the area which overlooked the Roman campagna, and consisted of a few thatched huts clustered together in a defensible position. Originally, life had been lived at a basic level, but the evidence from tombs suggests a period of considerable development beginning in the first half of the eighth century. Population appears to increase; there is growing contact with the outside world, particularly the Greek colonies of Campania; some of the tombs display an unprecedented richness; and defences are beginning to be built around some of the hilltop villages. Clearly the geographical advantages of Rome's position are now making themselves felt. Rome stands at the last feasible crossing-point of the Tiber before the river reaches the sea at Ostia, and on the natural route of the later Via Praenestina from the north to the south. She therefore offers access to the fertile plain of Latium (the southern part of the modern Lazio), and to the salt-beds at the mouth of the Tiber.

The regal period (753BC–c509BC)

Traditionally, Rome was ruled by a succession of seven non-hereditary kings in the first 250 years of her existence, the last one being expelled by an aristocratic faction in 509BC (or 510 – a date which, suspiciously, coincides with the date of the expulsion of the last tyrant of Athens). While the tradition has been embellished by many obviously fanciful details, there is much in it that has a surprising ring of truth. In particular, the tradition enables us to make a plausible reconstruction of the political and social organisation of the early city. Romulus is credited with having chosen an advisory body, the senate, of 100 or so 'fathers', whose descendants became patricians, and with having reorganised the city into three tribes. (The names of these tribes are Etruscan, but the extent of Etruscan influence on early Rome is a matter of much dispute.) Each tribe was subdivided into ten curiae and these were the basis of a primitive assembly, not at this stage with any executive authority, the comitia centuriata. The tribes were also the basis of the military organisation, each providing 1000 infantry and 100 cavalry to the city's army. Both the tribes and the curiae were probably local divisions based on kinship; and clearly the gens and the family were already the basic units of society, as they continued to be in historical times. The paterfamilias, the head of the family, had throughout his lifetime supreme power over the members of his family, including even the right to put them to death; the provision of the Twelve Tables whereby, when a paterfamilias died intestate and without heirs, his belongings went to the gens may suggest that property originally belonged to the gens, rather than the father. Proof of the importance of the gens is provided by an incident of 479BC, when the Fabian gens made its own private war on the Etruscan city of Veii; but there is no certainty as to the relationship of the gens to the tribe and the state.

When a king died, the choice of a successor, and his coronation, were matters in which religion played an all-important part; the role of the religious officials known as augurs is the source of our word 'inaugurate'. It is clear that religion was already a central feature of the state, as it continued to be in historical times; and the second of the kings, Numa Pompilius (traditionally 715–673BC; his name suggests a Sabine origin), was particularly remembered for his contributions to the religious development of the new city. Roman religion ascribed great importance to vows, and to obtaining the favour of the gods, the pax deorum, through the observance of the proper ritual. In historical times it became a source of great wonder to non-Romans. One Greek observer, Polybius, wrote 'The quality in which the Romans most excel is in my view the nature of their religious convictions', and another, Dionysius of Halicarnassus, 'To understand the success of the Romans you must understand their piety'.

Archaeology has shown that in the seventh century the original Palatine community expanded into the valley of the forum, and then into the Quirinal, Esquiline and Viminal hills. By the end of the century, thatched huts give way to houses with stone foundations, timber frames and tiled roofs; public buildings, especially temples, are being laid out; both the forum and the Sacred Way (Via Sacra) which connected it with the rest of the city receive permanent pavements; and the Forum Boarium, the cattle market by the river, is established. To this period also probably belong the systematic draining of the forum and the first building of the Cloaca Maxima.

In the sixth century, Rome had, traditionally, only three kings. The number is probably an over-simplification; but with the Etruscan Tarquin I, Lucius or Tarquinius Priscus (traditionally 616–579BC), Servius Tullius (578–535BC), and the son, or grandson, of Tarquin I, Tarquinius Superbus, or Tarquinius the Proud (534–509BC), we are probably face to face with historical figures. All three seem to have been autocrats, along the lines of contemporary tyrants in Greece. They pursued ambitious building programmes, with Servius allegedly building earthworks round the northern, exposed, part of the city (this has not been confirmed by archaeology; the so-called 'Wall of Servius Tullius' (Agger Servii Tulli) is a fourth-century structure), and Tarquin II beginning the temples of Jupiter Optimus Maximus and of Juno and Minerva on the Capitol – the former 180 feet wide and 200 feet long, quite the largest building Rome had yet seen. He also established a shrine of Diana on the Aventine hill, which became a common cult-centre for a federation of Latin states under Roman leadership. Servius is credited with significant political and military reforms. He appears to have accepted immigrants as citizens on the basis of residence. These new citizens would not have been members of the curiae; but Servius arranged a classification of citizens on the basis of property into centuries, and the resulting comitia centuriata, while retaining the distinctive Roman feature of voting by groups, soon displaces the Romulan comitia centuriata in importance. Wealth also seems to have been the basis of the Servian military organisation. He is credited with the creation of a middle-class army, and the re-equipping of the infantry with the armour of the Greek heavy infantryman, the hoplite. An early sixth-century find in a tomb on the Esquiline of a bronze shield of the Greek type confirms this reform, which may have been suggested to Rome by Etruscan examples, rather than directly from Greece.

Tradition has it that Tarquin II (Tarquinius Superbus) was driven from Rome by a group of noblemen after he had raped the wife of one of them, Lucretia, who had then

3

committed suicide. But the noblemen may have had more overtly political aims. The Tarquins had been their enemies, and seem to have introduced political and economic measures to benefit the less-privileged members of the state at the expense of the nobles. It is noteworthy that 'king' became a hated word at Rome after the Tarquins, but it is regularly directed against upper-class politicians who try to disturb the status quo with reforms aimed at the relief of the poor. In the first century and a half of the republic, these would-be reformers pay with their lives for this offence.

The Roman republic (c510BC–c31BC)

Origins

The aristocrats who expelled Tarquin II replaced him with a system that seems to have no close parallel with any known institution of the time. Supreme power was exercised by two men, at first called praetors (from *prae-ire*, to go before), and later consuls.

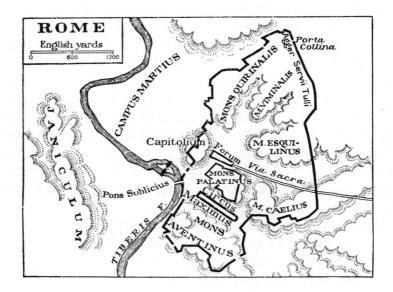

Rome

These officials were elected from members of the senate by the comitia centuriata; they held office for one year, with re-election for the following year forbidden; and either of them could veto the proposals of the other. On finishing their year of office, they returned to the senate. This system of collegiate magistracies, subject to time-limits, and with restrictions on re-election, was extended to all subsequent offices. Throughout her history Rome regularly confronted new situations by the creation of new officials to deal with them; the sources tell of quaestors being created in 447BC, and censors four years later. The one officer who was free of these restrictions was the dictator, an office apparently instituted in the earliest days of the republic. He had no colleagues, and against his decisions there was no appeal. But a dictator was only appointed to deal with specific emergencies, and after six months his power automatically lapsed.

Officers were immune from prosecution while in office, and this system of strong public authorities, with power vested in them, rather than in the legislature, remained a dominant feature of the Roman constitution. But, as individuals held power for only one year, it was the senate, though still officially a purely advisory body, which was responsible for such continuity of policy as there was; and, since consuls were elected by the comitia centuriata, and this assembly was organised in a way which favoured the richer members of the community, it might be said that government was in the hands of the rich – though we cannot tell how often or how far the rich were sufficiently united among themselves to exploit the opportunities that the system offered them. Writing in the second century BC, the Greek observer Polybius greatly admired the equilibrium of the Roman system.

The struggle of the orders

It is clear that in the early years of the republic the sacred and secular offices were dominated by a small group of so-called patrician families, who also exercised predominant control over Rome's economic resources. These patricians were probably the descendants of the original Romulan senators, and of those persons who had subsequently been conscripted into the senate, and they may have numbered no more than about ten per cent of the total citizen population. It is also clear that there soon emerged an alternative group, the plebeians; its struggle to obtain from the patricians a fairer distribution, both of the extensive offices of the state and of its economic resources, is the dominant theme of the internal history of the first two centuries of the republic. This so-called struggle of the orders, which is remarkable for the lack of bloodshed that it involved, may be said to have ended in 287BC, when it was enacted that the recommendations – plebiscita – of the assembly that the plebeians had by then won for themselves should have the force of law. This assembly, the concilium plebis, from which the comitia tributa was formally distinct, was grouped by tribes, and thus designed to eliminate the advantages of wealth that the comitia centuriata offered.

There are no literary sources remotely contemporary with the struggle of the orders, and those that survive are probably wrong in ascribing to the struggle the circumstances of their own times when they represent the plebeians as comprising all the non-patrician citizens of Rome – the original plebeians were probably a group within the non-patrician body. They would express their protest by withdrawing to the Aventine hill, outside the original boundaries of Rome, and there setting up their own state within a state, with their own religious officials, aediles (see Aediles plebeii), and their own cult of Ceres, Liber and Libera; five such secessions are recorded between 493 and 287BC. In their pursuit of political equality, the plebeians were successful; in the second century Cato could write that there were no formal disqualifications on any citizen from attaining to the highest office. Rome incorporated into the state the offices and institutions that the plebeians created. The most important of these offices was the tribunus plebis (see Tribuni), or tribune of the plebs, who became in effect another magistrate of the state. The tribune could bring public business to a standstill by exercising his right of veto (intercessio), and he could bring help to any citizen against a decision of the consul. Thus, the result of the struggle was to replace the domination of the patricians by a patrician-plebeian nobility, which, as far as we can tell, governed effectively, and reasonably harmoniously, throughout the dangerous foreign wars in which Rome was engaged in the third and the first half of the second centuries BC. The plebeians were crucial to Rome's manpower; and they used the political importance that this gave them to protest effectively against the deterioration in their economic situation that military service away from home imposed upon them.

One of the plebeians' demands had been for the codification and publication of the civil law, so that in their dealings they should not be at the mercy of arbitrary patrician officials; the result was the publication, traditionally in 451BC, of the Twelve Tables. These Tables formed the basis of the civil law for the next four centuries at least, and, though they do not now survive themselves, there are sufficient surviving quotations of them to permit their reconstruction: see p37 et seq. While they do not present a systematic code in the modern sense, they do seek to regulate equitably the relations of citizens in matters of the family, inheritance, property ownership and debt, leaving it to the individual to get his opponent to court and to execute judgment on him. The clause forbidding intermarriage between patricians and plebeians was hardly published before it was hurriedly repealed.

The unification of Italy

Closely contemporaneously with the struggle of the orders, Rome was steadily developing her influence throughout Italy, and after winning the battle of Sentinum, in Umbria, against Umbrian, Samnite, and Etruscan forces, had no rival to fear south of the Po valley, on a line from Pisa to Ariminum (Rimini). Beyond this line lay Gallia Cisalpina ('Gaul on this side of the Alps'), whose tribes crushingly defeated Rome at the Allia battle and then sacked Rome in 390BC, and whose time for absorption by Rome still lay some time in the future.

Our sources for Rome's expansion are all written three centuries or more after the events, and are all entirely Rome-focused. They do not present us with any clear picture, either of the step-by-step developments, or of Roman policy. The repeated theme of Rome reluctantly responding to external aggression looks simplistic – although in the early period the fertile plain on Latium may well have attracted intruders from the mountainous areas of the interior. Nor do the sources do justice to the great range of ethnic, religious, political and social differences over which Rome imposed herself, from the developed Greek communities of the coast from Cumae to Tarentum and the Etruscans to the north of Rome to the backward peoples of eastern Italy in such areas as Picenum and Apulia. But Rome's success is to be measured by the loyalty with which her allies stood by her, and fought in her armies, in the great wars against overseas powers in the third century; the success must, at least in part, be attributed to the skill and generosity with which she exported her institutions and her culture to the most far-flung parts of the peninsula.

During the regal period, and principally in the reigns of Servius Tullius and the Tarquins, Rome had clearly extended her influence over her immediate neighbours. But this influence seems to have declined during the early period of the republic, and a battle with the Latin states was fought at Lake Regillus in 499BC, to be followed by a treaty with them in 494. In the ensuing period, it appears that the Volscians and the Etruscans were the main opponents. The Volscian wars, impossible to trace in detail, gave rise to the story of Coriolanus; and this phase of the Etruscan campaigns culminated in the capture of Veii, fifteen miles from Rome, after a siege which reputedly lasted ten years, in 396. This success doubled Roman territory at a stroke; and the land thus acquired was settled with four new tribes of colonists from the lower classes at Rome.

Expansion, and colonisation, continued in the fourth century BC. A key date is 338, when the Romans defeated a force of resurgent Latins, Campanians and Volscians. This led to the dissolution of the old Latin league. Some of the defeated Latin cities were incorporated directly into the Roman state, with their inhabitants becoming full members of the Roman citizen body. Other states were instituted as self-governing communities; such epigraphic evidence as there is suggests that the Roman model of government may well have been followed here, even to the extent of the peculiarly Roman institution of voting by groups. The citizens of these communities were liable to military service with Rome, but enjoyed the rights of inter-marriage, and of business dealings on an equal footing, with Romans; they could apparently move from their original community to another, including Rome, and enjoy the same status in their new community as they had enjoyed in their original one. The non-Latin peoples who had fought against Rome were incorporated into the Roman state as 'citizens without the vote'. They were required to meet the same financial and military obligations as Roman citizens, but they could not vote in the Roman assemblies or hold office in Rome.

Rome at the same time continued to plant colonies of her own lower-class citizens at strategically vital areas such as Fregellae (328BC) and Cales (324). The colonists would give up Roman citizenship in exchange for a grant of land in the new colony, which would then become an independent community, with the members enjoying the same rights of connubium and commercium as the old Latin cities now enjoyed. Further colonies were established in consequence of the second (327–304) and third (298–290) Samnite wars; and this period also saw the beginning of another instrument of Romanisation, road-building. Appius Claudius 'the Blind', himself of Sabine origin, began the Via Appia, from Rome to Capua, in 312; the Via Valeria, which linked Rome with the Adriatic coast via the Central Apennines, followed six years later. Appius Claudius also began an aqueduct, the Aqua Appia, in 312.

The foreign wars of the third and second centuries

Pyrrhus. Rome's victory at Sentinum in 295BC brought the Italian wars to a close, but within 15 years she found herself face-to-face with an enemy from overseas. Many of the old-established Greek cities of Italy had welcomed association with Rome, but one of them, Tarentum, was reluctant to accept a new relationship, and in 280 called in against Rome the Greek mercenary commander Pyrrhus of Epirus. This was Rome's first taste of a fully trained Hellenistic army, but she offered stern resistance, and Pyrrhus' successes were won at a heavy cost – hence the expression 'Pyrrhic victory'. Eventually he was defeated at Beneventum, and in 278 returned to Greece, where he was soon afterwards killed in an accident. Rome overcame Tarentum in 272, and this success brought the whole of the Italian peninsula south of the valley of the Po into the control of Rome. This control duly led, by a process which it is not now possible for us to trace in much detail, to the disappearance of linguistic, ethnic, and cultural differences throughout the peninsula; one of the most important factors in this must have been the service of the Italians in the Roman army. At the same time, the name of Rome was becoming known overseas. In the years following the war with Pyrrhus, at least three Greek writers – Callimachus, Lycophron, and Tinacus – wrote of Rome, and in 273 there were diplomatic exchanges between Rome and Egypt.

Carthage. The state of Carthage, in what is now Tunisia, was older, and better known to the Greek world, than Rome. Traditionally, it had been first settled by refugees from Phoenicia. Early relations between Rome and Carthage had been peaceable.

   A non-aggression pact between the two states from the earliest days of the republic is the earliest Roman document that is known to us in its entirety, and this was shortly followed by two further agreements along similar lines. More recently, Carthage had shared Rome's hostility to Pyrrhus of Epirus. But in 264BC a small local incident in north-east Sicily involved the two states in the first Carthaginian, or Punic, war, which became a war for the control of Sicily. There is nothing to suggest that Rome entered the war in consequence of a long-term expansionist policy, but her ultimate success in it left her with her first overseas possession, Sicily, to which were added soon afterwards Sardinia and Corsica. The war lasted from 264 to 241, and was fought with unprecedented ferocity. The Greek historian Polybius wrote of it: 'In terms of its intensity, and of the scale of operations, this was the greatest war in history.' The outbreak of the war presented Rome with the task of building her first navy, a task to which she addressed herself with characteristic vigour and success. After a disaster in 249, the navy had to be built all over again (the land operations had meanwhile featured a disastrous expedition to Africa under M Atilius Regulus), and it was this second navy which played the decisive part in the ultimate victory in a battle off the Aegates islands in 241. It has been estimated, inevitably somewhat speculatively, that Roman losses in the war may have amounted to about 100,000 men and 500 warships.

Italy and Sicily in the Hellenistic age

Under the terms of the peace by which the war was concluded, Carthage was to evacuate Sicily altogether, return all prisoners, and pay in ten equal instalments a massive indemnity of 3,200 talents. In 238BC, Rome further took to herself – with no justification at all, according to Polybius – Sardinia and Corsica. But with these first three overseas possessions Rome did not apply the model that she had used in Italy, where the defeated community was left with a large measure of autonomy and provided manpower as required to the Roman army. Instead, she followed what for the ancient world was the more usual procedure, whereby, save for a few privileged communities in Sicily, the three islands were to become subjects and pay taxes. They were assigned to the control of Roman magistrates; since the sphere in which a Roman magistrate exercised his imperium was a provincia, they became a provincia. The model thus established became the usual one for Rome's overseas conquests in the years to come.

During the course of the war, two domestic developments took place of especial significance to the student of Roman legal affairs. In 253BC the office of chief priest, or pontifex maximus, was being held for the first time by a plebeian, Titus Coruncanius; he then initiated the practice of admitting his legal students, and possibly members of the general public as well, to his legal consultations. This innovation gave rise in due course to a body of trained jurists, who would not normally practise in courts themselves but would be available for expert consultation, advice and instruction on legal matters. The courts were still presided over by the public officials, but these officials would not necessarily have any training in law at all, and so the jurists would sit in on the hearings, and offer their expert contributions, and would likewise be available out of court to provide non-partisan judgments and advice. They, therefore, played a vital part in the construction and maintenance of the mighty edifice of Roman law.

Another development occurred in 247BC, with the establishment of a new Roman magistrate, the praetor peregrinus (see Praetors), whose task it was to hear and judge cases where at least one of the parties was a non-Roman (peregrinus), ie either a foreigner, or a subject of Rome who did not hold Roman citizenship. Hitherto, Roman law had confined itself entirely to relations between Roman citizens, so that the praetor peregrinus was a significant extension, giving rise in due course to the Roman idea of jus gentium, or 'law of the nations'. This term originally defined the sphere of the praetor peregrinus, namely, those parts of the law that were open to non-citizens as well as citizens, and in thus recognising the rights of non-citizens Rome could not claim to be treading a path that some Greek city-states had not trodden many years before. But in its development it gave rise to a belief in a body of law that was valid on a worldwide basis, a code of 'natural law' (see Jus gentium) which governed, or should govern, the relations between all the different states of the world; and thus the creation of the praetor peregrinus was the first step in the process that ultimately made the law of the Romans more nearly of universal application than any other system that has ever been devised.

In 225BC, aggression by the Gauls obliged Rome to turn her attention to Cisalpine Gaul. The Gallic invasion was repulsed, in 222 Mediolanum was captured, and in 218 colonies were established at Placentia and Cremona. Rome's arrangements for Cisalpine Gaul did not follow the liberal pattern that had been followed with the Italian communities in the previous century. But by now Carthage was once more demanding Rome's attention. Deprived by Rome of Sicily, Sardinia and Corsica, she had been seeking, since 237, to establish an empire for herself in Spain, attracted by the wealth of precious metals there. It is possible — though our chief source for this period, the Roman historian Livy, is manifestly chauvinistic and tendentious — that in the early 220s Carthage accepted a Roman demand that she confine her activities to the area south of the river Ebro, and also that the attack by the Carthaginian commander on Saguntum in 219 was the immediate casus belli, in that Saguntum, while well south of the Ebro, was at that time an ally of Rome. So, at least, Livy, but also the Kriegsschuldfrage, the question of which state was responsible for the second Punic war, have been endlessly, and quite inconclusively, debated in ancient and modern times alike.

Once he had crushed Saguntum, Hannibal started on his epic journey from Spain to Italy via the Alps. He took with him perhaps 20,000 infantry and 6,000 cavalry, to which were added Gallic reinforcements once he had reached the plains of northern Italy. In the years 218–216BC he inflicted four crushing and bloody defeats on the Roman armies, culminating in the battle of Cannae, in Apulia, at which Rome lost both the consuls and perhaps about 30,000 men — though the sources put it higher than that. But, while several of the states of Italy, notably Capua, defected to Hannibal, he was frustrated by the unanticipated loyalty to Rome of the great majority of her Italian allies. Once the Roman high command renounced outright confrontation with Hannibal, he was left without resource. Polybius' account of the Gallic invasion of 225 makes it clear that Rome must by then have been able to call on a very large reserve of manpower indeed; and this proved adequate both to confining Hannibal to Bruttium and to prosecuting the war successfully on the other fronts at the same time. So Capua was recovered in 211, in the same year the Carthaginian attempt to re-establish herself in Sicily was defeated when M Claudius Marcellus recovered Syracuse for Rome, and in a crucial engagement on the river Metaurus in 207 Hannibal's brother Hasdrubal, who was attempting to join forces with him, was defeated and killed. Meanwhile, Publius Scipio was eliminating the Carthaginian influence in Spain; with this accomplished, he took the war to Africa in 204, whither Hannibal, after a fifteen-year stay in Italy, was obliged to follow him the next year. The generals met at Zama in 202. Scipio's victory obliged the Carthagians to sue for peace, and confirmed Rome's control over the whole western Mediterranean area; Scipio established a significant precedent by taking the name 'Africanus' in honour of his victory.

The second century. The war with Hannibal, and the narrowness of Rome's escape from total disaster in 216BC, left a deep and lasting impression on the Roman consciousness. But the war had other effects as well. Military service from now on might involve long periods of service overseas; the Roman and Italian soldier was now very much more of a professional. At the same time, the war, and its consequences, led to a vast influx of wealth into Italy — from booty, indemnities paid by the defeated, and the administration of the newly acquired territories. Much of this wealth would find its way into the hands of the Roman and Italian élite, who would invest it in land. Increasingly, the farming of central Italy was done by large-scale enterprises, worked by slaves acquired by military conquest. But for the moment the strains that these developments put on the existing social and political system remained latent. As far as our deplorably inadequate sources allow us to tell, the senate emerged with credit from the Hannibalic war, and political control was firmly in the hands of the patrician and plebeian nobility.

The period following Hannibal was one of warfare and expansion. It again seems that Roman actions were the response to circumstances as they arose, rather than the consequence of long-term policy decisions. Further campaigns were undertaken in Cisalpine Gaul until about 175BC, with landmarks being the beginning of the Via Aemilia in 187 and the planting of a colony at Aquileia in 181. Spain required a continual military presence, and, though Scipio Aemilianus destroyed Numantia, the stronghold of the Celtiberians, in 133, it was another 100 years before the country was finally conquered. Narbonese Gaul was conquered in 125–121. In the east, Roman armies were operating in both Greece and Asia within 15 years of defeating Hannibal. Macedonia became a tributary state of Rome in 168, and after further trouble twenty years later was made into a province. The rest of Greece was treated likewise, and the ancient city of Corinth sacked, in 146BC; and in the same year, after another, but much shorter, Punic war, Carthage was obliterated and a new province of Africa, corresponding to the modern Tunisia, created.

The extent of Rome's expansion after the first province was acquired in 241BC is indeed impressive. However, just as the map of her overseas possessions at the end of the second century would suggest an absence of systematic planning in the acquisition of these possessions, so the history of the following century makes clear that Rome had not adequately anticipated the strains with which her internal system would be confronted by her new role as the major imperial power of the Mediterranean world.

Revolution

Ancient historians saw the fall of Carthage and the sack of Corinth in 146BC as a turning-point in Rome's history. The Romans, they liked to maintain, were now freed from the fear of attack from overseas, and in consequence lost the virtues of self-restraint, self-sacrifice and devotion to duty by which their ancestors had made Rome great. Certainly, the period after 146 was one of revolution, violence in politics, civil war and anarchy, which was not brought to an end until the victory of C Octavius (the subsequent Augustus) over M Antonius ('Mark Antony') at the battle of Actium in 31BC.

The later part of the revolutionary period is uniquely well documented for us, thanks largely to the voluminous writings of the extraordinary Marcus Tullius Cicero (AD106–43) – politician, statesman, orator, philosopher, letter-writer, even poet – whose greatest achievement, perhaps, was that, while not even from Rome (his birthplace was Arpinum, south-east of Rome), and with no ex-Roman magistrates among his ancestors, he yet managed to become consul in the earliest year (63) at which he was legally able to do so. The revolution is to be ascribed to the very profound changes that Rome's conquest of the Mediterranean were causing to the political, economic, and social life of Rome and Italy. But, if the effect of these changes is most clear to us in the violence and anarchy of the first century BC, we should not lose sight of how, at the same time, Roman art and architecture, literature and philosophy were all adapting to and profiting from the new influences, principally Greek ones, that the empire opened up to them.

Cicero looked back on the century that followed the stormy tribunate (see Tribunes) of C. Flaminius in 232 as a golden age of senatorial authority; and as far as our very inadequate sources allow us to tell, it does seem that the senate's handling of the Hannibalic war, and of the subsequent involvements with Greece and the east, commanded general assent. The revolutionary period is marked by a series of challenges to the senate's authority, which led in due course to the breakdown of this authority. But one must remember that the leading figures of the revolution were themselves senators, and often, as in the case of Julius Caesar, from the old families of the ruling élite. The senate was undermined from within, not from without. And, while such figures would

The senate house as it is today

make great use of the less privileged members of the citizenry in their clientelae (see Clientelae), and would from time to time propose legislation for the benefit of such groups as, for example, the peasant ex-landholders who had been dispossessed by years of continuous military service away from home, or Italians who served in the Roman army but without enjoying the full benefits of Roman citizenship, it is far from certain that these proposals were made in a spirit of genuine reform, rather than for the immediate political advantage of the proposer. It would be a mistake for us to think of there having been at Rome anything eqivalent to parties in the modern sense, or to

13

underestimate the extent to which the Roman politician was driven by self-interest and by the desire to promote his own gloria. Political power was pursued for its own sake.

One of the major losers of Rome's enlarged military activity overseas was the peasant smallholder. While he was on service overseas, his family would be driven out by the rich investor, who was using the influx from the new empire of wealth and slaves for the development of latifundia, vast farming estates owned by absentee landlords and worked by slaves under the supervision of a resident manager. The accelerating displacement of the smallholder, quite apart from the human misery it caused, had serious consequences for military manpower as well; for the dispossessed peasant was reduced to proletarian status, and was thus no longer liable for military service. There are a number of recorded recruitment difficulties in the years following 150. These problems were addressed in his tribunate of 133 by Tiberius Gracchus, who proposed that a commission of three men should arrange the settling of the dispossessed on small allotments of public land. The proposal seems a moderate one, but it threatened the vested interests of the wealthy landowners, from whose holdings the new allotments would be drawn. Tiberius gave further offence when he had a tribune who was attempting to veto his proposals voted out of office, and then, his law passed, formed his land-commission out of his brother, his father-in-law, and himself. Further, having not consulted the senate over his law, he flouted its authority when he proposed that an unexpected legacy from the estate of an eastern king be distributed among his new smallholders; finally, he gave notice that he intended to stand for a second tribunate for the following year.

How far Tiberius' actions and proposals were outside the law is by no means certain. The question is anyhow a largely academic one; Tiberius' actions were untraditional, and they threatened the political and economic privileges of the ruling oligarchy. On the day of the elections, a party of leading senators broke up the assembly; in the ensuing riot Tiberius and 300 of his supporters were killed. It was the first time in the republic's history that political dispute had ended in bloodshed.

But Tiberius had established an example; and in the years that followed there were further attacks on the established order by radical tribunes. The first of these was Tiberius' brother, Gaius Gracchus, who did manage two successive tribunates in 123 and 122BC. His proposals included another agrarian bill, but they were altogether more far-reaching than his brother's. Two of his proposals were especially significant. He attacked the senate's control of its own officials by establishing a regular criminal court to be manned not by senators but by equestrians (see Equites), the propertied class whose members were not senators (and who were free, therefore, from the restraints on business activity that the Lex Claudia had imposed on senators). By this measure, it was later said, Gracchus had split the ruling class, and given the state two heads. He also proposed measures to benefit Rome's allies in Italy, who were already liable to full military service in the Roman army. The Latin allies were to have full Roman citizenship rights, and the other Italian allies were to have Latin rights. But this proposal seems to have forfeited Gracchus his support, which had previously been great, with the plebs; and in another massacre Gaius and 3,000 of his supporters lost their lives.

Gaius' legislation was unique in its range and set the pattern of Roman politics for the next 50 years and more, both in the problems which it confronted and in its style. The role of the tribune as protector of the people was revived and the unchallenged government of the senatorial oligarchy was at an end.

In the years following Gaius Gracchus, the senatorial oligarchy succeeded in having his legislation repealed; but military defeats in Macedonia, and at the hands of two Germanic tribes, the Cimbri and the Teutones, and a crisis in Africa provoked by the ambitious king of Numidia, Jugurtha, thoroughly discredited their leadership in military matters. After a disaster against the Cimbri and the Teutones at Arausio in 105BC, the ex-consul Q Servilius Caepio became the first man to have his imperium abrogated since the Tarquins. The military emergency was successfully overcome by C Marius, a man who, like Cicero, came from Arpinum, and boasted no Roman magistrates among his ancestors. He made political capital out of the discredit of the nobility, held the consulship – quite illegally – six times between 108 and 100, and met the strains on Rome's manpower that the current wars were imposing by abandoning the property qualification for military service and opening the army to any volunteers who presented themselves. The army thus offered a career to the most needy; but the men thus recruited would become crucially dependent on their commander for resettlement in civilian life once their military service was over. The problem of the army and its commander in politics became a recurring one for the remaining period of the republic, and one of the major factors in the collapse of the republic. It made its first appearance in 100, when proposals for the resettlement of Marius' own veterans led to renewed bloodshed and rioting in the assembly.

Rome's wars were also imposing severe strains on her relations with her Italian allies, who, while liable to military service in Rome's armies, still lacked full Roman citizenship. In 91BC, the allies rose in revolt and the bitter 'Social War' was only brought to an end two years later by Rome conceding full citizenship to all communities which had remained loyal to her, and all which would now lay down arms. But this war was no sooner over than news arrived that Rome's by now extensive trading interests in the eastern Mediterranean and throughout Asia were under severe threat from King Mithridates VII of Pontus, who in a single day in 88 reportedly massacred 80,000 Romans in Asia. The appointment to this war of a dissolute patrician, L Cornelius Sulla, provoked unprecedented civil bloodshed, not only at the time it was made, but throughout the period of his absence and on his return. In 83, he marched on Rome with his army, which was now supplemented by three legions that the young Pompey had raised on his own initiative, had himself appointed dictator, and hunted down his enemies throughout the whole Roman world with remorseless ferocity. He also passed a series of measures designed to remove the political troubles that had arisen in the last half century; but these were more adept in seeing what these problems were than in

15

establishing a realistic cure for them. Sulla retired in 79, and died in the following year; and his measures hardly outlived him by more than ten years.

After Sulla's death, Pompey, by taking one military command after another, gradually became the most powerful man in Rome. The campaign in Asia by which he finally ended the threat of Mithridates (66–62BC) was particularly successful. He annexed Syria (Jerusalem was captured in 63), enlarged Cilicia, added Pontus and Bithynia, and surrounded Rome's possessions with a network of client-kingdoms. Domestic politics remained incurably fractious. In 63 the debased patrician Catiline, having failed to get himself elected consul on a programme of agrarian reform and the cancellation of debt, resorted to armed insurrection against the state. His attempts were foiled by the prompt action of the consul Cicero, but they show us, though our sources for Catiline are lamentably one-sided, how serious the problems of debt and poverty had now become.

Cicero in the senate accusing Catiline of treason

Pompey returned from the east at the end of 62BC; and amid universal relief he disbanded his army when he landed at Brundisium. But the unrelenting opposition of his political opponents drove him in 60 into forming an informal alliance with two other politicians, the immensely wealthy Crassus and the shrewd and ambitious Julius Caesar. Political alliances of this sort had, from the earliest days of the republic, been a regular feature of Roman politics; but this one, which came to be known as the First Triumvirate, was made distinctive by the immense resources that its members commanded. Its power was irresistible, and later observers would look back on 60BC as the year when the free state came to an end. Caesar became consul in 59, when he had himself voted a five-year command in Gaul, for which he left in the following year. In 55, he had this command renewed for a further five years, and similar commands were also granted to Crassus in Syria and Pompey in Spain. But the alliance between the three was broken by the death of Julia, Caesar's daughter and Pompey's wife, in 54, and the death of Crassus at the disastrous battle of Carrhae (Harran) the following year. Anarchy meanwhile prevailed at Rome. Both 53 and 52 opened with no consuls in office; and, as Caesar's command approached its end, his political enemies manoeuvred to prevent him passing directly from his command to another consulship. On 10 January 49 Caesar crossed the Rubicon river with his army and entered Italy; he claimed that his opponents had left him with no alternative.

In the civil wars that followed, Caesar's success was complete. His opponents had recruited Pompey as their military leader, but after evacuating Italy he was defeated by Caesar in Greece at Pharsalus in 48BC, and murdered when he fled to Egypt immediately afterwards. The remainder of the opposition Caesar then mopped up in Africa and Spain. In politics Caesar behaved as the complete autocrat. He had himself appointed dictator in 49, dictator for ten years in 46, and for life in 44. He was called 'Father of the Fatherland', had the month of his birth renamed 'July' after him, had his statue placed among those of the old kings on the Capitol, and issued coins with his own portrait on them. His military activities, and his liaison with Cleopatra, whom he placed with her brother on the throne of Egypt, left him little time for legislation; nevertheless, he began a massive programme of reform, which included the initiation of the Julian calendar from 1 January 45. He also began a major building programme, which included a new forum built around the temple of Venus Genetrix, from whom his family claimed descent.

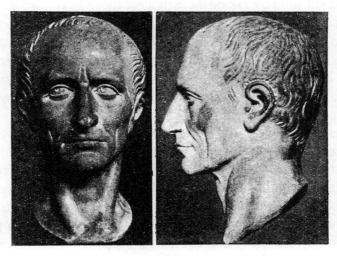

Julius Caesar

Caesar's high-handed disregard for the republican constitution was bound to cause bitterness – it offended Cicero deeply – but his murder on 15 March 44BC by a clique of noble senators solved nothing. The years that followed were ones of almost unbroken civil war. Important early developments were the emergence of C Octavianus, the subsequent Augustus, who in 44 was but 19 years old (he was the grandson of Caesar's sister, but his father's family was quite obscure; Caesar's will nominated him as his heir and adopted him as his son); the callous murder of Cicero, engineered by M Antonius (Mark Antony) in collusion with Octavianus, in 43; and the defeat of Caesar's murderers at the battle of Philippi in 42. In 31, Octavianus, having received an oath from all the towns of Italy, undertook a national crusade against Antonius, who had by now become infatuated with Cleopatra and was staying in Alexandria. At the battle of Actium, Octavianus was victorious. Antony and Cleopatra escaped to Alexandria, where they committed suicide; Octavianus was left in complete control of the empire.

The principate

Augustus (31BC–AD14)

Octavianus had displayed great skill throughout the civil war period; and he displayed no less now that the civil war was won. In the 44 years between his victory at Actium in 31BC and his death in AD14, he reigned supreme, restoring stability and prosperity, ensuring a dynastic succession, and establishing the monarchical rule that was to last for centuries. He took the title Augustus in 27BC, but was careful to avoid the open autocracy of Caesar. He retained control of the army by taking for himself as a 'province' those provinces where the bulk of the army was stationed; but he laid the greatest emphasis on tradition, constitutionality and republicanism, and so was able to maintain the appearance of a constitutional princeps. In 23BC he was able to resign as consul, taking instead the powers of the tribunes; these gave him an absolute right of veto, which as far as we know, he never needed to exercise. In his own account of his achievements, the *Res Gestae*, Augustus claimed that he had no greater legal powers than the other magistrates but was pre-eminent in auctoritas. This seems right. Such was his auctoritas that he did not need to resort to his legal powers. Elections, and senatorial debate, continued, but increasingly became formalities; by the end of his reign Augustus was in practice appointing the chief magistrates.

Augustus paid great attention to the administration of the state, and created a host of new administrative offices, such as prefect of the corn-supply, and curator of aqueducts, generally filling these posts with men from the equestrian, rather than the senatorial, class. Coming from a municipal family himself, he did much to promote new families of Italian origin in public life; he also set forth a national programme of moral and spiritual regeneration, reviving the traditional state religion, and legislating to promote morality and restore the sanctity of family life. He actively supported literature and the arts; the lyric poetry of Horace, Virgil's epic poem *The Aeneid*, and the sculpture of the Altar of Augustan Peace are achievements which Rome never again equalled. All three of these works are heavily imbued with the spirit of the Augustan age; but to call them propaganda would be simplistic. Augustus also transformed the city of Rome by his building programme, and while much of this was concentrated on public works such as a new forum, and the Theatre of Marcellus, he also improved the quality of life for the lower classes in the city, chiefly by the building of two new aqueducts.

In the provinces, too, Augustus brought the benefits of peace, stamping out the corruption of Roman governors that had been a common feature of the late Republic. Early in his reign he pacified north-western Spain, and then advanced Roman power in central Europe northwards to the Danube, thereby improving communications with the crucial province of Illyrium. In Asia, he safeguarded Roman interests by establishing client kings, of whom Herod of Judaea is the best-known example; Egypt, after the death of Cleopatra, became virtually Augustus' personal province. In northern Europe, Augustus clearly at one stage must have entertained hopes of pushing eastwards from the Rhine to the Elbe, but this had to be abandoned following the catastrophic loss of three legions in the Teutoberg Forest in AD9, and thereafter the Roman army fell back to the left bank of the Rhine.

The later Julio-Claudians (AD14–68)

For 50 years after Augustus' death, the principate was continued by four emperors who came from his family, but all of whom to a greater or lesser extent lacked his auctoritas. Tiberius (AD14–37) and Claudius (41–54) made serious, and often successful, attempts to maintain the firm and beneficial rule of Augustus, but neither had Augustus' facility for commanding apparently universal assent for what he did. Gaius (Caligula) (37–41) apparently became deranged, and Nero (54–68), who succeeded through the machinations of his villainous mother, seems purely frivolous. Under Claudius Britain was invaded in 43 (Augustus may have had earlier plans for invading Britain, but these were never executed); otherwise provincial affairs under the Julio-Claudians are distinguished by two bloody revolts bloodily suppressed – that of Boudicca in Britain in 60–61, and that of the Jews in 66–73 (the Temple was destroyed in 70). But we should not overlook the 'civilisation' of the western empire that was now well under way. Rome freely exported her own culture to the western provinces – the Maison Carreé at Nîmes, and the Pont du Gard nearby, are conspicuous examples – and, without using coercion, she also encouraged Roman habits in dress, the learning of the Latin language, and the adoption of her own civic and political institutions. Claudius admitted provincials from Gaul to the senate, and both the imperial cult, and the Roman army, were powerful Romanising influences. But these developments did not prejudice local traditions in language, art or religion, and they were at this period to be found only in the western empire, not in the Greek east.

The murder of Gaius in AD41, and the appointment of the unexpected Claudius to succeed him, were both due to the Praetorian Guard, the élite corps which Augustus had created as the bodyguard of the emperor and garrison of Italy. On Nero's suicide in 68 the army once more appeared in politics. All the major army groups, except for that in Britain, sought to establish their own claimant to the throne; after short-lived reigns by Galba (from Spain), Otho (the nominee of the Praetorian Guard), and Vitellius (from

Lower Germany), Vespasian, with the armies of the east, finally established himself as emperor in 70.

From the Flavian to the Severan dynasties (AD70–235)

It is generally agreed that the period which began with the accession of Vespasian and ended with the death of the last of the Severans, Alexander Severus, in 235 represents the highest point of Rome's political and cultural achievement. The period is much less well known to us, at least from the literary sources, than the revolutionary and Julio-Claudian periods that preceded it. But it was clearly a period of steady, rather than spectacular, development, in which firmly-founded dynasties produced emperors who, apart from Domitian (81–96) and Commodus (180–192), ruled with prudence and restraint. While the Flavians came to power as a result of a military coup d'état in 69–70, such civil war did not reappear until 193, when it brought the Severans to the throne; in 98, a threat of something similar was averted by the childless Nerva's hurried adoption of Trajan, who was then the army commander of Upper Germany.

The period was one of great military expansion – undertaken, it would appear, more for strategic reasons than for conquest for its own sake. After the Jewish revolt, Titus (79–81) increased the occupation of Syria, and, to improve communications with the upper Euphrates, garrisoned Cappadocia and introduced extensive roadworks into the area. The awkward Rhine-Danube salient was annexed and fortified, and the Dacian wars of Trajan (98–117), uniquely recorded for us on Trajan's Column in Rome, by leading to the annexation of Dacia, secured Rome's grip on the Danube. In the east Septimius Severus (193–211) established the new province of Mesopotamia, and thereby ensured the security of the Roman cities of Syria, while in Numidia he advanced Roman power to the edge of the Sahara desert. On the other hand, the wars which Marcus Aurelius (161–180) fought against the Marcomanni marked a new development for Rome, in that they were purely defensive, with the object of maintaining the Danube frontier. But such wars became increasingly common from now on, and so demanded of an emperor more and more that he should be a military man. When the last of the Severans, Alexander Severus (222–235), was murdered at Moguntiacum, the reason was his inadequacy for the military crisis then facing the empire; he was succeeded by a military officer, C Julius Maximinus.

The period is also one when both a great extension of the Roman citizenship takes place, and the fruits of the earlier extensions make themselves felt.

The literary men of the period come from outside Italy – the historian Tacitus from Gaul, the rhetorician Quintilian from Spain, and the biographer Suetonius from Africa – and the emperors do not come from Rome. After the Flavians from old Sabine territory, Trajan and Hadrian (117–138) came from Spain, Antoninus Pius (138–161) from Nemausus (Nîmes), and Septimius Severus from Africa. This widening provincial background of the emperors is paralleled by the background of the members of the ruling classes generally, and reflects the growing wealth and romanisation of the empire.

It is from this period that the monuments most impressively reflect the prosperity of the empire, and led Gibbon to conclude that the provinces had been 'the seat of a polite and powerful empire'. At Rome, we have the forum and baths of Trajan, the bronze equestrian statue of Marcus Aurelius (the only such surviving statue from the classical period), the arch of Septimius Severus, and the massive Baths of Caracalla, which were in fact instituted by Caracalla's father Severus. In the provinces, the best evidence comes from the buildings with which Severus endowed his birthplace, Leptis Magna, an originally Punic settlement in the province of Africa. The town was already well developed before Severus – it drew great wealth, not only from trade and commerce, but also from the olive- and wheat-farming of the immediately surrounding area – but Severus built a new forum and basilica, modernised the harbour, and instituted a massive colonnade from the harbour to the baths of Hadrian in the heart of the city. The monuments of the age also attest the devotion to public duty that made such magnificence possible. The wealthier individuals in one city after another would undertake public building and the provision of civic amenities in the spirit of self-sacrificing generosity; the sense of collective responsibility can seldom have been higher.

Two legal developments of the period deserve notice. Under Hadrian (117–138) the African jurist Salvius Julianus collected, revised, and published the edicts (see Edicta magistratuum) which from the earliest times successive praetors had pronounced at the start of their year of office. This move must have facilitated a much more widespread understanding of the Roman law and it also led to the Institutes of Salvius' pupil Gaius, which is the only legal work to have come down to us from the classical period substantially in its original form. The work suggests that Gaius was particularly interested in the application of Roman law to the provinces, and is further proof of the steady undermining of the distinction that had once existed between Roman and provincial. On the other hand, another distinction is becoming more and more clear, that between the honestiores, the superior, land-owning class, and everyone else, the humiliores, who had inferior legal rights and were liable to heavier penalties in the courts, ones which in some cases had previously been applied only to non-citizens. This division of society into two distinct groups was to have ominous consequences for the future.

Marcus Aurelius' legal adviser, Quintus Cervidius Scaevola, left extensive written works behind, and thus gave impetus to a practice that in origin was Greek rather than Roman. The practice of writing down, and working out, the principles of the entire field of Roman law reached its climax under Septimius Severus, who had been taught by Cervidius. The importance that Severus attached to law is made clear by his regular appointment of the leading jurists as his praetorian prefects (see Prefects), in which capacity they exerted great influence in financial and judicial matters. Papinian, who was prefect from 203 to 212, made considerable collections and summaries of legal decisions; he was followed by Ulpian, who came from Tyre, and was joint praetorian

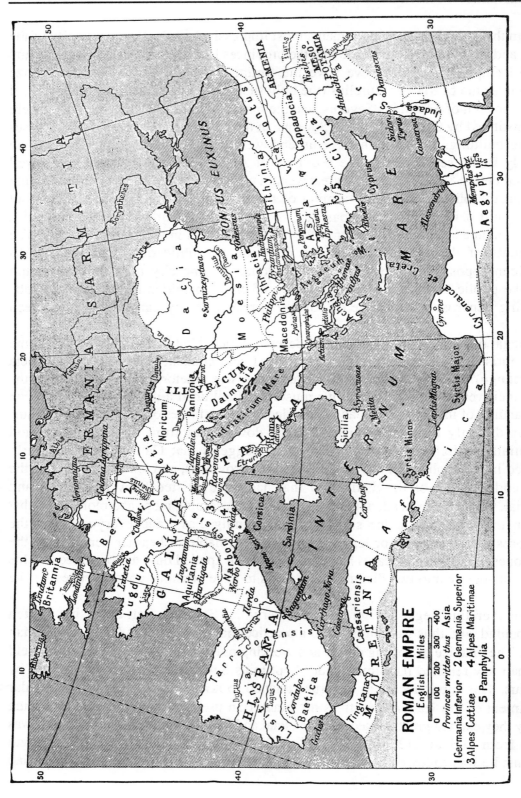

The Roman empire during the reign of Trajan

prefect in 222–223. Ulpian's monumental work covers, with impressive ease, the entire range of Roman law; even more massive were the works of the third great praetorian prefect/jurist of the day, Paulus. Between them, these three writers provide more than half of the Digest of Roman Law that Justinian was to publish 300 years later.

Crisis and recovery

The later third century

The end of the Severan dynasty in 235 was followed by fifty years of anarchy, in which at least eighteen 'official' Roman emperors jostled for position with countless usurpers and pretenders. Our literary sources are now abysmal, but it seems clear that increasing pressure on the frontiers of the empire was at the least one very important cause of the anarchy. With the province of Asia now threatened by the Goths, and Gaul and Spain by the Alamanni and Franks, the local commander was obliged to take control. So the usurper Postumus established an independent Gallic empire in the 260s, and in the same decade the emperor Gallienus (260–268) was obliged to entrust the defence of the eastern frontier, where his own father Valerian (253–260) had already been captured in battle, to the local dynast Odaenathon, who with his successors established a quasi-independent empire that stretched from Egypt to Asia Minor.

At the same time, the empire was afflicted by economic crisis. Increased government expenditure, and a shortage of precious metals, led to a progressive debasing of the coinage, and so to hyper-inflation. The main loser was the government, whose tax revenues became less and less valuable in real terms, and which, therefore, more and more resorted to the direct requisitioning of goods and services in place of taxes. There followed a marked decline in the civic munificence that had characterised the preceding age – public buildings would be inhabited by squatters, or incorporated into the city's defences. Another significant development was a shift in economic resources to the frontier areas where the military threat was greatest. Towns such as Trier on the Moselle and Serdica in the Danube area assumed an importance which owed its origin to military factors; Rome, while still a flourishing centre, began to become isolated from the empire which she supposedly governed.

Diocletian and the tetrarchy (AD284–312)

In 284–285 Diocletian, an army commander from Dalmatia, seized power by military coup, and his vigorous government for the next twenty years laid the foundations of the later Roman state. Crucial to his success was his devolution of imperial power. While Diocletian concentrated on the eastern frontier, he appointed Maximian as co-emperor in the west; in 293 the 'Tetrarchy' was instituted, when Galerius and Constantius were appointed Caesars below Diocletian and Maximian, and adopted by them. The tetrarchs promptly won a series of military successes over Rome's enemies, and then launched a wide-ranging series of reforms designed to confront the problems of the previous half-century. In the army, a mobile force was developed to support the frontier garrisons, and manpower was greatly increased. New gold and silver coins were introduced in an attempt to stabilise the currency, and in 301, to stem inflation, Diocletian passed his remarkable Edict of Maximum Prices. This may seem to us economically naive, and it was alleged at the time to have driven goods off the market; but the willingness of the Roman government to address itself to the problem of inflation in such detail must surely have seemed significant at the time, just as it does today. Taxation was also revolutionised. A standard unit of taxation was introduced, based on the area of the taxpayer's land and the labour and animal stock used on it, and a number of supplementary taxes were also introduced. The provinces, and even Italy, were divided into smaller, and more manageable, units, arranged in regional groups, 'dioceses', each under the authority of a vicarius.

The Tetrarchs also cloaked themselves in much more elaborate ceremonial than their predecessors. Subjects granted an audience would begin by kissing the imperial robe; petitions were addressed to the 'sacred ears' of the emperor, and replies came from the 'sacred mouth'. Official pronouncements were riddled with such abstractions as 'Our Majesty', 'Our Serenity', and 'Our Eternity', and the staff of the imperial palace was vastly increased. As the public art of the period shows — the sculpture on the Arch of Constantine at Rome is the best-known example — the age is characterised by an increasing formalism; the emperor is less an individual than a symbolic abstraction.

Diocletian's Great Persecution of the Christians was begun in AD303. There had been official persecutions of the Christians in the previous century by Decius (249–251) and Valerian, and these may have been provoked by the belief that the spread of Christianity was alienating the favour of the traditional state gods and thereby causing the misfortunes of the times. But it is difficult to tell what were the motives of Diocletian, whose own wife and daughter were among those punished as Christian sympathisers; it may be that the persecution was imposed on him, for personal reasons, by Galerius. Nor can we properly assess the impact of the persecution, which was anyhow very unevenly applied throughout the provinces. It was officially ended in 313, after the deaths of both Diocletian and Galerius, when Constantine and Licinius granted freedom of worship and restored its confiscated property to the Christian church — thereby beginning the peace of the church and the conversion of the empire to Christianity.

Constantine (AD312–337)

In 305 Diocletian and Maximian resigned, Galerius and Constantius succeeded them, and two new Caesars were appointed. This new arrangement was not successful. In 306 Constantius died, and his son Constantine systematically eliminated his rivals, and became master of the western empire by his victory at the battle of the Milvian Bridge in 312. In 324 he defeated Licinius, the emperor of the east, at Hadrianople and Chrysopolis, and from then until his death in 337 he was the sole ruler of the entire empire, with his three sons as his Caesars.

After his victory in AD312, Constantine repeatedly emphasised his conversion to Christianity and attributed his successes to it. He had dreamed before the crucial battle, so he said, first of a vision of the cross with the inscription 'Conquer with this', and then that he was being admonished to paint the Christian Chi-Rho monogram on his soldiers' shields. On the Arch of Constantine he declared that he owed his victory to 'the inspiration of the Divinity and the greatness of his own mind'. His religious convictions again make themselves clear in his infinitely significant foundation of Constantinople on the site of the ancient Byzantium. This was dedicated in 330, and, though built on seven hills and having its own senate, it from the outset excluded pagan worship, and replaced the old pagan temples with splendid Christian churches, such as those of the Apostles and of Holy Peace, Hagia Eirene. The church of Santa Sophia was probably begun by his son Constantius. After his deathbed baptism and death in 337, Constantine was buried in Constantinople.

Other church-building by Constantine included the Holy Sepulchre in Jerusalem, supposedly on the spot where Christ had been buried, and in Rome the Lateran basilica and St Peter's. He also promoted Christianity by the appointment of Christians to prominent positions at court; thus Ablabius became praetorian prefect, and in 326 Acilius Severus became the first known Christian prefect at Rome.

Constantine also introduced many administrative reforms, including a new, and very unpopular, monetary tax, and a new basic unit of gold currency, the solidus, which was to retain its value for many years to come. And he campaigned successfully against the German tribes and against the Goths and Sarmatians on the Danube frontier.

Constantine's successors

Constantine was succeeded by his sons, but in AD355 renewed threats from Germany obliged Constantius to appoint his nephew Julian as Caesar in Gaul. On Constantius' death in 361 Julian became emperor, and in two years did all he could to restore the worship of the ancient gods at the expense of Christianity. On his death, while he was campaigning in Persia in 363, the rule was continued by military men, who were increasingly preoccupied with foreign wars. Valentinian (364–375) faced trouble in Gaul and in Britain, and Valens (364–378) from the Goths. In 376 Valens was induced to admit Visigoths to the empire as a solution to Rome's manpower problems; but the policy misfired, and in 378 Valens, and more than half his army, were killed in battle against the Goths at Hadrianople. He was succeeded in the east by Theodosius I, who restored the military situation there, and then, in the face of renewed civil war in the west, established his court at Milan in 394. But at his death in the following year the empire passed jointly to his young sons, Honorius in the west, and Arcadius, ruling from Constantinople, in the east. From henceforth the Roman empire was effectively divided into an eastern and a western part.

Theodosius also consummated the triumph of Christianity by his legislation abolishing pagan sacrifice, closing the ancient temples and confiscating their estates. Meanwhile

Gratian (emperor of the west, AD367–383) renounced the title of pontifex maximus, and took other measures to eliminate the traditional state religion from Rome. It seems probable that by now Christians predominated in the Roman senate, and that throughout most of the empire the lower classes were by the end of the fourth century largely Christian. The church, though enjoying no formal position within the state, was nevertheless influential in state affairs; Bishop Ambrose of Milan in 389–390 forced Theodosius first to rescind legislation directed against the church in Syria, and then to do penance for a massacre perpetrated by his soldiers in Greece.

Collapse

The fall of the western empire

Theodosius I was the last emperor for fifty years to exercise effective control over the empire. His successors came from his own family, but they all came to the throne at an inappropriately young age, and power lay more and more in the hands of ministers and military commanders. The division of the empire between the courts of Constantinople and Milan (the latter transferred in AD402 to Ravenna), hardened; the Visigoths, under their own leaders, became an increasingly important influence within the empire.

After Theodosius' death the military commander Stilicho, himself a half-Vandal, sought the help of Alaric the Visigoth. Alaric complied, but after Stilicho had been executed by the emperor he turned on Rome, and captured and sacked it in AD410. Meanwhile, a massive German invasion had swept over the Rhine, overrun Gaul, and even penetrated into Spain, and Britain was abandoned in the face of repeated Saxon invasions. And in 429 Vandal forces crossed from Spain to Africa, and worked their way steadily towards Carthage. There was little that the government could do about these developments; manpower was chronically short, and few military leaders could be trusted.

From about AD420, the Huns, having established themselves north of the Danube, pushed southwards, and thereby disrupted land communications between the eastern and western empires. Roman territory south of the Danube was lost, and in 451 Attila led the Huns westwards to Gaul and Italy, where he sacked Milan. But he was persuaded by diplomacy to leave Italy, and the Hunnish empire did not outlive his death in 453.

The eastern court did what it could to restore the precarious position in the west. It installed Valentinian III as emperor in AD425, and in 437 his marriage to a daughter of Theodosius took place in Constantinople. It was on this occasion that western envoys brought back from Constantinople copies of the Theodosian Code (see Codex Theodosianus), the compilation of the imperial legislation of the fourth and early fifth centuries that had been made on the order of Theodosius II (emperor of the east, 408–450), one of the last examples of east-west co-operation.

The dynasty of Theodosius ended in the east in AD450 and in the west in 455, the year in which Rome was sacked again, this time by the Vandals. The eastern government attempted to install its own men in Rome but its nominee Nepos was displaced by his general Orestes, who made his son Romulus emperor; when Romulus was supplanted in 476 by the German general Odoacer, the Roman empire in the west was at an end. Henceforth, Italy was under the control of Germanic kings from their court at Ravenna.

The Ostrogothic kingdom and the Byzantine reconquest

In AD493 Ravenna was captured and Odoacer killed by Theoderic the Ostrogoth. Both Odoacer and Theoderic respected the traditions of Rome. Odoacer restored and revived the Colosseum and the senate continued as a considerable force in ecclesiastical politics. But relations between Theoderic and the senate were soured by developments in the east. When Justin I became emperor of the east, he departed from his predecessors by following a vigorous 'orthodox' policy in religious affairs, a policy which was maintained and developed by his nephew and successor Justinian (527–565). This drew the western church towards the eastern, and away from the Arian Theoderic, who became increasingly suspicious of this new development. In 526, in an attempt at rapprochement, he allowed Pope John I to make the first visit by a pope to the eastern capital, but after John's rapturous welcome in Constantinople Theoderic put him under house arrest on his return.

Justinian presenting his code to Tribonian

27

Theoderic died in the same year, and his successors quarrelled among themselves. By AD535 the Visigothic dynasty was at an end, and Justinian's general Belisarius was heading the reconquest of the west. Justinian, an immensely energetic man, had already begun his reorganisation and codification of Roman law, by which three million lines of earlier Roman law-books were condensed into 150,000 lines; he had also made terms with Persia. The reconquest of the west began with the recovery of Africa from the Vandals in 533; but Italy was not fully conquered until 553. Thereafter, the Roman senate immediately disappears from history; the new government, or Exarchate, establishes itself in great splendour at Ravenna, and throughout Rome and the rest of Italy impoverishment takes over, and brings the classical world to an end. The Byzantine empire lasts for another 900 years, but when the Lombards over-run Italy in the late 560s there is little that can be done to stop them.

2 Reception and Continuing Influence

A 'second life'

Quite apart from the fact that Roman law is one of the great things which have happened in the world and that it is part of a liberal education to know something about it, as with many other 'great things', its influence has survived the passing of the years. Indeed, for Ihering, writing in the last century, it was to become 'an element of the civilization of the modern world'.

Of course, for lawyers and law students Roman law has served, and continues to serve, a particular purpose as an introduction to jurisprudence, the study of the science of law. In England, Roman law has been seen in this light since Vicarius, a Lombard, began teaching it here in Oxford in 1149, or thereabouts; he also published a book based on Justinian's Code and Digest.

After Justinian, Roman law (along with the Roman state) declined, and it could so easily have become just a fascinating aspect of the history of its time. Whether it would have survived simply as an introduction to jurisprudence can only be a matter of conjecture. However, Roman law was not to pass from the scene; far from it. As Vinogradoff said, it is, in a sense, a 'ghost story' telling of a 'second life ... after the demise of the body in which it first saw the light'.

The 'reception'

Why should Roman law have come to life again from the eleventh century or, as it is said, to have experienced its 'reception' in 'the first renaissance'? In large measure, schools and universities provide the answer. There, Roman law (including canon law) was read by students from many European countries and, as practitioners and judges, they applied it, if only to fill gaps in their local law, in their native lands. Law schools at Provence, Pavia (emphasising Lombard law), Ravenna and (particularly) Bologna led the way. Scholars ('glossators', so called because of their glosses or notes on Roman law texts), believing Roman law to be of universal application, gave it much emphasis. The glossators were followed, in the fourteenth century, by another school of lawyers, the 'post-glossators' or 'commentators', and they concentrated upon Roman law's practical application in the courts.

As has been inferred, Roman law's reception was not uniform or everywhere immediate: it took place over several centuries and, according to a country's history and present circumstances, to a greater or lesser extent. Switzerland and the Scandinavian countries were, perhaps, the least affected by Roman law's reception; in no case was it complete. Certain aspects of Roman law were received more readily than others; some, for example criminal law, made little impression. Universities, as and when, and wherever in Europe established, were always a key factor. Roman law was the basis of their legal teaching and, in most cases, national law was not taught there until the eighteenth century, although Swedish law was taught at Uppsala from 1620.

By the seventeenth century it could be said that Justinian's corpus juris, as perceived by the glossators and interpreted by the commentators, allowing canon law and the clergy to play its and their considerable part, had become the common law of much of Europe, supplementing (at least) local law and custom. As Gierke said, 'living Italian law ... had passed beyond the Alps'.

Holland

Reception in Holland – in the fifteenth century – is particularly noteworthy because it gave rise, in the seventeenth century, to that combination of Roman and local customary law known to this day as Roman Dutch law. Where the local law did not apply, the Court of Pleas of Holland, the earliest Dutch court, turned to Justinian's corpus juris. In course of time the jurists of Holland set down the resulting undigested mass, concisely and authoritatively, and Roman Dutch law received its lasting form.

England

As for England (and Ireland), much Roman law influence is to be found in the works of Glanvil, *Tractatus de Legibus*, published about 1188, and Bracton, *Tractatus de Legibus et Consuetudinibus Angliae*, published in the following century. Both books made a deep and enduring impression on the development of English law. Attempts were made to replace the common law of the land by Roman law, especially during the reign of Henry VIII. The movements were defeated, but many Roman law principles continued to be applied in relation to commercial transactions (the law merchant) and admiralty (maritime) matters and to have a lasting effect. In *Baylis* v *Bishop of London* [1913] 1 Ch 127 Farwell LJ was able to say that 'the jus naturale of Roman law ... has had a considerable influence in moulding our common law'.

As will be seen, Roman law has left its mark on other aspects of English law as well; canon law made a significant contribution, particularly on the chancellor's equitable jurisdiction. It is possible, indeed likely, that the law applied by the Romans during their occupation, or some of its rules, had an abiding influence. In relation to England W S Holdsworth summed up the position as follows: 'We have received Roman law; but we have received it in small homoeopathic doses, at different periods, and as and when required. It has acted as a tonic to our native legal system, and not as a drug or a poison. When received it has never been continuously developed on Roman lines. It has been naturalized and assimilated; and with its assistance, our wholly independent system has, like the Roman law itself, been gradually and continuously built up, by the development of old and the creation of new rules to meet the needs of a changing civilization.'

Scotland

In Scotland the position was much clearer, although Roman law was never formally received there. During the thirteenth and fourteenth centuries Scotland's customary law was similar to that of England, but in the next century continental influence began to be felt north of the Tweed and Roman law doctrines were beginning to spread, not least because many Scottish lawyers were starting to receive much of their training in the universities of Holland and other Continental countries. Roman law was also taught in the universities of St Andrew's and Glasgow, both of which were founded in the fifteenth century, but it was the next century which was of the greatest significance. Writing towards the end of it, Sir John Skene bemoaned the fact that 'those who are in daily practice in the courts consume their days and nights in learning the civil law of the Romans, and give their whole labours to the practising of it'. Indeed, when the Court of Session was founded in 1532 it was provided that one half of the fourteen ordinary judges should be clerics, ie trained in Roman law. It was the institution of this court, with this constitution, which proved to be decisive. Where the local customary law was uncertain or inadequate, the judges turned to Roman law to supply the need. Roman doctrine and discipline had made a lasting impression.

Western Europe – and far beyond

Looking at western Europe and its reception of Roman law as a whole, W S Holdsworth helpfully summarised the position when he said: 'However much we may minimize, however much we may deplore the reception, it is clear that the political theories and institutions, the organisation of industry and commerce, and the rules of law public and private ... would not have been what they are today, if the leading European states had not at different times and to a varying extent received the Roman law.'

As those same European states extended their power and influence to other parts of the world, so, again to a varying extent, they extended the influence of Roman law. For example, by the middle of the eighteenth century, Roman Dutch law was administered in the Netherlands; at the Cape of Good Hope; at Java, in Borneo, Sumatra, Celebes, Moluccas, Sunda, and part of New Guinea, in the East Indies; at Curaçao in the West Indies; and at Guiana, in South America. Less directly, of course, the British colonies came under the influence of Roman law as the English common law was applied within their boundaries.

Codification

During the period of the reception Portugal and Spain introduced codes of law and their contents bore many marks of Roman influence. Indeed codification was itself a Roman phenomenon: Roman law began with a code (the Twelve Tables) and ended with one, Justinian's corpus juris. The seventeenth century saw codifications in Scandinavian countries, but there was little evidence of Roman influence in those cases.

In the eighteenth century codification received fresh emphasis – and the need for it was clear. In France, for example, different laws applied to different aspects of life; the Frenchman's will would be governed by canon law, his contracts by Roman law. Add to this the immense variety of local or customary laws and it will be readily appreciated why Voltaire once reflected that a traveller through France changed his law as often as he changed his horses. Much the same was true of Germany, where Roman law was supplemented and modified by local customary law, and, no doubt, of other European countries at that time.

Bavaria led the way in the new round of codification, followed by Prussia, but the most significant – and the most needed? – was Napoleon's Code Civil which came into force in 1804. The Code Civil drew significantly upon Roman law and its terminology; it adopted, for example, the distinction in Justinian's Institutes between persons and things. Sir Henry Maine once said that the Code Civil 'may be described without great inaccuracy as a compendium of the rules of Roman law then practised in France cleared of all feudal admixture, such rules, however, being in all cases taken with the extensions given to them and the interpretation put upon them by one or two eminent French jurists, and particularly by Pothier'. Napoleon's Code applied throughout the French empire (including, at that time, Holland); the Code Civil, like other European systems of law, also served as a basis for, or influenced the law of, many other countries. The Dutch (replacing the Code Civil) and German civil codes took effect in 1838 and 1900 respectively. The influence of Roman law in Holland remained strong and, although its influence on the German code may not have been as obvious as it was on the Code Civil, it was at least as real. As to Germany, Saleilles said at that time: 'To want to eliminate the Roman law by creating a code would have been to create a German code without German law.'

It will be readily appreciated, therefore, why Sir John Salmon once remarked that 'when an English lawyer with any knowledge of the terminology of Roman law comes to the study of a practical law-book of France or Germany he finds himself on ground not wholly unfamiliar'. No doubt the same could be said of the legal tomes of many other countries as well.

Influence today

The reception over the centuries of Roman law by western European countries, and through them by many other lands, is clear, although a detailed study of it is beyond the scope of this book. The question arises as to the extent to which this influence is obvious today. Just a few examples must suffice.

English law

In his Institutes, Book II, Title VII, Justinian referred to donations mortis causa as follows: 'A donation mortis causa is that made under an apprehension or suspicion of death, eg, when a thing is given upon condition that if the donor dies the donee shall possess it absolutely, or that the thing shall be returned if the donor survives the danger which he apprehends. As far as possible gifts mortis causa are treated in the same way as legacies. In brief, a donation mortis causa is made when a man so gives as to show that he would rather possess the thing than that the donee should possess it, and yet that he is more willing that it should go to the donee than to his heir.'

This concept, and its very name, has passed into English law. In *Sen v Headley* [1990] 2 WLR 620 Mummery J found that the essential conditions for a valid donation mortis causa are:

'(1) There must be a clear intention to give, but only if the donor dies, whereas if the donor does not die then the gift is not to take effect and the donor is to have back the subject matter of the gift. The gift must, therefore, be conditional in that sense, either expressly or by inference. (2) The gift must be made in contemplation of death, by which is meant not the possibility of death at some time or other, but death within the near future, which may be called death for some reason believed to be impending ... (3) The donor must effectively part with dominion over the subject matter of the gift. Mere words of gift are not enough. There must be some clear act taken towards a transfer of the property.'

In the case which was then before him Mummery J had to decide whether there could be a valid donation mortis causa of real property – a house – by delivery of the title deeds. His answer was in the negative but, for present purposes, it is more important to recall that, in argument, reference was made to textbooks on Scots and South African law and to Justinian's Institutes.

Another clear example is to be found in the law relating to easements. The basis for acquiring an easement, such as a right of way, by prescription is continuous user as of right for the necessary period of time. In Roman law, where a servitude had been enjoyed nec vi, nec clam, nec precario (without force, without secrecy, without permission) for ten or twenty years, according as to whether the owner of the servient tenement had been present or absent, a valid and legal servitude was deemed to exist. The origin of this rule is to be found in the Twelve Tables: see Twelve Tables, Table VI, and Institutes, Book II, Title VI.

In determining the meaning of the phrase 'user as of right', English courts have adopted the Roman test nec vi, nec clam, nec precario. For example, in *Sturges* v *Bridgman* (1879) 11 Ch D 852 Thesiger LJ said: 'Consent or acquiescence of the owner of the servient tenement lies at the root of prescription, and the fiction of a lost grant, and hence the acts or user, which go to the proof of either the one or the other, must be, in the language of the civil law, nec vi, nec clam, nec precario.' Again in *Dalton* v *Angus & Co* (1881) 6 App Cas 740, after recalling that the Roman praetor had forbidden any one to disturb, by force, any possession which had been obtained nec vi, nec clam, nec precario, Lord Blackburn said that 'the English law as to prescription was, beyond controversy, greatly derived from the Roman law, the very words of which are often quoted in the earliest English authorities'.

The words of Thesiger LJ in *Sturges* v *Bridgman* above were noted with approval by the Court of Appeal in *Mills* v *Silver* (1990) The Times 13 July. In that case it was decided that sporadic vehicular use of a track by a neighbouring farmer without the landowner's permission, but with his knowledge and acquiescence, had been user as of right creating a prescriptive easement by the presumption of a lost grant. In other words, the user of the track had been nec vi, nec clam, nec precario: toleration of the user without objection was not the same as giving permission for it.

A third example is to be found in relation to the rule that a barrister cannot sue to recover his fees. As Lord Morris of Borth-y-Gest explained in *Rondel* v *Worsley* [1967] 3 WLR 1666, 'this inability rests on a rule of etiquette which has now hardened into a rule of law'. It is a rule of considerable antiquity; certainly it was well acknowledged by the eighteenth century. In his *Commentaries on the Laws of England*, Sir William Blackstone wrote: '... it is established with us, that a counsel can maintain no action for his fees ...' Indeed, in *Thornhill* v *Evans* (1742) 2 Atk 330, Lord Hardwicke LC had asked: 'Can it be thought that this court will suffer a gentleman of the bar to maintain an action for fees ...?'

However, the rule was challenged – unsuccessfully – in *Kennedy* v *Brown* (1863) 32 LJ (NS) CP 137 where a barrister sued to recover a fee of £20,000 – a sizeable sum even today! Kennedy, the plaintiff barrister, argued that the civil law of Rome had allowed an advocate to sue for his fee and that Blackstone had made a mistake in referring to it to support a contrary opinion. Erle CJ dismissed this argument out of hand. 'In this, 'he said, 'it appears to us that the mistake is on the part of the plaintiff.

Throughout the whole growth of the civil law, from the foundation of Rome to the Digest of Justinian, not only was the advocate always under incapacity to make any contract for his remuneration but also throughout a part of that time he was under prohibition from receiving any gain for his services.' He added: '... the Roman jurists are entitled to be gratefully remembered, because their intuitive sense of right showed to them where right was in the conflicts of interests perpetually arising as the relations of man to man multiplied, and their works have helped to guide succeeding generations in their search for right when similar conflicts arose.'

Scots law

As has been seen, the influence of Roman law was greater north of the border than to the south of it. Writing in 1882, George Watson observed that the principles of Roman Law 'are so remarkably incorporated with those of the law of Scotland'. A recent example of its continuing importance there is to be found in the case of *Upper Crathes Fishing Ltd* v *Barclay*, a decision of the Court of Session on 23 October 1990. Salmon fishings on the river Dee had once been owned by a Mr Lamyman and a Mr Baillie in two equal pro indiviso shares. Mr Lamyman's share had been acquired by the pursuers (plaintiffs); Mr Baillie's share was now vested in his executors, the defenders (defendants). Could the plaintiffs insist on the sale of the fishings and the division of the proceeds of sale?

Resisting the plaintiffs' claim, the defendants contended, inter alia, that they (the plaintiffs) had not acted in good faith in acquiring the fishings and that they were interested only in their commercial exploitation. In other words, the defendants argued, essentially on grounds of equity, that the plaintiffs should be denied the ordinary remedy of division and sale.

The Lord Ordinary took the view that this defence was irrelevant and that, as a general rule, a pro indiviso proprietor had an absolute right of sale. In particular, he recalled that in *Brock* v *Hamilton* (1857) 19D 700 Lord Rutherford had said:

'That law [referring to Roman law] and our common law proceed upon the principles that no one should be bound to remain indefinitely in communione with another or others as proprietors of a common property ...'

On appeal, the Lord Ordinary's view was upheld. Here the defendants relied first on Roman law, referring to the works of Gaius and Justinian and to modern Roman law textbooks, but Lord Allanbridge said:

'In this situation I agree with the Lord Ordinary's view that the Roman texts require to be treated with some reservation when considering the Scottish action as it has now developed. There is no doubt, however, the Roman law does indicate that a co-owner has the "right" of division … Thus an examination of the Roman law does not give any clear support to the [defendants'] contentions in this case.'

It should also be noted that the defendants' second and equally unsuccessful argument was based upon a passage from *Stair's Institutes*, a work much influenced by Roman law.

Future influence?

As new systems and facets of law continue to emerge, nationally and internationally, it may be asked to what extent they, in their turn, will be influenced by Roman law. While it is impossible to give an answer to that question which even approaches precision, it is difficult to believe that the Roman concepts and principles which have influenced, to a greater or lesser extent, directly or indirectly, the laws of so many nations will not make an impression. Put another way, it is reasonable to suppose that this 'element of the civilization of the modern world' will continue to bring its influence to bear.

Indeed, in the fourth edition of his book *Principles of Public International Law*, published in 1990, Ian Brownlie wrote, in relation to territory sub judice: 'The analogy here is perhaps with the right of possession which the sequester or stakeholder had in Roman law. The existing regime rests on acts in the law which in principle could not create sovereignty in the existing holder but which do not render the region terra nullius.' At the height of their power it is doubtful whether the Romans ever regarded the title to any territory in which they were interested as being sub judice, far less a terra nullius; nevertheless, an international lawyer of today finds their concept of depositum sequestre (see Real contracts), involving juristic possession, to be of help, if only by analogy.

3 The Twelve Tables – a Reconstruction

Table I	Of summoning before the magistrate
Table II	Of judicial proceedings
Table III	Of execution
Table IV	Of paternal power
Table V	Of inheritance and tutelage
Table VI	Of ownership and possession
Table VII	Of the law concerning land
Table VIII	Of wrongs
Table IX	Of public law
Table X	Of sacred law
Table XI	Supplementary laws
Table XII	Supplementary laws

Table 1: Of summoning before the magistrate

If a person be summoned to appear before the magistrate, he must go: if he does not go the plaintiff may call witnesses and take him by force.

If the defendant evades the notice to appear, or takes to his heels, the plaintiff may detain him by force.

If the defendant is prevented from attending by reason of illness or old age, the plaintiff must find him a conveyance, although he is not obliged to provide a covered carriage.

The surety for a landowner (or taxpayer) must also be a landowner (or taxpayer); for anyone other than a landowner (or taxpayer) anyone who is willing may be his surety.

Where the parties come to terms, the judge shall announce the settlement.

Where the parties do not come to terms, the plaintiff must state his case before noon in the consilium, or in the forum, in the presence of the defendant.

After midday, if one of the parties has not appeared, judgment shall be given by default in favour of the party present.

If both parties are present, the proceedings terminate at sunset.

Both parties must enter into recognizances for re-appearance.

Table II: Of judicial proceedings

In the sacramental action 500 (or 50, where the amount involved in the dispute is less than 1000) pound pieces of copper (asses) must be deposited in court as security for costs.

The case may be adjourned on account of the serious illness of the judge or arbitrator or one of the parties, or if one of the parties is an alien.

He who wants a person as a witness must go to his house and summon him in a loud voice to attend on the third market day following.

If a theft has been compromised the action is extinguished.

Table III: Of execution

Thirty days are allowed for the payment of debts admitted or adjudged due by pronouncement in court.

After this period has elapsed, the defaulter may be seized by the creditor and brought before the magistrate.

If the judgment is not satisfied, and no one offers as surety on the debtor's behalf, the creditor may take his debtor and bind his hands or feet with fetters not exceeding fifteen pounds in weight, or less if the creditor so desires.

If he wishes the debtor may find his own sustenance; otherwise the creditor must give him one pound of bread a day, or more if he (the creditor) pleases.

In default of payment or satisfactory security, the debtor may be kept in bonds for sixty days, and during this time the debtor shall, on three successive market days, be brought before the praetor and the amount of the debt shall there be publicly declared.

After the third market day the debtor may be punished with death, or sold beyond the Tiber. If there is more than one creditor the debtor's body may be divided between them, and if the parts be greater or less than they should be, no liability is entailed.

Table IV: Of paternal power

Monstrous or deformed offspring may be immediately destroyed by the father.

A father has absolute power over his legitimate children throughout their life: he may imprison, flog, chain or sell them, or even take their life, however exalted their position and however meritorious their public services.

Three consecutive sales of a son by his father releases the son from the father's power.

A posthumous child born within ten months after the death of the mother's husband is deemed legitimate.

Table V: Of inheritance and tutelage

All females are in perpetual tutelage, except vestal virgins who are free from this tutelage and from paternal power.

Such property of a woman, under the tutelage of her agnates, as requires a formal conveyance for its transfer, cannot be acquired by use unless alienated by the woman herself with the authority of her tutor.

A father may dispose of his entire property as he pleases and may appoint such tutors as he thinks fit.

On intestacy the property of a father goes to the proper heirs and, in default of proper heirs, the nearest agnate takes the inheritance.

Failing an agnate, the inheritance goes to the gens.

In default of tutors appointed by testament the nearest agnate becomes the statutory tutor.

If a lunatic or spendthrift is not provided with a curator, the care of his person and property falls to the agnates or, in default, to the gens.

If a freedman dies intestate and without a proper heir his patron succeeds to his property.

Debts due to or from a deceased person are divided by operation of law between the heirs in proportion to their respective shares in the inheritance.

A division of the inheritance may be achieved by an action for its partition.

A slave freed by testament, on condition of giving a certain sum to the heir, may, if alienated by the heir, obtain his freedom by paying such sum to the alienee.

Table VI: Of ownership and possession

The legal effect of every contract and of every conveyance made with bronze (copper) and scales is determined by the verbal declaration made at the time.

A person who denies that he used the words actually spoken is liable to a penalty of double the value of the subject-matter of the contract or conveyance.

A vendor may make good any faults which have been expressly mentioned, but for any faults which he has expressly denied he must pay a penalty of double damages.

Land may be acquired by use after two years' possession; in the case of other property one year is sufficient.

A husband acquires marital power over a woman by cohabitation for one year, but by absenting herself from her husband's house for three consecutive nights in each year a woman prevents her husband from acquiring marital power over her.

Title by possession, however long, to a Roman citizen's property can never be acquired by an alien.

After the preliminary inquiry as to the right to property, interim possession is given to the party who already possesses; but, if the suit concerns personal freedom, interim possession must be given in favour of the party asserting freedom.

Stolen timber built into a house, or forming supports for vines, cannot be removed, although the owner may bring an action to recover double the value of the timber. If the timber becomes separated it may then be claimed by its owner.

The property in a thing sold and delivered does not pass until the purchaser has paid or otherwise satisfied the vendor.

Conveyances by surrender in court and by bronze and scales are confirmed.

Table VII: Of the law concerning land

A space of two and a half feet must be left around every house.

Boundaries are regulated in accordance with the laws of Solon: thus a fence must be kept within the boundary line; a foot of space must be left outside a wall, two feet outside a house; a space must be left as broad as a ditch or trench is deep and, in the case of a well, six feet must be left. Olives and fig-trees must be kept within nine feet, other trees within five feet, of the boundary.

Conditions relating to villas, farms and country cottages:

A space of five feet must be left between neighbouring fields for the purpose of access and the turning of the plough: this vacant land cannot be acquired by use.

If neighbours disagree on the subject of boundaries, three arbitrators are to be appointed by the magistrate to settle the dispute.

Roads must be at least eight feet broad where straight, and sixteen feet round bends.

Adjoining owners must keep the road free and, if the road becomes impassable, a person may cross their land where he pleases.

If rain-water threatens to cause damage, or the owner of property is prejudiced by the construction of an aqueduct, he may demand a guarantee against threatened damage and recover compensation for damage actually sustained.

Overhanging branches must be lopped 15 feet from the ground. Action can be taken for the removal of a tree leaning over a neighbour's land.

Fruit which falls from a tree onto a neighbour's land may be collected by the owner of the tree.

Table VIII: Of wrongs

If anyone libels another by imputing criminal or immoral acts to him, he shall be scourged to death.

If a man breaks another's limb, and does not offer compensation to the injured party, he is liable to retaliation.

For a broken bone the penalty (if the injured party is a free man) is 300 pound pieces of copper (asses): if the injured party is a slave the penalty is 150.

If a man otherwise injures another the penalty is 25 pound pieces of copper (asses).

In the case of damage accidentally caused compensation is recoverable for the damage sustained.

If a four-footed animal has caused damage compensation is recoverable from its owner or he must surrender the animal to the party aggrieved.

An action lies against anyone who pastures his animals on another's land.

Anyone who by magic arts destroys crops or removes them from one field to another is liable to be punished with death.

For cutting or pasturing on a neighbour's crops by stealth at night the penalty is death, but if the culprit is under the age of puberty he may, at the magistrate's discretion, be scourged, and made liable for double the value of the damage actually caused.

If a man wilfully sets fire to a house or a haystack near a house, if of sound mind he is to be punished by scourging and burning alive. If the fire was the result of negligence, he must make compensation but, if he is too poor, he must be moderately chastised.

The penalty for unlawfully felling another's trees is 25 pound pieces of copper (asses) for every tree.

If a theft is committed at night, and the owner kills the thief, the killing is deemed lawful. If the theft is in the daytime the killing of the thief is not lawful unless he defended himself with a weapon.

A freeman taken in the act of theft in the daytime, and not having defended himself with a weapon, is to be scourged and delivered over to the person from whom he has stolen; if under the age of puberty he is, at the discretion of the magistrate, to be scourged and compelled to compensate for the theft. A slave is to be scourged and then hurled from the Tarpeian rock.

If stolen property is discovered in the thief's possession after a solemn search, wearing only a girdle and holding a plate, the penalty is the same as for a thief taken in the act; but for theft discovered without the prescribed formalities, or for the clandestine deposit of the stolen property on the premises of another, the penalty is three times the value of the thing stolen. For any other kind of theft the penalty is double the value of the thing stolen.

Stolen property cannot be acquired by use.

A person exacting more than the legal interest of eight and a half per cent per annum is liable to fourfold damages.

For fraudulent conduct on the part of a bailee the penalty is double the value of the deposit.

Any citizen may bring an action for the removal of a suspected tutor, and the latter incurs a penalty of double the value of any of the property which he has misappropriated.

A patron who defrauds his client shall be sacrificed to the gods.

A person who has acted as a witness or a scale-bearer, and who refuses to give his evidence, is to be branded infamous and declared incapable of being a witness and of calling upon others to be a witness for him.

False witnesses are to be hurled from the Tarpeian rock.

Anyone who practises magic arts or uses poisonous drugs incurs the penalty of death.

Seditious gatherings in the city by night are forbidden under penalty of death.

Members of corporate bodies may make their own rules provided such rules do not conflict with public law.

Table IX: Of public law

No law shall be passed affecting an individual only: all laws must be of general application.

Only the comitia centuriata has the right of legislating so as to inflict a punishment on a citizen involving his life, his liberty or his citizenship.

A judge or arbitrator appointed by a magistrate to decide a case is to be put to death if he receives a bribe.

There is a right of appeal to the people in cases where a death sentence is passed.

A person who has incited an enemy to make war against the Roman people, or who has delivered up a citizen to the enemy, is to be punished with death.

No one may be put to death except after a formal trial and sentence.

Table X: Of sacred law

Dead bodies must not be buried or burned within the city.

The wood of a funeral pyre must not be smoothed with the axe.

Not more than three mourners wearing mourning robes, or more than one wearing a purple tunic, may attend a funeral, and not more than ten flute players may be hired.

Women must not disfigure their faces, tear their hair or indulge in excessive wailings.

The bones of a deceased person are not to be collected for the purpose of a second funeral unless he died on the field of battle or in a foreign country.

Slaves' bodies must not be embalmed, and drinking bouts, costly besprinklings of the funeral pyre, long garlands and incense boxes are forbidden. However, the deceased is entitled to have placed on his body at the funeral a wreath won by himself or his slaves or horses, or his father may wear it.

No person shall have more than one crier.

Gold must not be buried with the dead, but if teeth are fastened with gold it is not unlawful to bury or burn it with the body.

A funeral pyre or sepulchre must not be placed within sixty feet of another man's house, except with his consent.

Neither a tomb nor its enclosure can be acquired by use.

Table XI: Supplementary laws

Marriage between a patrician and a plebeian is forbidden.

Table XII: Supplementary laws

A creditor may levy distress for the unpaid price of an animal bought for sacrifice, or for the hire of a beast of burden when the amount of the hire was to be spent on a sacrifice.

If a slave commits theft, or does any other damage, his owner may, as an alternative to paying damages, surrender the slave to the party aggrieved.

If a person wrongfully acquires interim possession of a thing which is the subject of litigation, he is to be condemned in double the value of his temporary possession of the thing by the three arbitrators appointed to investigate the case.

A penalty of double its value is payable by a person who consecrates a thing which is the subject of litigation.

Subsequent legislation repeals previous laws inconsistent with it.

(For the circumstances of the publication of the Twelve Tables, see Historical Background, p6.)

4 The Institutes of Justinian - Book One

Title I: Of justice and of law

Justice is the constant and perpetual desire of giving to every man that which is due to him. Jurisprudence is the knowledge of things divine and human, and the exact discernment of what is just and unjust. The precepts of the law are these: to live honestly, not to hurt any man, and to give to everyone that which is his due. The law is divided into public and private. Public law regards the constitution of the state, but private law, with which we are here concerned, is collected from natural precepts, from the law of nations, and from the civil law of any particular city or state.

Title II: Of natural law, the law of nations, and the civil law

The law of nature is not a law to man only, but likewise to all other animals, whether they are produced on the earth, in the air, or in the waters. From hence proceeds the union of male and female, which we call matrimony; from hence arises the procreation of children, and our care in bringing them up. We perceive, also, that the rest of the animal creation are regarded as having a knowledge of this law, by which they are actuated.

Civil law is distinguished from the law of nature because every community (including the people of Rome) uses partly its own particular laws, and partly the general laws which are common to all mankind. That law which a people enacts for the government of itself is called the civil law of that people; but that law which natural reason appoints for all mankind is called the law of nations, because all nations make use of it. All civil laws take their name from that city in which they were established; thus the law which the Roman people make use of is styled the civil law of the Romans. Whenever we mention the words 'civil law' without addition we emphatically denote our own law.

The law of nations is common to mankind in general, and all nations have framed laws through human necessity; for wars arose, and the consequences were captivity and servitude, both which are contrary to the law of nature, for by that all men are free. But almost all contracts, eg, buying, selling, letting and hiring, were at first introduced by the law of nations.

The Roman law is divided into written and unwritten. The written law consists of the laws, the plebiscites, the decrees of the senate, the constitutions of the emperors, the edicts of magistrates, and the answers of the sages of the law.

A law is what the Roman people enact at the request of a magistrate of the Roman people, eg, a consul.

A plebiscite is what the plebeians enact, when requested by the plebeian magistrate, ie, a tribune. The plebiscites, by the Hortensian law, acquired the same force as the laws themselves.

A decree of the senate is what the senate commands and appoints; for, when the people of Rome were increased to a degree which made it difficult for them to assemble for the enacting of laws, it seemed right that the senate should be consulted instead of the whole body of the people.

The constitution of the prince has also the force of a law, for the people, by a law called lex regia, make a concession to him of their whole power. Therefore whatever the emperor ordains by rescript, decree, or edict, it is a law. These acts are called constitutions. Of these some are personal, and are not to be drawn into precedent: other constitutions are general and undoubtedly bind all people.

The edicts of the praetors are also of great authority. These edicts are called the honorary law, because those who bear honours in the state have given them their sanction. The curule aediles also, upon certain occasions, published their edicts, which became part of the honorary law.

The answers of the sages of the law are the opinions of those who were authorised to give their answers concerning matters of law. For anciently they were persons who publicly interpreted the law, and to these the emperors gave a licence for that purpose.

They were called jurisconsulti, and their opinions obtained so great an authority that it was not in the power of a judge to depart from them.

The unwritten law is that which usage has approved, for all customs which are established by the consent of those who use them obtain the force of a law.

The laws of nature, which are observed by all nations, inasmuch as they are the appointment of divine Providence, remain constantly fixed and immutable. But those laws, which every city has enacted for the government of itself, suffer frequent changes, either by tacit consent or by some subsequent law repealing a former.

The laws which we make use of relate either to persons, things, or actions.

Title III: Of the law of persons

The first general division of persons, in respect to their rights, is that all men are either free or slaves. Freedom, from which we are called free, is that natural power which we have of acting as we please, if not hindered by force or restrained by the law. Slavery is that by which one man is made subject to another, according to the law of nations, though contrary to natural right.

Slaves are called servi, or mancipia, and they are either born such, or become so. They are born slaves when they are children of female slaves, and they become slaves either by the law of nations, ie, by captivity, or by the civil law, which happens when a free person, above the age of 20, allows himself to be sold for the sake of sharing the price given for him. In the condition of slaves there are no distinctions, but among those who are free there are many: thus some are ingenui (born free), others libertini (made free, ie, libertines or freedmen).

Title IV: Of persons born free

The term 'ingenuous' denotes a person who is free at the instant of his birth, by being born in matrimony of parents who are both ingenuous, or both libertines, or of parents who differ in condition, the one being ingenuous and the other a libertine. But when the mother is free, although the father is a slave, or even unknown, the child is ingenuous; and when the mother is free at the time of the birth of her infant, although she was a slave when she conceived it, yet such infant will be ingenuous. Also if a woman who was free at the time of conception is afterwards reduced to slavery, and delivered of a child, her issue is, notwithstanding this, freeborn. The child of a woman who is made free during pregnancy, but becomes a slave again before delivery, is also ingenuous.

When any man is by birth ingenuous, it will not injure him to have been in slavery, and to have been afterwards manumitted; for there are many constitutions by which it is enacted that manumission shall not prejudice free birth.

Title V: Of persons made free

'Libertines', or freedmen, are those who have been manumitted from lawful slavery. Manumission implies the giving of liberty: for whoever is in slavery is subject to the hand and power of another; but whoever is manumitted is free from both.

Manumission took its rise from the law of nations, for all men by the law of nature are born in freedom. It is effected in various ways; either in the sacred churches in accordance with the imperial constitutions, or by the vindicta, or in the presence of friends, or by letter, or by testament, or by any other last will. Liberty may also be properly conferred upon a slave by diverse other methods, some of which were introduced by the constitutions of former emperors, and others by our own. Slaves may be manumitted by their masters at any time, even whilst the praetor, the governor of a province, or the proconsul is going to the baths, or to the theatre.

The libertines were formerly distinguished by a three-fold division: some obtained 'the greater liberty' and became Roman citizens; some obtained 'the lesser liberty' and became Latins, according to the law Junia Norbana; and some obtained only 'the inferior liberty' and became dedititii by the law Aelia Sentia. We have entirely abolished the name of dedititii by a constitution and made all the freedmen in general citizens of Rome, regarding neither the age of the person manumitted nor the manumitter, nor any of the forms of manumission as they were anciently observed. We have also introduced many new methods by which slaves may become Roman citizens, and the liberty of becoming such is that alone which can now be conferred.

Title VI: Of those who may not manumit, and why

It is not in the power of every master to manumit at will, for whoever manumits with an intent to defraud his creditors may be said to commit a nullity, the law Aelia Sentia impeding all liberty thus granted. The law Aelia Sentia allows a master who is insolvent to appoint a slave to be his heir with liberty, that thus the slave may obtain his freedom, and become the only and necessary heir of the testator, provided that no other person is also heir by the same testament, and this may happen either because no other person was instituted heir, or because the person so instituted is unwilling to act as such.

By a new act of our humanity a slave also becomes free by being instituted an heir, although no mention was made of liberty in the testament, for it is highly improbable that a testator would be willing that the person whom he hath instituted should remain a slave, since the testator would thus defeat his own purpose and be without an heir.

A man may be said to manumit in order to defraud creditors if he is insolvent at the time when he manumits, or if he becomes insolvent by manumitting. Liberty, when granted, does not fail to take effect unless the manumitter had an intent to defraud, although his goods are insufficient for the payment of his creditors: it only fails to take effect when creditors are doubly defrauded, ie, both by the intention of the manumitter and in reality.

By the law Aelia Sentia a master under the age of twenty years cannot manumit, unless a just cause is established. Such a just cause must be approved by a council appointed for that purpose, at whose command liberty is conferred by the vindicta. A just cause is established when it is alleged that the person to be manumitted is his father or mother, his son or daughter, his brother or sister, his teacher, his nurse, his foster-child or his foster-brother or foster-sister; or when he alleges that he would manumit his slave in order that he might manage his (the manumitter's) affairs; or a female slave, with intent to marry her, on condition that the marriage is performed within six months. A slave under 17 years of age cannot be manumitted for the purpose of managing the manumitter's affairs.

While any person who was 14 complete might make a testament, institute an heir, and bequeath legacies, by the law Aelia Sentia no person under twenty could confer liberty by this method. This could not be tolerated and we therefore permit all who are in their 18th year to confer liberty by testament.

Title VII: Of the repeal of the law Fusia Caninia

By the law Fusia Caninia all masters were restrained from manumitting more than a certain number by testament, but we have thought proper to abrogate this law, judging it inhuman that, whilst persons in health should have power to manumit a whole family if no just cause impedes the manumission, those who are dying should be prohibited from doing the same thing by testament.

Title VIII: Of those who are free from power, and of those who are in the power of others

We now proceed to another division of persons, for some are independent, and some are subject to the power of others. Of those who are subject to others, some are in the power of parents, others in the power of their masters. Our first inquiry concerns those who are in the power of masters.

All slaves are in the power of their masters, which power is derived from the law of nations, by which law masters have the power of life and death over their slaves and whatsoever is acquired by the slave is acquired for the master. Today all men subject to our rule are prohibited to inflict any extraordinary punishment upon their slaves without lawful cause or with excessive severity. A constitution of the emperor Antoninus provides that whoever kills his own slave without a just cause is not to be punished with less rigour than if he had killed a slave who was the property of another. By another constitution of the same emperor it was ordained that if the severity of masters should appear at any time excessive, they might be compelled to sell their slaves on equitable terms, the price paid being given to the masters. This constitution is just and reasonable because the welfare of the state demands that no person should be permitted to misuse even his own property.

Title IX: Of paternal power

The children whom we have begotten in lawful wedlock are under our power. Matrimony is a social contract between a man and woman, obliging them to an inseparable cohabitation during life. The issue of yourself and your legal wife are immediately under your own power. Also issue of a son and son's wife, ie, either grandsons or granddaughters by them, are equally in your power; the same may be said of great-grandchildren, etc. But children born of a daughter will not be in your power, but in the power of their own father, or father's father, etc.

Title X: Of marriage

The citizens of Rome contract valid matrimony when they unite according to the law, the males having arrived at puberty, and the females having attained to a marriageable age: if they are children of a family they must first obtain the consent of the parents under whose power they are. A constitution of ours allows the son as well as the daughter of a madman to marry without the intervention of his father.

Matrimony must not be contracted between parents and their children, a grandfather and his granddaughter, a grandmother and her grandson: the same prohibition extends to all ascendants and descendants, including those by adoption and even after the adoption is dissolved. A brother and sister are forbidden to marry, whether they are the children of the same father and mother, or of either. If any person becomes your sister by adoption, as long as such adoption subsists a marriage contracted between her and you cannot be valid, but when the adoption is destroyed by emancipation, she may then be taken to wife. If you yourself are emancipated, there will not then remain any impediment, although your sister by adoption is not so. From hence it appears that if a man would adopt his son-in-law, he should first emancipate his daughter, and that whoever would adopt his daughter-in-law should previously emancipate his son.

It is unlawful to marry the daughter of a brother or a sister; neither is it lawful to marry the granddaughter of a brother or sister, although they are in the fourth degree. There is not any impediment against the marriage of a son with the daughter of her whom his father has adopted, for they bear not to each other any relation either natural or civil. The children of two brothers or two sisters, or of a brother and sister, may legally be joined together in matrimony.

A man is not permitted to marry his aunt on the father's side, although she is only so by adoption; neither can a man marry his aunt on the mother's side because they are both esteemed to be the representatives of parents. And for the same reason no person can contract matrimony with his great-aunt, on either his father's or his mother's side.

It is unlawful to marry a wife's daughter or a son's wife, in that both are in the place of daughters; and this rule must be understood to relate not only to those who actually are, but also to those who have been, our daughters-in-law at any time. It is unlawful for a man to have two wives at the same time.

A man is forbidden to marry his wife's mother and his father's wife, because they both hold the place of mothers: this rule must be observed even when the relationship by affinity is dissolved. No woman may have two husbands at the same time.

The son of a husband by a former wife, and the daughter of a wife by a former husband, or vice versa, may lawfully contract matrimony, even though a brother or sister is born of such second marriage between their respective parents. If a wife, after divorce, brings forth a daughter by a second husband, such daughter is not to be reckoned a daughter-in-law to the first husband, although Julian thought that we should abstain from such marriages.

The relationship between slaves is an impediment to matrimony, as when a father and daughter, or a brother and sister, are manumitted.

There are, besides these already mentioned, many other persons who, for diverse reasons, are prohibited to marry with each other, all of whom we have caused to be enumerated in the Digest, collected from the old law.

If any persons presume to cohabit together in contempt of the rules which we have here laid down, they shall not be deemed husband and wife, neither shall their marriage, or any portion given on account of such marriage, be valid; and the children born in such cohabitation (spurii, or spurious children) shall not be under the power of their father. After the dissolution of any such marriage no portion can be legally recovered, and those who contract such prohibited matrimony must undergo the further punishments set forth in our constitutions.

It sometimes happens that the children who at the time of their birth were not under the power of their parents are reduced under it afterwards. Thus a natural son who is made a decurion (ie, a member of a local council) becomes subject to his father's power, and he also who is born of a free woman with whom marriage was in no way prohibited by law, but with whom the father was merely cohabiting, will likewise become subject to the power of his father as soon as the marriage instruments are drawn up in accordance with the provisions of our constitution.

Title XI: Of adoption

Not only are all natural children subject to paternal power, but those also whom we adopt. Adoption is made either by a rescript from the emperor or by the authority of a magistrate. The imperial rescript empowers us to adopt persons of either sex who are sui juris and not under the power of parents: this form of adoption is called adrogation. By the authority of the magistrate we adopt persons actually under the power of their parents, whether they are in the first degree, as sons and daughters, or in an inferior degree, as grandchildren and great-grandchildren.

But today, by our constitution, when the son of a family is given in adoption by his natural father to a stranger, the right of paternal power in the natural father is not dissolved, neither does anything pass to the adoptive father, neither is the adopted son in his power, although such son is allowed by us to have a right of succession to his adoptive father if he dies intestate. But if a natural father should give his son in adoption not to a stranger, but to the maternal grandfather of such son – or if a natural father, who has been emancipated, should give his son, begotten after emancipation, to his paternal or maternal grandfather or great-grandfather – then, the rights of nature and adoption concurring, the power of the adoptive father is established both by natural ties and legal adoption, so that the adopted son would be both in the family and under the power of his adoptive father.

When any person not arrived at puberty is adrogated by the imperial rescript, the cause is first inquired into, that it may be known whether the adrogation is justly founded and advantageous for the pupil; for such adrogation is always made on certain conditions, namely, the adrogator must give security to a public notary that if the pupil should die within the age of puberty he will restore all the goods and effects of such pupil to those who would have succeeded him if no adrogation had taken place. The adrogator is also forbidden to emancipate the one whom he has adrogated, unless he has given legal proof that his adrogated son deserves to be emancipated; even then he is bound to make full restitution of all things belonging to such son. Also, if a father upon his death-bed disinherits his adrogated son, or when in health emancipates him without just cause, the father is commanded to leave the fourth part of all his goods to his son, in addition to that which such son brought to him at the time of adrogation and acquired for him afterwards.

A person is not permitted to adopt a person older than himself and he who would adopt or adrogate should be senior to his adopted or adrogated son by full puberty, ie, by 18 years. It is lawful to adopt a person, either as a grandson or granddaughter, great-grandson or great-granddaughter, or in a more distant degree, although the adopter has no son, and a man may adopt the son of another as his grandson, and the grandson of another as his son. However, if any man who has already either a natural or an adopted son wishes to adopt another as his grandson, the consent of his son, whether natural or adopted, should first be obtained, but if a grandfather is willing to give his grandson in adoption, the consent of the son is not necessary.

He who is either adopted or adrogated is in many respects in a similar position to a son born in lawful matrimony, and may be given in adoption to another.

It is a common rule, both in adoption and adrogation, that an impotent person may adopt, but those who are castrated cannot adopt. Women cannot adopt as they cannot have even their own children under their power, but when death has deprived them of their own children the emperor may allow them to adopt others as a comfort and recompense for their loss.

If a person having children under his power gives himself in adrogation, both he as a son and his children as grandchildren would become subject to the power of the adrogator.

Ancient lawyers approved the view that slaves adopted by their masters obtain freedom by the adoption. Guided by this opinion we have enacted by our constitution that a slave whom any master nominates to be his son in the presence of a magistrate becomes free by such nomination, although it does not convey to him the rights of a son.

Title XII: Of the means by which persons are released from the powers of others

Those who are under the power of a parent become independent at his death, but by the death of a grandfather his grandchildren do not become independent, unless it happens that there is an impossibility of their ever falling under the power of their father. Therefore, if their father is alive at the death of their grandfather, and they are till then under his power, the grandchildren become subject to the power of their father; but if their father is either dead or emancipated before the death of their grandfather, they then cannot fall under the power of their father, and they become independent.

If a man upon conviction of some crime is deported into an island, he loses the rights of a Roman citizen and his children cease to be under his power. Likewise, if a son is deported, he ceases to be under the power of his father; but if, through the clemency of the emperor, a criminal is wholly restored, he regains instantly his former condition. A father who is relegated to an island (a less serious punishment than deportation) retains his paternal power, and a son who is relegated remains under the power of his father.

A man judicially pronounced to be the slave of punishment (ie, condemned to the mines or sentenced to be destroyed by wild beasts) loses his paternal power.

The son of a family who becomes a soldier, a senator or a consul remains under the power of his father, but it is enacted by our constitution that the patrician dignity, conferred by our special diploma, shall free every son from all paternal subjection.

If a parent is taken prisoner by the enemy, although he becomes a slave, he does not lose his paternal power which remains in suspense by reason of the right of postliminium: when captives obtain their liberty they are repossessed of all their former rights, including paternal power. If a prisoner dies in captivity his son is deemed to have become independent from the time when his father was taken prisoner. When a son or grandson becomes a prisoner the power of the parent is only in suspense.

Children also cease to be under the power of their parents by emancipation. Emancipation was effected, according to our ancient law, either by imaginary sales and intervening manumissions, or by the imperial rescript, but now by an express constitution parents may have immediate recourse to the proper judge or magistrate and emancipate the children, grandchildren, etc, of both sexes. By a praetorian edict the parent is allowed to have the same right in the goods of those whom he emancipates as a patron has in the goods of his freedmen. Further, if the children emancipated are within the age of puberty, the parent by whom they were emancipated obtains the right of wardship or tutelage by the emancipation.

A parent having a son under his power, and by that son a grandson or granddaughter, may emancipate his son and yet retain his grandchild in his power. He may also manumit his grandchild and still retain his son under his power, or he may make them all independent.

If a father gives his son in adoption to the natural grandfather or great-grandfather of such son, strictly adhering to the rules laid down in our constitutions for that purpose, the right of parental power passes wholly from the natural father to the adoptor.

Where a son's wife has conceived, and you emancipate that son or give him in adoption during the wife's pregnancy, nevertheless the child which she brings forth will be born under your parental authority.

Children, either natural or adopted, can rarely compel their parents by any method to dismiss them from their power.

Title XIII: Of tutorship

Of those who are not in the power of their parents, some are under a tutor, some are under a curator, and some are not under either.

Servius defined tutelage (tutorship) as an authority and power given and permitted by the civil law and exercised over such independent persons who are unable, by reason of their age, to protect themselves. Tutors are those who have such authority and power.

Parents are permitted to appoint tutors by testament to such of their children who have not reached the age of puberty and are under their power. This privilege of parents extends without exception over sons and daughters, but grandfathers can only give tutors to their grandchildren when it is impossible that such grandchildren should ever fall under the power of their father after the death of their grandfather. Therefore, if your son is in your power at the time of your death, your grandchildren by that son cannot receive tutors by your testament, although they were actually in your power, because at your decease they will become subject to the power of their father.

Tutors may be given by the testament of a parent to a posthumous child as well as to those already born if such posthumous child, had he been born in the lifetime of his father, would have been his proper heir and under his power. If a father gives a tutor by testament to his emancipated son, such tutor must be confirmed by order of the governor of the province.

Title XIV: Of those who can be appointed tutors by testament

Not only the father of a family may be appointed by testament to be a tutor, but also the son of a family. A man may by testament appoint his own slave to be a tutor, at the same time giving him his liberty, but if no mention is made of liberty, the slave tacitly receives immediate liberty and may therefore lawfully act as a tutor; the opposite is the case where a testator erroneously imagines that his slave whom he has appointed tutor is a free person. The unconditional appointment of another man's slave to be a tutor is invalid, but if the appointment is made upon condition that the person appointed obtains his freedom, it is good. However, if a man by testament appoints his own slave to be a tutor 'when he shall obtain his liberty', the appointment is void.

If a madman or a minor is by testament appointed to be a tutor, the one shall begin to act when he becomes of sound mind, and the other when he has completed his 25th year. A testamentary tutor may be appointed up to a certain time, or from a certain time, or conditionally, or before the institution of an heir.

A tutor appointed for 'sons' and 'daughters' is also tutor to a posthumous son or daughter, but not to grandchildren; the general term 'children' would include grandchildren.

Title XV: Of tutorship by the law of agnates

By the law of the Twelve Tables agnates (agnati) are appointed to be tutors to those to whom no testamentary tutor was given: such tutors are called statutory tutors.

Agnates are those who are collaterally related to us by males, as a brother by the same father, or a son of a brother, or by him a grandson; also a father's brother, or the son of such brother, or by him a grandson. Those who are related to us by a female are cognates, ie, they bear only a natural relation to us. Thus the son of a father's sister is not related to you by agnation, but by cognation; and you are related to him in the same manner, ie, by cognation.

This provision of the law of the Twelve Tables applies equally to those who are intestate and to those who are intestate only in respect of tutelage, ie, where a tutor appointed by testament dies during the testator's lifetime.

The civil law right of agnation (but not the natural right of cognation) is taken away by almost every diminution or change of status.

Title XVI: Of changes in status

Diminution is the change of a man's former condition which is effected in the following three ways:

The greatest diminution when a man loses both the rights of a citizen and his liberty; this occurs in the case of those who by the rigour of their sentence are pronounced to be the slaves of punishment, when freedmen are condemned to slavery for ingratitude to their patrons, and where men suffer themselves to be sold in order to share the price.

The less or mesne diminution when a man loses the rights of a citizen, but retains his liberty; this occurs when a man is forbidden the use of fire and water or is transported into an island.

The least diminution when the condition of a man is changed without the forfeiture either of his civil rights or his liberty; this occurs when he who is independent becomes subject to the power of another by adoption or when the son of a family is emancipated by his father.

The manumission of a slave does not effect any change of status because before manumission a slave has no status or civil capacity: those whose dignity is changed, eg, by being removed from the senatorial dignity, do not suffer diminution.

Rights of cognation are destroyed by the greatest and the less diminution, but remain after the least diminution.

Although the rights of tutelage belong to agnates, they do not belong to all agnates in common, but to those only who are in the nearest degree. If there are many in the same degree, eg, several brothers, the rights of tutelage belong to them all within that degree.

Title XVII: Of tutelage (tutorship) by the law of patrons

By the same law of the Twelve Tables, the tutelage of freedmen and freedwomen is adjudged to belong to their patrons, and to the children of such patrons; this tutelage is called statutory, because it is firmly established by interpretation as if it had been introduced by express words. For, since the law commands that patrons and their children shall succeed to the inheritance of their freedmen or freedwomen who die intestate, it was the opinion of the ancient lawyers that tutelage also by implication should belong to patrons and their children. However, when any person not arrived at puberty is manumitted by a female, such female is called to the inheritance, but not to the tutelage.

Titles XVIII, XIX: Of tutelage by the law of ascendants and fiduciary tutelage

Similarly, if a parent emancipates a son or a daughter, a grandson or a granddaughter, or any other of his children not arrived at puberty, he is then their statutory tutor, but at his death his male children of age become the fiduciary tutors of their own sons, or of a brother or sister, or of a brother's children emancipated by the deceased. But when a patron who is a statutory tutor dies, his children also become statutory tutors because they do not fall under the power of their father's brothers and therefore cannot be under their statutory tutelage. The condition of a slave is not changed by the death of his master because he becomes a slave to the children of the deceased.

The persons above mentioned cannot be called to be tutors unless they are of full age, a rule which, by our constitution, applies generally to all tutelage (tutorships) and curations (curatorships).

Title XX: Of the Atilian and Julia-Titian tutors

By virtue of the law Atilia, the praetor of the city, with a majority of the tribunes, had authority to assign tutors to all such who were not otherwise entitled to tutors, but in the provinces tutors were appointed by the respective governors of each province, in consequence of the law Julia and Titia. Thus if a tutor had been given by testament conditionally, or from a certain day, another tutor might have been appointed by virtue of the above-named laws whilst the condition was unfulfilled or till the day came. Again, if a tutor was taken by the enemy, another tutor was requested under the provisions of these same laws, but his office ceased when the first tutor returned from captivity, for he then resumed the tutelage by his right of return.

Appointments were no longer made under the Atilian and Julia-Titian laws when the consuls began to give tutors to pupils of either sex, after inquiry: the praetors were afterwards given the same authority by the imperial constitutions. Under the Atilian and Julia-Titian laws no security was required from tutors that property would be kept intact for the benefit of their pupils, and tutors could not be compelled to perform the duties of their office.

Under our present practice at Rome the prefect of the city, or the praetor, according to his jurisdiction, and in the provinces the governors, may appoint tutors after inquiry into their morals and circumstances; an inferior magistrate, at the command of a governor, may also appoint tutors, if the possessions of the pupil are not large.

We, however, have ordained by our constitution that the judge of Alexandria, and the magistrates of every city, together with the chief ecclesiastic, may give tutors or curators to pupils or adults whose fortunes do not exceed 500 aurei, without waiting for the command of the governor to whose province they belong. All such magistrates must take from every tutor so appointed the security required by our constitution.

It is agreeable to the law of nature that those who have not arrived at puberty should be put under tutelage, to the intent that all who are not adults may be under the government of proper persons. Tutors may be compelled to render an account, by the action of tutelage, when their pupils arrive at puberty.

Title XXI: Of the authority of tutors

When a man stipulates to make a gift to a pupil, the authority of the tutor is not required, but the opposite is the case when a pupil enters into a contract because it is an established rule that pupils may better their condition, but not impair it, without the authority of their tutors. Thus in the case of all contracts which give rise to mutual obligations, eg, buying and selling, he who contracts with a pupil is bound by the contract, but the pupil is not bound unless the tutor has given his authority.

However, no pupil without the authority of his tutor can enter upon an inheritance, or apply for the possession of goods, or take an inheritance in trust: in these cases there is a probability of profit – there is also a possibility of loss.

A tutor must be present at the negotiations in order to give his authority; it is of no effect if given by letter, by messenger, or after a contract has been concluded.

When an action is to be commenced between a tutor and his pupil, as a tutor cannot exercise his authority as tutor against himself, a curator (not a praetorian tutor as was formerly the custom) is appointed, by whose intervention the suit is carried on. When the action is concluded the curatorship ceases.

Title XXII: Of the termination of tutorship

Pupils, both male and female, are freed from tutelage when they arrive at puberty. The ancients judged of puberty in males not by years only, but also by their physical development; by our sacred constitution we have enacted that puberty in males should be reputed to commence immediately after the completion of their fourteenth year. In relation to females we leave unaltered the ancient law by which they are esteemed marriageable after the completion of their twelfth year.

Tutelage is determined before puberty if the pupil is either adrogated, or suffers deportation; it also determines if he is reduced to slavery, or becomes a captive. If a testamentary tutor is given upon a certain condition, the tutelage ceases after that condition is fulfilled. Tutelage is also determined by the death either of the tutor or of the pupil.

When a tutor suffers the greatest or the less diminution of status every kind of tutelage comes to an end, but if the least diminution only is suffered, only statutory tutelage is extinguished. Every diminution of status in pupils takes away all tutelage.

Testamentary tutors for a term only are discharged from the tutelage at the expiration of that term. Tutorship is also determined where a tutor is removed from office upon suspicion of misconduct, or where he exempts himself from the burden of tutelage for just reasons.

Title XXIII: Of curators

Males arrived at puberty and females of marriageable age receive curators until they have completed their 25th year; until they reach that age they are not old enough to take a proper care of their own affairs.

Curators are appointed by the same magistrates who appoint tutors. A curator cannot be absolutely given by testament as such an appointment must be confirmed by either a praetor or the governor of a province. No person can be obliged to receive curators except for a law suit, for a curator may be appointed for a special purpose.

By a law of the Twelve Tables all madmen and prodigals, although of full age (ie, over 25), must nevertheless be under the curation of their agnates. But if there are no agnates, or those who exist are unqualified, curators are appointed at Rome by the prefect of the city, or the praetor, and in the provinces by the governors, after the requisite inquiry. Those who are of feeble mind, or deaf or mute or subject to any continual malady, must be placed under curators.

Sometimes even pupils receive curators, eg, when the statutory tutor is unqualified, because a tutor must not be given to him who already has a tutor. If a testamentary tutor, or a tutor appointed by a praetor or the governor of a province, appears afterwards to be incapable of executing his trust, it is usual, although he is guilty of no fraud, to appoint a curator to act with him. It is also usual to appoint curators in place of such tutors who are not wholly excused, but excused for a time only.

If a tutor, by illness or any other cause, is prevented from personally executing his office, and the pupil is absent or an infant, the praetor or the governor of the province shall appoint by decree any person whom the tutor approves to be the pupil's agent, for whose conduct the tutor must be answerable.

Title XXIV: Of the security to be given by tutors and curators

The praetor must ensure that tutors and curators give sufficient security for the safety and indemnification of their pupils. However, this is not always necessary, for a testamentary tutor is not compelled to give security, and the same exemption applies to tutors and curators appointed after inquiry.

If two or more are appointed by testament, or by a magistrate, after inquiry, to be tutors or curators, any one of them, by offering security, may be preferred to the sole administration, or cause his co-tutor or co-curator to give security in order to be admitted himself to the administration. When no security is offered, if the testator has appointed any particular person to act, such person must be preferred, but if no particular person is specified by the testator, the administration must be committed to such person or persons whom a majority of the tutors shall elect, according to the praetorian edict; if they disagree in their choice, the praetor must interpose his authority. The same rule applies when many, either tutors or curators, are nominated to the magistrate, ie, a majority of them may appoint one of their number to administer.

Tutors and curators are liable to an action on account of the administration of the affairs of pupils, minors and others under their protection, because a subsidiary action, which is the last remedy to be used, lies against a magistrate either for entirely omitting to take sureties, or for taking such as are insufficient. Such an action extends even against the heir of any such magistrate, but does not lie against the prefect of the city, nor the praetor, nor the governor of a province, nor any other person who has power to appoint tutors; it lies only against those magistrates who are liable to extract the security. By the same constitutions which enable a subsidiary action to be brought against heirs of such magistrates it is expressly enacted that all tutors and curators who refuse to give security may be compelled to do so.

Title XXV: Of grounds of exemption of tutors and curators

Persons nominated to be either tutors or curators may, for various reasons, excuse themselves; but the most general excuse is that of having living children, whether they are in power or emancipated. At Rome, if a man has three children living (in Italy four, in the provinces five) he may be excused from tutelage and curation as from other public offices. Adopted children will not excuse the adopter, although they will excuse their natural father who gave them in adoption. Also grandchildren by a son, when they succeed in the place of their father, will excuse their grandfather; yet grandchildren by a daughter will not excuse him. Normally only those children who are living can excuse from tutelage and curation, but children who have fallen in battle count for this purpose.

The emperor Marcus Aurelius declared by rescript that whoever is engaged in the administration of affairs relating to the treasury may be excused from tutelage and curation whilst he is so employed. Those who are absent on the affairs of the state are exempt from tutelage and curation; if they have already been appointed a tutor or curator then a curator is appointed in their place, but when such tutors return they must again take up the burden of the tutelage.

By a rescript of the emperor Marcus all superior magistrates may, as such, excuse themselves, but they cannot abandon a tutelage once they have undertaken it. No man can excuse himself from taking the office of a tutor or curator by alleging a law suit with a pupil or minor, unless the suit is for all the goods or the whole inheritance of such pupil or minor. Three tutelages or curatorships, which are not acquired merely for advantage, will exempt a man during their continuance from the burden of a fourth, but the tutelage or curation of several pupils, eg, of brothers, counts only as a single tutelage or curation.

Additional grounds of excuse are:

poverty, when it can be proved to be such as must render a man incapable of the burden imposed upon him;

illness, when it is so great as to prevent a man from transacting his own business;

illiteracy, although in some cases an illiterate man may not be incapable of the administration;

enmity, ie, where a father through enmity appoints any particular person by testament to be tutor to his children, unless such person has promised the father that he would so act;

deadly enmity, unless there has been a reconciliation;

that the person appointed has had his status called in question by the father of the pupil;

age, ie, that the person appointed is above 70 years of age.

Minors, as such, were formerly excusable, but by our constitution they are now prohibited from being tutors or curators. The fact that the person appointed was unknown to the father of a pupil is not in itself a sufficient excuse, but no military person, although willing, can become a tutor or curator. Both at Rome and in the provinces all grammarians, teachers of rhetoric and physicians, who exercise their professions within their own country, are exempted from tutelage and curation.

A person who can bring forward many excuses, but has failed in those which he has already given, may yet give others within the time prescribed. A person living within 100 miles of the place where he was appointed must make his excuses to the proper magistrate within 50 days of learning of his appointment; if the distance is more than 100 miles the time is one day for every 20 miles, and 30 days besides, but this time is calculated so as never to be less than 50 days.

When a tutor is appointed he is considered to have the care of his pupil's whole estate.

He who has been the tutor of a minor cannot be compelled to become his curator, and by the rescript of the emperors Severus and Antoninus, although the father of a family should by testament appoint any person to be the first tutor of his children, and afterwards their curator, if the person so appointed in unwilling to undertake the curation, he is by no means compellable. The same emperors also enacted that a husband may excuse himself from being a curator to his wife, even after he has begun to act.

If any man succeeds by false allegations in getting himself dismissed from the office of tutor he is not released from the burden of the office.

Title XXVI: Of suspected tutors or curators

Proceedings by way of accusation of suspected tutors or curators are derived from the law of the Twelve Tables. At Rome the power of removing suspected tutors belongs to the praetor, and in the provinces to the governors or to the legate of the proconsul.

All tutors may become suspected, whether testamentary or otherwise; anyone may accuse them. By rescript of the emperors Severus and Antoninus even women are allowed to be accusers, yet only those who are impelled to it by their duty or by their relation to the minor. Thus a mother, a nurse or a grandmother may become accusers, as also may a sister. Indeed, the praetor can at his discretion admit any woman who appears to have no other motive than to relieve the injured. No pupil can bring an accusation of suspicion against his tutor, but adults are permitted, when they act by advice of persons related to them, to accuse their curators.

Although he is solvent, a tutor may be pronounced suspected if he does not faithfully execute his trust. A tutor may be removed from his office as suspected even before he has begun to execute it. Any person removed upon suspicion on the ground of fraud is stigmatised with infamy, but this is not so if he is removed for negligence.

If any tutor is accused upon suspicion, according to Papinian his administration is suspended while the accusation is being considered. If he dies while the proceedings are pending, the accusation is dropped.

If a tutor fails to appear, with the intent to defer the making of an allowance for the maintenance of his pupil, the pupil is put into possession of his tutor's effects and a curator is appointed in order that those things which would deteriorate by delay may be sold. Therefore, any tutor who, by absenting himself, impedes the grant of an allowance to his pupil, may be removed as suspected. If a tutor makes a personal appearance, and falsely avers that the effects of his pupil are insufficient for an allowance, such tutor shall be remitted to the prefect of the city, and punished by him in the same manner as if he had acquired a tutelage by bribery. A freedman who is proved to have fraudulently administered the tutelage of the son or grandson of his patron must be sent to the prefect to be punished.

Lastly, they who unfaithfully administer their trust, must be immediately removed from it, although they offer sufficient security. We also deem every man suspected whose immoralities give cause for it, but a tutor or curator cannot be removed as a suspected person merely on account of poverty.

5 The Institutes of Justinian - Book Two

Title I: Of the division of things

Let us now inquire concerning things, which may be divided into those which can and those which cannot come within our patrimony and be acquired; for some things are in common among mankind in general, some are public, some universal, and some are such to which no man can have a right. Most things are the private property of individuals, by whom they are variously acquired.

Those things which are given to mankind in common by the law of nature are the air, running water, the sea and the shores of the sea. No man is prohibited from approaching any part of the sea-shore, provided he does not commit any acts of violence in destroying houses, etc, which are private property.

All rivers and ports are public and the right to fish in ports and rivers is common to all. All land over which the highest winter tide extends is sea-shore. By the law of nations the use of the banks of rivers is also public and all persons may bring their vessels to the land to unload them, and fasten ropes to trees upon the bank. Nevertheless, the banks of a river are the property of those who own the adjoining land and trees growing on the banks are also their property.

The use of the sea-shore is also public and common by the law of nations, as is the use of the sea: therefore any person may build a hut there or dry his nets, for the shores are not the property of any man.

Theatres, race-courses and similar things which belong to the whole city are universal or corporate property and not the property of any particular person. Things sacred, religious and holy (or sanctioned) cannot be vested in any person as his own. Those things which have been consecrated by the pontiffs are deemed sacred; they include churches and all moveable things which have been properly dedicated to the service of God. By our constitution sacred things cannot be alienated or pledged, except for the purpose of the redemption of captives. According to Papinian, the very ground on which a sacred edifice has once been erected will continue to be sacred although the edifice is destroyed.

Anyone may make any place of his own religious by making it the repository of a dead body, but if the land is jointly owned the other joint owner must consent to the land being used in this way. However, in the case of a sepulchre held in common one joint owner may make use of it without the consent of the others. Where there is a proprietor and a usufructuary of the same place, the proprietor cannot without the consent of the usufructuary render it religious. It is lawful to lay the body of a dead person in a place belonging to any man who has given his consent and, although he dissents after the burial, the place will have become religious.

Holy things also, eg, the walls and gates of a city, are in a way of divine right, and therefore the property of no man. The walls of a city are said to be sanctioned, or holy, because any offence against them always leads to capital punishment.

There are various means by which things become the property of private persons. Of some things we obtain ownership by the law of nature which, as we have already said, is also called the law of nations; we acquire ownership of other things by the civil law.

Wild beasts, birds and fish do, as soon as they are taken, become instantly, by the law of nations, the property of the captor; it is not material whether they are taken by a man upon his own ground or upon the ground of another, although that other could have prohibited him from entering upon his ground had he foreseen the intent. If wild beasts or birds escape and recover their natural liberty the right of the captor ceases and they become the property of the first who seizes them; they are said to have recovered their natural liberty if they have run or flown out of sight, or cannot without difficulty be pursued and retaken. If a wild beast is wounded so that it can easily be taken, it does not become the property of the person who wounded it until he actually takes it.

Bees are also wild by nature and they do not become your property until you enclose them in a hive; it is not sufficient to show that they swarmed on your tree. Honeycombs become the property of him who takes them, although you may forbid a person to enter upon your land for this purpose. A swarm which has flown from your hive remains yours as long as it remains in sight and may easily be pursued; in other cases it becomes the property of the first occupant.

With regard to wild birds and animals which have the habit of going and returning, eg, peacocks and pigeons and even tame deer, the rule is that they remain yours as long as they appear to retain an inclination to return; if this inclination ceases, ie, they lose the habit of returning, they are no longer yours and they become the property of him who takes them.

Geese and fowls are not wild by nature and if they take flight they remain yours wherever they may be found and although you lost sight of them. Whoever detains such animals with a view to profit is guilty of theft.

All those things which we take from our enemies in war become instantly our own by the law of nations, but if they (including a freeman taken as a slave) afterwards escape and return to their own people, they obtain again their former state.

Precious stones, pearls and other things which are found upon the sea-shore become instantly by the law of nations the property of the finder. The product of those animals of which we are the owners and masters is by the same law deemed to be our own.

The ground which a river has added to your land by alluvion, ie, by an imperceptible increase, is property acquired by you according to the law of nations, but if a river severs a portion of your land, and adjoins it to that of your neighbour, such part continues to be yours. However, if it remains for a long time joined to your neighbour's land and trees carried off with it take root in his land, from that time both the land and the trees are deemed to have become acquired by your neighbour's estate.

When an island rises in the sea the property of it is in the first occupant, but if an island rises in a river and is placed exactly in the middle of it, such island belongs in common to those who own the lands near the banks on each side of the river, according to the proportion of the length of each man's estate along the bank. If the island is nearer to one side than the other, it belongs to them only who own lands next to the bank on that side to which the island is nearer. If a river divides itself, and afterwards unites again, having reduced a tract of land into the form of an island, the land still remains the property of him whose it was.

If a river begins to flow in a new channel, the original channel belongs to the riparian owners in proportion to the length of their estate next to the banks; the new channel acquires the character of a river and becomes public. If the river returns to its original channel the new channel becomes the property of those who own land along its banks. Ownership of land is not affected by temporary flooding.

Where a man has made a thing out of materials belonging to another, eg, wine out of grapes, flour from corn, a vessel out of gold, a garment out of wool or a ship from timber, if the thing can be reduced to its original raw material, the owner of the material is also the owner of the thing made out of it, but if the thing cannot be so reduced, he who made it is the owner. If a man makes a thing partly with his own materials and partly with the materials of another, eg, where a man makes a garment using his own and another's wool, he who made it is also the owner as he not only gave his labour but also provided part of the material. If any man interweaves the purple of another into his own vestment, the purple appertains to the vestment by accession and he who was the owner of the purple may have an action of theft and a personal action (a condiction) against the one who took it. A condiction for the recovery of the value of the purple may be brought against the thief or against any other possessor.

If the materials of two persons, eg, wine or gold, are with their consent or by accident mingled together the resulting mass or composition is common to both. Where, eg, the corn of one person is mixed with the corn of another, if the mixture was by consent the result will be common, but if the intermixture was accidental or without consent the result is not common because the corns of grain still remain distinct in substance; in this latter case if one person retains the whole of the corn the other has an action in rem for the recovery of his portion.

If a man constructs a building on his own land he is the owner of the building even if he used the materials of another and by the law of the Twelve Tables he cannot be compelled to restore such materials. However, that other remains the owner of the materials and by an action de tigno juncto he may recover double the value. Should the building at any time be destroyed, unless he has already recovered double the value, he may claim the actual materials which are his and sue for their production.

On the other hand, if a man knowingly builds a house with his own materials on another's land, the house and the materials become the property of the owner of the land; even if the house falls he cannot claim the materials. However, if the builder was in possession of the land and acted in good faith and the owner refuses to pay the price of the material and the wages of the workmen, the owner may be repelled by an exception of fraud.

If you set another man's plant in your own ground the plant becomes yours; conversely, if you set your plant in the land of another, the plant becomes his. In either case until the plant takes root it remains his whose it was. Trees become the property of him in whose ground they have cast their roots; if a tree planted near a boundary extends its roots into the land of another, such tree becomes common to both landowners.

Similarly, grain belongs to the owner of the soil in which it is sown, but – as with houses – he who at his own expense and acting in good faith has sown in another's land may protect himself by an exception of fraud.

Letters, although written with gold, appertain to the paper or parchment upon which they are written, and if you write a poem upon the paper or parchment of another the whole belongs to that other; but if he demands his books or parchments from you, and at the same time refuses to defray the expense of the writing, you may defend yourself by an exception of fraud, provided you obtained possession of the papers or parchments in good faith, ie, honestly, and believing them to be your own.

If a man paints a picture on the tablet of another, the tablet accedes to the picture, but if the painter fails to offer the price of the tablet, his claim to the work may be defeated by an exception of fraud. However, if the painter is in possession of the work, the owner of the tablet has an action called utilis, and if the owner of the tablet omits to tender the value of the picture, he may be repelled by an exception of fraud if the painter possessed the tablet in good faith. If the tablet was taken feloniously, the owner has an action for theft.

If a person purchases land or obtains it by way of gift or any other lawful means in good faith from a person who is not the owner, the fruits of that land which he has gathered shall be his own, and if the true owner of the land afterwards appears, he has no action for those fruits. However, if a person knowingly takes possession of another's land, he may be compelled to account for the fruits even though they have been consumed.

A usufructuary of lands gains no property in the fruits of such lands until he has actually gathered them; therefore ungathered fruits would not belong to his heir but to the owner of the soil. A tenant farmer is in a similar position.

The product of animals, eg, milk, wool, lambs and calves, appertains by natural right to the usufructuary, but the offspring of a female slave belongs to the owner of the slave. According to Julian the usufructuary of a flock must replace those which die out of the produce of the flock and thereby preserve the original number of sheep; similarly, he must replace dead vines or trees and act in every respect like a good husbandman.

Following the rules of natural equity the emperor Hadrian allowed that any treasure which a man finds in his own land should be the property of the finder; the same rule applies to things found by chance in sacred or religious places. If a man finds treasure by chance in the ground of another, half belongs to the owner of the soil and half to the finder: thus if treasure is found in land belonging to the emperor, half belongs to the emperor and half to the finder. Similarly, if a valuable thing is found in a place belonging to the treasury, the public or the city, half belongs to the finder and half to the treasury, the public or the city.

Things are also acquired, by the law of nature, by tradition or delivery; therefore corporeal things may be delivered and when delivered by the true owner are absolutely alienated. Stipendiary and tributary lands, ie, those situated in the provinces, may be transferred in this way, and by our constitution we have now removed the distinction between these lands and Italian estates.

Although things have been sold and delivered, they are not acquired by the purchaser until he has either paid for them or given the seller satisfaction in some other way, eg, by giving a pledge. This rule is to be found in the law of the Twelve Tables and it also arises from the law of nations, that is, from the law of nature. However, if the seller gives the buyer credit, the thing becomes instantly the property of the buyer.

It is immaterial whether the owner delivers the thing himself or whether another delivers it with the owner's consent. Thus if a person entrusts another with the free and universal management of his affairs, if that other sells and delivers any of his goods they become the property of the receiver.

In some cases, even without delivery, the mere consent of the owner is suffcient to transfer the property in a thing; thus if a person lends, hires or deposits a thing in your possession, and afterwards sells or gives it to you, as soon as it is by consent reputed to be yours you acquire the property in the thing as fully as if it had been delivered to you as a thing sold or given.

Again, if a person sells merchandise deposited in a warehouse, he transfers the property in the merchandise as soon as he delivers the keys of the warehouse to the buyer.

The property in a thing may be transferred to an uncertain person: thus when praetors or consuls throw largesse to the crowd, it is their intention that what every man receives shall be his own and it therefore instantly becomes his property.

A thing abandoned by its owner becomes the property of the first occupant, but it is otherwise in the case of things thrown overboard in a storm in order to lighten a ship: such things remain the property of the owners and anyone who takes them, even at sea, is guilty of theft. Goods dropped from a carriage in motion without the knowledge of the owner are in a similar position.

Title II: Of things corporeal and incorporeal

Things corporeal are those which may be touched, eg, land, slaves, garments, gold, silver, etc. Things incorporeal are those which are not subject to the touch, but consist in rights and privileges, such as inheritances, usufructs, uses and all obligations. It is the right which is incorporeal, although those rights might exist in respect of a thing which is corporeal. Incorporeal rights include rights over rural and city (urban) estates, which are also called servitudes.

Title III: Of servitudes

Servitudes over rural estates are: a path, a road, a highway, and an aqueduct or free passage of water. A path denotes the right of passing and repassing on foot over another man's land, but not of driving cattle or a carriage over it. A road implies the liberty of driving either cattle or carriages, and he who has a road has also a path. A highway is a servitude which imports the right of passing, driving cattle, etc, and it includes both a path and a road. An aqueduct is a servitude by which one man may have the right of a free passage or conduit for water through the grounds of another.

The servitudes of city estates are those attaching to buildings, because we call all buildings city estates, although they are situated on farms or in villages. By these servitudes neighbours bear the burdens of neighbours; thus one neighbour may be entitled to place a beam upon the wall of another, or be compelled to receive – or be exempt from receiving – water from his neighbour's gutter, or may be restrained from raising his house in height lest he should darken his neighbour's house.

Some believe that rural servitudes include the right of drawing water, watering and feeding cattle, making lime, digging sand, etc, in the land of another.

All these servitudes are called servitudes of estates because no man can either owe or acquire a rural or city servitude unless he possesses either a house or lands. Such servitudes may be created by either contract or stipulation. A man may also by testament prohibit his heir from heightening his house so as to obstruct his neighbour's view, or oblige his heir to permit the rafter of another man's house to be laid upon his wall, to receive water from his neighbour's gutter, or to allow any person to walk, drive cattle or draw water in his grounds.

Title IV: Of usufruct

Usufruct is the right of using and enjoying, without altering the substance, the things which are the property of another; if the things perish the usufruct ceases.

The usufruct of things is often separated from the ownership, eg, where the usufruct is bequeathed by testament, the heir has only the bare ownership vested in him, while the legatee possesses the usufruct. Conversely, a testator may bequeath his lands without the usufruct and the legatee will receive only the bare property while the heir enjoys the profits, ie, has the usufruct. Again, the usufruct may be bequeathed to one man and the lands, without the usufruct, to another.

Usufruct may also be created by pacts and stipulations, but in order that ownership of lands should not be made wholly unbeneficial by deducting the usufruct for ever, by certain means the usufruct will be extinguished and revert to the ownership.

In addition to lands and houses there may also be a usufruct of slaves, cattle, and other things, except those which would be consumed by use, eg, wine, oil and clothes. However, the senate has ordained that there may be a usufruct of money if sufficient security is given to the heir for the repayment of a like sum. A usufruct of other things which may be consumed by use may be bequeathed, but the legatee must give security for the payment to the heir of their value either on the death of the legatee or in the event of his diminution. The senate has not thereby created a usufruct of consumable things: it has established a quasi-usufruct, ie, a right in the nature of a usufruct.

The usufruct of a thing determines on the death of the usufructuary or when he suffers either the greatest or the less diminution; it also determines if it is not used according to the manner and during the time prescribed. All this is set forth in our constitution. Usufruct also determines if the usufructuary surrenders it to the owner of the property, or by consolidation, ie, where the usufructuary becomes owner of the thing. Again, if a house is destroyed by fire, earthquake or decay, the usufruct is extinguished and no usufruct exists in respect of the land on which the house stood.

When the usufruct of a thing is determined it reverts to the owner of the property who from that moment has complete power over the thing.

Title V: Of use and habitation

The usufruct and bare use of a thing are both created and determined by the same means.

Use is less beneficial than usufruct, for he who has simply the use of lands can do no more than use such quantity of herbs, fruit, flowers, hay, straw and wood as may be sufficient to supply his daily needs, and he may remain on the land only on condition that he does not become troublesome to the owner or impede his husbandmen. Unlike a usufructuary, he who has a mere use can neither let, sell nor give away his right to another.

He who has the mere use of a house may only inhabit it himself together with his wife (or husband, as the case may be), children, freedmen and such other free persons who are there as servants; he cannot transfer his right to another and it is hardly thought allowable that he should receive a guest or lodger.

He who has the use of a slave or a beast of burden cannot transfer his right to another. If the use of cattle is left by testament, the usuary cannot use the milk, the lambs or the wool as these are included in the produce, but he may use the cattle to soil and improve his lands.

A habitation (ie, a right of habitation), whether created by testament or any other means, is neither a use nor a usufruct. He who has a habitation may not only live in it but also let it to another.

Having examined the ways in which things are acquired by the law of nations, we now consider how things are acquired according to the civil law.

Title VI: Of acquisition by use and long-standing possession

In order to remove uncertainty as to the ownership of things, the civil law provided that he who by purchase, donation or any other lawful means had obtained a thing from another whom he mistakenly believed to be the true owner and, if it was moveable, possessed it in good faith for one year either in Italy or the provinces, or, if it was immoveable, possessed it for two years in Italy, should acquire the thing by use. However, by our constitution it is provided that things moveable may be acquired by use after the expiration of three years; in the case of immoveables by long-standing possession, the period being ten years if the parties are present, ie, in the province, and twenty years if either of them is absent. These rules apply throughout our dominions, provided the possession was justly founded.

Certain things, eg, free persons, things sacred or religious and fugitive slaves, cannot be acquired by use, and things moveable which have been stolen and things immoveable which have been taken by force are in the same category. Even those who have purchased or otherwise received in good faith things stolen or taken by force cannot acquire them by use. However, if an heir, thinking a particular thing to belong to the inheritance which had only been lent, let to or deposited with the deceased, shall have sold, given or otherwise disposed of it to another who received it in good faith, the receiver may acquire that thing by use. In such a case the thing is not regarded as stolen property and the heir is not guilty of theft. Similarly, if he who has the usufruct of a female slave either sells or gives away the child of such slave, believing it to be his own property, he does not commit theft; for theft cannot be constituted without an intention to commit it.

In regard to things immoveable, if any man takes possession of an estate without force, by reason either of the absence or negligence of the owner, or because he died without heirs, although he has thus possessed the land dishonestly, he who receives it from him in good faith may acquire the same by use because he has not received a thing which was stolen or taken by force. The opinion of ancient lawyers that land and things immoveable might be stolen is now abolished and imperial constitutions provide that a long and undoubted possession of immoveable property ought not to be taken away.

There are occasions on which a thing which has been stolen or taken by force may be acquired by use, eg, when such a thing has fallen again under the power of its true owner, acquisition by use again becomes a possibility.

Things belonging to our treasury cannot be acquired by use, but when things escheatable have not been certified to the treasury, a purchaser in good faith may acquire them by this means after delivery. Lastly, if any man purchase a particular thing in good faith, or obtain possession of it by any other lawful means, he cannot acquire it by use unless the thing itself is free from vice.

A mistake as to the ground of possession does not give rise to acquisition by use, eg, when a person mistakenly believes that he has purchased a thing or that it has been given to him.

If things are possessed by any man in good faith, so that the possession is lawfully commenced, his heir, or the possessor of his goods, may continue the possession and acquire them by use although he knows that what he possesses is the property of another. If the possession was from the beginning in bad faith, or unlawful, possession does not help the deceased's heir or the possessor of his goods, even though he was himself ignorant of the way in which the deceased's possession began. In computing the years necessary to give rise to acquisition by use, the periods for which the thing is possessed by a seller and buyer are reckoned together.

An edict of the emperor Marcus provides that when a thing is purchased from the treasury, the purchaser, after five years' uninterrupted possession, may repel the true owner by pleading this fact, but by a constitution of the emperor Zeno those who by sale, donation, or any other title have received things from the public treasury may instantly be secured in their possession; those who think that they have a right of action in respect of such things may bring an action against the treasury within four years. Our recent constitution extends to those who have received anything from our palace or the palace of our empress the same rules as were laid down by the emperor Zeno concerning alienation by the treasury.

Title VII: Of gifts

Property may also be acquired by donation, of which there are two kinds: the one, mortis causa, ie, on account of death; the other, non mortis causa, ie, not on account of death, and this takes effect during the life of the donor.

A donation mortis causa is that made under an apprehension or suspicion of death, eg, when a thing is given upon condition that if the donor dies the donee shall possess it absolutely, or that the thing shall be returned if the donor survives the danger which he apprehends. As far as possible gifts mortis causa are treated in the same way as legacies. In brief, a donation mortis causa is made when a man so gives as to show that he would rather possess the thing than that the donee should possess it, and yet that he is more willing that it should go to the donee than to his heir.

Donations made without any thought or apprehension of death we call donations inter vivos, and these cannot be compared with legacies, because once they are made, they cannot be revoked without cause. Such gifts are completed when the donor has manifested his intention in writing or otherwise. Our constitution provides that, like a sale, a donation inter vivos requires delivery by the donor. Our predecessors enacted that donations exceeding 200 solidi should be publicly and formally enrolled and registered, but we have increased this figure to 500 solidi; up to that sum registration is not required, and there are certain cases where gifts are valid without registration, whatever the amount.

Nevertheless, there are cases when a donor may revoke a donation inter vivos on account of the ingratitude of the donee: these cases are set out in our constitution.

There is another kind of donation inter vivos, unknown to ancient lawyers, which was introduced by later emperors: this is called ante nuptias, ie, before marriage. Such gifts were conditional on the marriage taking place and could never be made after the celebration of the marriage. However, the emperor Justin allowed such gifts to be augmented during the marriage, and we have ordained that they may also originate at any time during the marriage. In view of this, such gifts are no longer called donations ante nuptias, but donations propter nuptias, ie, on account of marriage: they are thus made equal with portions and may now not only precede marriage but be augmented or even made after the marriage has been celebrated.

Formerly there was another way of acquiring ownership by civil law, ie, by accretion: thus if Primus and Titius owned a slave in common, and Primus gave him his freedom, the share of Primus in that slave would accrue to Titius. However, we have decreed that freedom, although granted by one partner only, shall immediately take effect, but the manumitter must indemnify his partner by giving him his share of the worth of the slave.

Title VIII: Of those who can, and those who cannot, alienate

It sometimes happens that the owner of a thing cannot alienate it, yet he who is not the owner may do so. For example, by the law Julia a husband cannot alienate lands in Italy which came to him in right of his wife, unless his wife consents to the alienation: even with her consent he cannot mortgage them. Lest the frailty of women should bring about the ruin of their fortunes, we have amended the law Julia so that now no husband can alienate or mortgage, even with the consent of his wife, any immoveable possession, whether provincial or Italian, obtained with her as a marriage portion.

A creditor, by virtue of the contract, may alienate a pledge, although the thing pledged is not his property. In order to protect both the debtor and the creditor our constitution has laid down a fixed procedure for the sale of pledges.

No pupil, whether male or female, has power to alienate anything without the authority of a tutor; eg, money lent without the authority of a tutor may be claimed by vindication, ie, by a real action, if it exists entire or unspent. If the money lent has been spent by the borrower in good faith (ie, believing that the lender was of full age) it may be recovered by condiction, ie, by a personal action; if it has been spent in bad faith an action ad exhibendum (for the production of the money) will lie against him.

On the contrary, the property of anything may be transferred to pupils without the authority of their tutors, but a debtor is not discharged unless the payment is authorized by the pupil's tutor. Our constitution provides that the debtor of a minor may lawfully pay any sum to his curator or tutor if a judicial decree permitting the payment is first obtained without expense to the minor; such decree gives the debtor complete security. Even if money has been paid to a pupil without first obtaining the consent of the court, if he afterwards requires that the money be paid to him again, his action could be defeated by an exception of fraud if it is shown that he has become richer by the increase of the money or even that he has preserved it safely. However, if the pupil has spent the money, or it has been stolen from him, the debtor will be compelled to make a second payment because he did not obtain the authority of the tutor or a decree of the court. Pupils cannot pay money without the authority of their tutors, and money so paid does not become the property of him to whom it is paid.

Title IX: Of persons through whom we can acquire

Things may be acquired not only by ourselves but also by those whom we have in our power, and also by slaves of whom we have only the usufruct. Acquisitions may also be made for us by freedmen, and even by slaves whom we possess in good faith, although they are the property of another.

Formerly, whatever property came to children of either sex who were in the power of the parents was acquired for the parents of those children: the peculium castrense (property gained in war) was an exception to this rule. Apart from this exception, any property so vested in parents could be applied by them in whatever manner they pleased. This seemed to be inhuman and we have ordained that if anything accrues to the son by means of the father's fortune, the whole shall be acquired for the father, but that whatever the son acquires in any other way shall remain the son's and the father shall have only the usufruct of such acquisition.

According to former constitutions, when a parent emancipated his children he might retain a third part of those things which were excepted from paternal acquisition as the price of emancipation. This also appeared to be inhuman and we have decreed that the parent shall now be entitled to a half-share not of the ownership but of the usufruct.

Whatever our slaves have acquired by any means is acquired by ourselves; we thus acquire things although we have no knowledge of, or are averse to, the acquisition. If a slave is instituted to an heir, he cannot enter upon the inheritance unless his master so commands; if the master does so command the legacy is acquired by the master as if he had himself been made the heir. Further, whatever is possessed by a slave is possessed by his master and upon such possession the master may found a claim by use or long-standing possession.

In regard to those slaves of whom the possessor has only the usufruct, whatever they acquire by means of his goods, or by their own work and labour, belongs to the usufructuary master; other acquisitions, eg, a legacy or gift, belong to the owner of the slave. The same rule applies to him who is possessed as a slave in good faith, whether he is a freeman or the slave of another. But a possessor in good faith who has acquired the slave by use becomes the owner of the slave and therefore of anything that the slave acquires. A usufructuary master cannot acquire by use because he can never be strictly said to possess, having only the power of using, and because he knows that the slave belongs to another. Nevertheless we may acquire not only ownership but also possession by means of the slaves whom we possess in good faith, or of whom we have only the usufruct, and even by means of a free person, of whom we have possession in good faith. In saying this we adhere to the distinction made above and speak only of those things of which a slave may acquire possession either by means of his master's goods or by his own industry.

It is therefore apparent that we cannot acquire by free persons who are not under our power or possessed by us in good faith; neither can we acquire property by another's slave of whom we have neither the usufruct nor the just possession. Thus it is said that nothing can be acquired by means of a stranger, but there is an exception because a constitution of the emperor Severus provides that possession may be acquired for us by a free person, eg, an agent, not only with, but even without, our knowledge, and by this possession ownership may be gained if delivery was made by the owner; and even if delivery was made by one who was not the owner, ownership may be acquired by use or long-standing possession.

We will now show how things come to us by universal acquisition, ie, wholly and in gross by one acquisition. We will now inquire into inheritances, which come either from a testacy or an intestacy; we will speak first of testaments.

Title X: Of the formalities of testaments

A testament is so called because it bears witness or testimony to the determination of the mind. Two kinds of testament were formerly in use; the one practised in times of peace, and named calatis comitiis, because it was made in the full assembly of the people; the other was used when the people were going forth to battle, and was styled procinctum testamentum. A third kind was added, which was called per aes et libram, because it was effected by emancipation, which was an alienation made by an imaginary sale in the presence of five witnesses, and the libripens, or balance-holder, all citizens of Rome above the age of fourteen, and also in the presence of him who was called the emptor familiae, or purchaser. The two former kinds of testament have for long been disused; the third continued longer, but has now ceased in part to be observed.

The three kinds of testament mentioned above arose from the civil law, but afterwards another kind was introduced by the edict of the praetor: by praetorian law the seals of seven witnesses were sufficient to establish a will without any emancipation or imaginary sale. The seals of witnesses were not required by the civil law.

When the civil and praetorian laws began to be blended together it became an established rule that testaments should be made at one and the same time, that they should be sealed by seven witnesses and that they should also be subscribed by the witnesses.

To these formalities we have added by our constitution the requirement that the name of the heir shall be expressed by the handwriting either of the testator or of the witnesses, and that everything shall be done in accordance with the tenor of that constitution.

According to Papinianus, every witness may use the same seal. It is also allowable to use another's seal. The witnesses must be persons who are themselves legally capable of taking by testament, but no woman, slave, or interdicted prodigal, no person under puberty, nor mad, mute or deaf person, nor anyone whom the laws have reprobated and rendered incapable of giving testimony, can be a witness. If, at the time of attesting, a witness was generally believed to be a free person but was in fact a slave, this fact would not render the testament invalid.

A father and a son in his power, or two brothers under the power of the same father, may be witnesses to a testament of a stranger, but no person can be a witness to a testament who is under the power of the testator, and neither the father nor anyone in his power can witness the testament by which his son disposes of property acquired in war.

An heir cannot witness the testament by which he is appointed heir, neither can anyone in his power, or his father in whose power he is, or his brothers in the power of the same father. The ancients accepted as witnesses the heir and those who were joined with him by ties of paternal power; the only precaution taken was the exhorting and persuading of such persons not to abuse their privilege. We have corrected this practice.

However, we permit legatees and trustees, and persons allied to them, to be witnesses because they are not universal heirs or successors. We have extended this privilege to those who are in their power and to those in whose power they are.

A testament may be written upon a table of wax, upon paper, or parchment or any other substance. A man may commit the same testament to more than one tablet, each of which will be an original if the requisite formalities are observed. If a man wishes to make a nuncupative testament, ie, a testament without writing, he may be sure that according to the civil law he makes a valid testament if, in the presence of seven witnesses, he declares his will by word of mouth.

Title XI: Of the military testament

Constitutions dispense with the formalities of making testaments in the case of all military persons. Witnesses, or any other formality, are not required if they are on actual service against the enemy; thus in whatever manner a military person declares his will, whether in writing or not in writing, it takes effect according to his intention. Soldiers who are not upon an expedition cannot claim this privilege; although such a soldier is a son in power, he may nevertheless make a testament, but he must observe the formalities required of those who are not soldiers. The emperor Trajan wrote that it is not sufficient for a soldier to say in the course of conversation 'I appoint you my heir', or 'I leave you all my estate'; he must (if he is to make a testament without writing), in the presence of witnesses purposely called, declare what person shall be his heir, and on which of his slaves he confers freedom.

A soldier, though mute and deaf, may yet make a testament. A testament made by a soldier without the usual formalities required for making a testament is valid for only one year after he leaves the army. If he dies within that year, and the condition upon which his heir is instituted is not fulfilled until after the expiration of that year, it is nevertheless a valid military testament. If a man makes a testament without observing the requisite formalities and then becomes a soldier, and when on active service shows an intention that his testament should be valid, eg, by adding to or subtracting from it, his testament would be valid as he would, in effect, have made a new military testament.

If a soldier is adrogated or, being the son of a family, is emancipated, his testament remains valid.

By our constitution we have extended the privilege whereby some persons in power may dispose by testament of peculia castrensia (property acquired in war) and peculia quasi castrensia (property analogous to that acquired in war) to all persons who possess property of this kind, on condition that they observe the usual formalities when making their testaments.

Title XII: Of persons who are not permitted to make a testament

The right of making a valid testament is not extended to all persons, eg, those in power do not normally have the right, even if their testament is made with their parents' consent. An exception to this rule has been noted above, ie, a soldier in power may dispose by testament of whatever he has acquired by military service, and the emperor Hadrian extended this right to those who were once soldiers. However, if a soldier or former soldier dies intestate without children or brothers his military estate passes to his father or other paternal ascendants. Although by the civil law peculia, or estates of those who are under power, are included in the wealth of the parents, it follows from what has been said that a soldier's military estate cannot be taken from him, even by his father or his father's creditors; it remains the sole property of him who acquired it, ie, the soldier. Apart from this exception (ie, in the case of military or quasi-military estates) a son in power cannot make a valid testament even though he is afterwards emancipated and dies sui juris.

Persons below the age of puberty and madmen cannot make valid testaments, and a minor's testament does not become valid if he reaches puberty before his death; similarly, a madman's testament does not become valid if he regains his senses, and then dies. However, a madman may make a valid testament during a lucid interval.

A prodigal who has been interdicted from managing his own affairs cannot make a valid testament, but a testament made before interdiction is valid. In certain cases our constitution allows deaf or mute persons to make a valid testament provided they observe the rules laid down in the constitution. A testament made before a person becomes deaf or mute remains valid. A blind person can only make a testament if he complies with the rules laid down by the emperor Justin. A testament made in captivity is invalid, even if the testator returns. A testament made before capture is valid by virtue of the jus postliminii (if he returns) or the law Cornelia (if he dies in captivity).

Title XIII: Of disinheriting children

Due observance of the formalities is not in itself sufficient to make a testament valid because a father who has a son under his power must either institute him his heir or disinherit him by name; if he omits to do either of these things the testament is of no effect, even if his son predeceases him. The ancients did not observe this rule in regard to daughters and grandchildren of either sex descended through the male line because by a right of accretion they were entitled to a certain portion of the inheritance. A child may be disinherited by name by the words 'Let Titus my son be disinherited'; where the testator has only one son it is sufficient for him to say in testament 'Let my son be disinherited'.

Posthumous children must either be instituted heirs or disinherited; if a posthumous son or any posthumous descendant of either sex is passed over in silence the testament is valid at the time at which it is made but is annulled if and when the child is born. Male posthumous children must be disinherited in express terms, eg, by the words 'Whatever son is hereafter born to me, I disinherit him': female posthumous children may be disinherited in express terms or by a general clause; if the latter they must have received a legacy to show that they were not omitted through forgetfulness.

The term 'posthumous children' includes those who succeed if the heir dies in the testator's lifetime. Therefore, just as a testator must either institute or disinherit his son if his testament is to be valid, so he must either institute or disinherit his grandson or granddaughter by that son lest, if the son should die in his (the testator's) lifetime, his grandson or granddaughter, succeeding to the place of his son, should make his testament void by a quasi-agnation. This has been introduced by the law Julia Velleia.

With regard to emancipated children, the civil law does not require that they be instituted or disinherited as they are not sui heredes, ie, proper heirs. However, the praetor commands that all children, whether male or female, if they are not instituted, shall be disinherited, males by name, females by name or under a general clause; if they are not instituted or disinherited in this way the praetor gives them possession of the goods in spite of the testament.

Adopted children, as long as they continue under the power of their adoptive father, have the same rights as children born in lawful marriage and therefore must either be instituted or disinherited in the same way as natural children. Children emancipated by an adoptive father are not numbered among his natural children. Adopted children, as long as they continue in adoption, are strangers to their natural parents who need not institute or disinherit them; when they are emancipated by their adoptive father they are in the same position as if they had been emancipated by their natural father.

These were the rules which the ancient lawyers introduced, but we have by our constitution made the same law in regard to both sons and daughters, and to all other descendants in the male line, whether in being or posthumous; so that all children, whether they are proper heirs or emancipated, must either be instituted heirs or disinherited by name. Regulations with regard to adopted children are contained in our constitution of adoptions. If a soldier makes his testament whilst upon a military expedition, knowing that he has children or will have a child, and passes them over in silence, such silence shall count as a disinherison by name.

Neither a mother, nor a grandfather on the mother's side, is under any necessity of either instituting their children heirs or of disinheriting them, but may pass them by in silence; such silence has the same effect as an actual disinherison by a father. The edict of the praetor gives possession of goods contra tabulas, ie, contrary to the disposition of the testament, to children who have been passed over in silence, and another remedy is available against the testament of a mother or maternal grandfather, as will be shown hereafter.

Title XIV: Of the appointment of heirs

A man may by testament appoint slaves as well as freemen to be his heirs, and may appoint the slaves of another (including those in whom he has a usufruct) as well as his own. Some preferred the opposite view, but by our constitution we have provided that a master may appoint his own slaves (including slaves of whom he has only the bare ownership) without giving them their liberty. If a mistress institutes a slave with whom she is alleged to have committed adultery, the institution is of no avail. This follows from a constitution of the emperors Severus and Antoninus that a slave alleged to have committed adultery with his mistress cannot, before a sentence of acquittal, be made free by that mistress.

When a slave has been instituted by his master, and remains in the same condition, he obtains his freedom at the death of his master by virtue of the testament, and becomes his necessary heir; if a slave is manumitted in the lifetime of his master, it is in his power either to accept or to refuse the inheritance. If a slave who has been instituted heir is alienated, he cannot enter upon the inheritance unless his new master so commands, and in this event the new master, by means of his slave, becomes the heir of the testator. A slave who has been instituted heir and given his liberty by his master's testament, and then sold, cannot take the inheritance to his own use and obtain his freedom under the testament. When the slave of another is appointed an heir, but remains in the same condition, he cannot take the inheritance except by his master's order; if he is alienated at any time before he actually takes the inheritance, he must either accept or refuse it at the command of his new master. If a slave is manumitted during the testator's lifetime or at any time before he enters upon the inheritance, he may decide for himself whether or not he will accept it. The slave of another may be instituted an heir after the death of his master and the slave of an unborn child may also be appointed. If a slave has many masters, all of whom are capable of taking by testament, and is instituted heir by a stranger, he acquires a part of the inheritance for each master who commands him to take it in proportion to their share in the ownership of him.

A testator may appoint one heir or as many as he pleases.

An inheritance is generally divided into twelve parts or ounces (unciae) which together make up an as or pound, although an as may consist of as many parts as a testator pleases. If a man appoints but one heir and appoints him heir for six parts, the whole as will be included because no man can die partly testate and partly intestate, unless he is a soldier in which case it is solely a question of what he intends.

When a testator institutes many heirs, they share equally in his inheritance unless he has indicated how his effects are to be divided. If the shares of some are indicated, but those of others are not, the residue is divided equally between those whose shares have not been expressed.

What happens if a part of an inheritance remains unbequeathed, but a certain portion of it is given to every nominated heir? The part of which no disposition has been made vests in each of the nominated heirs in proportion to the share bequeathed. On the other hand, if many are nominated heirs in portions which in total would exceed an as, each heir must suffer a reduction pro rata. Thus if four are instituted and a third is given to each, the disposition would take effect as if each had been given one quarter.

If more parts than 12 are bequeathed, he who is instituted without any prescribed share is entitled to what remains of a dupondius, ie, 24 parts; if more than 24 parts are bequeathed, he who is nominated without any prescribed share is entitled to the remainder of a tripondius, ie, 36 parts. But all these parts are afterwards reduced to 12.

An heir may be instituted simply or conditionally, but not from or to any certain period; thus if a testator says 'Be thou my heir after five years, to be computed from my death' such institution takes place immediately as if it had been a simple appointment. An impossible condition in the institution of heirs, the disposition of legacies, the appointment of trusts or the giving of freedom is treated as unwritten or void. If many conditions are jointly required in the institution of an heir, all must be complied with; if the conditions are placed separately and in the disjunctive, eg, if this or that be done, it is sufficient to comply with either.

A testator may appoint persons whom he has never seen, eg, his brother's sons, who are in a foreign country, even though he does not know where they are.

Title XV: Of vulgar substitution

A man by testament may appoint many degrees of heirs; for instance, 'If Titius will not be my heir, let Seius be my heir.' He may proceed in such a substitution as far as he pleases and, at last, he may institute a slave to be his necessary heir. A testator may substitute many in the place of one, or one in the place of many, or one in the place of each, or he may substitute even his instituted heirs reciprocally to one another. If a testator, having instituted several co-heirs in unequal portions, substitutes them reciprocally the one to the other, and makes no mention of their shares of the inheritance in the substitution, he gives the same shares by the substitution as he gave by the institution.

If a co-heir is substituted to an instituted heir, and a third person is substituted to that co-heir, such substituted person is admitted to the portions of both the co-heirs without distinction. Where a testator institutes the slave of another to be his heir, supposing him to be free, and adds 'if he does not become my heir I substitute Maevius in his place', if that slave should enter upon the inheritance at the command of his master, Maevius the substitute is admitted to a half share. Where a testator knew that the slave was under the power of another the words 'if he does not become my heir' mean if he will neither become my heir himself, nor cause another to be my heir.

Title XVI: Of pupillary substitution

A parent can substitute to his children who are within puberty and under his power not only in the way described above (ie, 'If my children will not be my heirs, let some other person be my heir') but also by saying 'If my children actually become my heirs, but die within puberty, let another become their heir'. Custom has ordained that parents may make wills for their children although the children are not of an age to make wills for themselves. Following this custom we have concluded in our code a constitution which enables a man who has children, grandchildren or great-grandchildren who are mad or disordered in their senses to make a substitution of certain persons to such children in the manner of a pupillary substitution although they have reached the age of puberty, but such a substitution becomes void as soon as they recover from their disorder in the same way as a pupillary substitution ceases to be effective when the minor attains to puberty.

If a testator fears that at the time of his death his son, being as yet a pupil, should be liable to fraud and trickery if a substitute is publicly given to him, he should insert a vulgar (common) substitution in the first tablet of his testament and write that substitution in which a substitute is named if his son should die within puberty in the lower tablet, which should be separately tied up and sealed. He should also insert a clause in the first part of his testament forbidding the lower part to be opened while his son is alive and within the age of puberty. Nevertheless, although it is unsafe and dangerous, a substitution to a son within puberty is valid even if it is written on the same tablet in which the testator has appointed him to be his heir.

Parents may also give a substitute to their disinherited children, and whatever a disinherited child who dies within the age of puberty may have acquired by inheritances, legacies and gifts from relations and friends becomes the property of the substitute. All that has been said concerning the substitution of pupils applies also to posthumous children.

No parent can make a testament for his children unless he has made a testament for himself, for the testament of a child within puberty is a part and consequence of the testament of the parent; if the testament of the father is invalid the testament of the son will not take effect. A parent may make a pupillary substitution to each of his children, or to him who shall die the last within puberty. A substitution may be made to a child within puberty either by name (eg, 'If my son becomes my heir and dies a pupil let Titius be my heir') or generally (eg, 'Whoever shall be my heir, let the same person be a substitute to my son if he dies within puberty'). Where there is a general substitution, all who have been instituted and become heirs to the father are entitled to a part of the son's inheritance if he dies within puberty in proportion to the share in which they were instituted.

A pupillary substitution may be made to males till they arrive at 14 complete, and to females till they have completed their 12th year; when these ages are passed the substitution becomes extinct. A pupillary substitution cannot be made to a stranger who is instituted, or even to a son who is instituted, if his age exceeds that of puberty, although a testator may oblige his heir to give another part, or even the whole, of the inheritance, by virtue of a fideicommissum, or gift in trust.

Title XVII: Of the ways in which testaments become invalid

A testament legally made remains valid until it is either broken or rendered ineffectual. A testament is broken or revoked when the force of it is destroyed, although the testator's status remains the same, eg, if the testator adrogates an independent person by licence from the emperor or adopts in the presence of the praetor a child under the power of his natural parent. In these cases the testament is broken by the quasi-birth of a proper heir.

A former testament, although legally perfect, may be broken or revoked by a subsequent testament; according to the emperors Severus and Antoninus the former testament would be broken even if the subsequent testament appointed an heir to some particular things only. However, we have commanded that even where the heir appointed by the subsequent testament is instituted to particular things only, it is as valid as if no mention had been made of the particular things, but the heir must content himself either with the things given him or with the fourth part allowed by the Falcidian law, and must restore the rest of the inheritance to the heirs instituted by the first testament. This follows from the insertion of words in the subsequent testament by which it is expressly declared that the first testament shall subsist.

Testaments legally made become irrata (ie, ineffectual) if the testator suffers diminution, ie, changes his status or condition. Testaments which are illegal are termed null; those which were at first legal but lose their force by some revocatory act of the testator are said to be rupta, or broken; and those since the making of which the testator has suffered a change of status are said to be irrata, or ineffectual.

However, testaments legally made and afterwards rendered void by diminution are not always without effect because the appointed heir is entitled to possession of the goods by virtue of the testament if it was sealed by seven witnesses and the testator was a Roman citizen and free from power at the time of his death. This exception does not apply if the testator had lost the right of a citizen or his liberty or had given himself in adoption and, at the time of his death, was under the power of his adopting father.

A testament cannot be invalidated simply because the testator was afterwards unwilling that it should subsist, and the emperor Pertinax said that it cannot be revoked by an imperfect second testament. The emperor Pertinax also declared that he would not take the inheritance of any testator who appointed him his heir because a law suit was pending or because the testament was not executed according to law; nor would he allow himself to be appointed heir by word of mouth or by any writing which did not satisfy the strict rules of the law. As the emperors Severus and Antoninus have said, 'Although we are certainly not subject to the laws, yet we live in obedience to them.'

Title XVIII: Of inofficious testaments

Children who have been unjustly disinherited, or unjustly omitted in the testaments of their parents, may complain that such testaments are inofficious on the supposed or fictitious ground that their parents were not of sane mind when the testaments were made. In fact it is acknowledged that such a testament was well made, and the only exception to it is that the testator had not made his testament in accordance with his duty as a parent. Had the testator really been insane the testament would be void.

Parents may also complain that the testaments of their children are inofficious and, although they cannot complain, brothers and sisters are, by virtue of the imperial constitutions, preferred to infamous persons if any such have been appointed by the deceased to be his heirs. Collaterals (blood relations) beyond brothers and sisters can only benefit if the testament is annulled and they are nearest in succession upon intestacy.

Adopted children and natural children can only complain that a testament is inofficious if they can obtain the effects of the deceased in no other way. Posthumous children are in the same position.

However, if any single thing, or the least part of an inheritance, has been bequeathed to those who have a right to a fourth part or legitime portion of the testator's estate, they cannot bring a querela or complaint that the testament is inofficious. In such cases they may bring an action to recover the balance of their legitime, even though there is no direction in the testament to this effect.

If a tutor accepts a legacy in the name of his pupil in consequence of a bequest made by the tutor's father, the tutor may nevertheless complain in his own name that the testament of his father is inofficious. On the other hand, if a tutor complains unsuccessfully in the name of his pupil against the testament of his pupil's father, the tutor is not barred by virtue of this proceeding from taking whatever was left him in that testament.

No person can be prevented from bringing a complaint of undutifulness unless he has received his fourth or legitime part by being appointed heir, by having a legacy, by means of a trust for his use, or by donation mortis causa or inter vivos, but in those cases only mentioned in our constitution, or by any other means set forth in our ordinances. Where there are more persons than one entitled to complain of undutifulness, only one-fourth is given to them to be divided amongst them all in equal portions.

Title XIX: Of the different kinds of heirs

Heirs are necessary, or proper and necessary, or strangers.

A slave instituted by his master is a necessary heir and he is so called because at the testator's death he becomes instantly free and can be compelled to take the heirship. Persons who suspect that they are insolvent often institute a slave to be their heir so that if they die insolvent the goods which are seized and divided amongst their creditors appear to be those of the heir rather than their own. However, in such a case the slave is allowed to keep whatever he has acquired after the death of his patron; such goods cannot be sold to make up a deficiency in the testator's estate.

Proper and necessary heirs are sons, daughters, grandsons or granddaughters by a son, or any other descendants in the direct line, who were in the power of the deceased at the time of his death. In the case of grandchildren it is not sufficient that they were in the power of their grandfather at the time of his decease; their father should have ceased to be a proper heir in the lifetime of his father by having been freed from paternal authority, for then it is that the grandson or granddaughter succeeds in the place of their father.

Such heirs are called proper, or sui, because they are family heirs and even in the testator's lifetime are, in a way, owners of the inheritance. From this it follows that if a man dies intestate his children are preferred before all others to the succession. They are called necessary heirs because, whether or not they are willing, they become the heirs of their parent either by virtue of a testament or in consequence of an intestacy. However, the praetor allows them to abstain from the inheritance in order that the effects of their parents rather than their own may be seized by creditors.

All heirs not subject to the power of the testator at the time of his death are called strangers. Children instituted heirs by their mother are regarded as strangers because a woman is not allowed to have her children under her own power. A slave instituted by his master's testament and afterwards manumitted is also a stranger.

Strangers must be capable of taking under the testament, whether they are themselves instituted heirs, or whether those in their power are instituted. This requirement must be satisfied both at the time of making the testament and at the time of the testator's death. Further, whether an heir is appointed simply or conditionally, he must be capable of taking under the testament at the time of entering upon the inheritance, but the heir will not be prejudiced by a change of status between the making of the testament and the testator's death, or the completion of the condition of the institution. The three particular times already mentioned are the times to take into account. It is not only persons who are capable of giving their effects by testament who are said to be capable of taking under a testament: the expression includes anyone who is capable of taking for the benefit of himself, or of acquiring by testament for the benefit of another. Thus persons who are mad or mute, posthumous children, infants, sons in power or the slaves of another are all capable of taking under a testament.

Strangers may deliberate whether they will or will not enter upon an inheritance, but a stranger who at once takes an inheritance, or a family heir who has been allowed to abstain intermeddles with the property, loses the right to renounce the inheritance, unless he was under the age of 25: in this case the praetor comes to his aid if he has rashly taken upon himself an injurious inheritance. The emperor Hadrian once allowed a person over the age of 25 to relinquish an inheritance when it afterwards appeared that it was encumbered with a great debt which had been concealed from him. This was a special case, but the emperor Gordian extended the privilege to soldiers in general. However, if heirs comply with the terms of our recent constitution, they may enter upon their inheritance and not be liable beyond the value of the estate. If an heir chooses to deliberate rather than take advantage of our constitution, he exposes himself to the danger attending the acceptance of an inheritance according to the ancient law.

A stranger who is instituted by testament, or called by law to take a succession in the case of an intestacy, may make himself accountable as heir either by doing some act as heir, or by simply signifying his acceptance of the heirship. A man is deemed to act as heir if he treats the inheritance as his own, eg, by selling part of it or cultivating or letting the land, or even if he declares his intention of entering upon the inheritance, either by act or speech, knowing that the person with whose estate he intermeddles is dead testate or intestate, and that he himself is the heir. Just as a stranger may become heir by bare consent, so by a mere dissent he can bar himself from an inheritance. A person who is deaf or dumb may, by acting as heir, acquire an inheritance, provided he understands what he is doing.

Title XX: Of legacies

Although we are considering the legal methods by which things are acquired universally, it is not altogether out of place to say something about legacies.

A legacy is a kind of donation which is left by a deceased person. Formerly there were four kinds of legacies, namely, per vindicationem, per damnationem, sinendi modo, and per praeceptionem. Each had its own form of words, but those fixed forms were removed by imperial ordinances. We have composed a constitution which provides that the nature of all legacies shall be the same and that legatees, by whatever words they are constituted, may sue for what is left them, not only by a personal but also by a real or hypothecary action.

Our constitution extends still further: formerly, legacies were confined within very strict rules while gifts in trust were treated with greater indulgence, and we have thought it necessary to make all legacies equal to gifts in trust so that no difference in effect remains between them, and whatever is lacking in one may be supplied by the other.

A testator may bequeath his own property, that of his heir or that of others. If a thing bequeathed belongs to another, the heir must either purchase and deliver it or, if he cannot purchase it, pay its value. If the thing in question is one that cannot be purchased, eg, the Campus Martius or the temples, the heir cannot be required to pay its value. The goods of another can only be bequeathed if the deceased knew that the goods belonged to another. It is for the legatee to prove that the deceased knew that what he bequeathed belonged to another because it is a general rule of law that the burden of proof always lies upon the person who is suing.

If a man bequeaths a thing which he has pledged to a creditor, the heir must redeem it, but only if the deceased knew that it was pledged. Nevertheless, if it appears to have been the express will of the deceased that the legatee should himself redeem the thing, the heir is relieved of this liability.

If a thing bequeathed is the property of another, and the legatee becomes owner of it in the testator's lifetime, if he bought it he can recover its value by an action founded on the testament; however, if he received it as a gift no such action will lie. Further, if the same specific thing is left by two testaments to the same person, when he sues upon one of the testaments his action will fail if he is already possessed of the thing, but if he has obtained only its value he may bring an action for the thing itself.

Things which do not exist may be bequeathed if there is a possibility that they will exist; thus a man may bequeath fruit which shall grow on a particular piece of land or the offspring which shall be born of a particular slave.

When the same specific legacy is left to two persons either conjunctively or disjunctively, if they are both willing to accept the thing must be divided between them. If one legatee dies in the testator's lifetime, renounces his legacy or is by any means prevented from taking it, the whole vests in his co-legatee. An example of a conjunctive legacy is 'I bequeath my slave Stichus to Titius and Seius'; 'I bequeath my slave Stichus to Titius: I bequeath my slave Stichus to Seius' would be a disjunctive legacy even though the testator says that he gives the 'same slave Stichus to Seius'.

If a man bequeaths the land of another, and the legatee has purchased that land without the usufruct and afterwards the usufruct accrues to him, Julianus said that the legatee might bring an action by virtue of the testament and claim the land because the usufruct is regarded as a servitude. However, the judge must order to be paid the value of the land less the value of the usufruct.

If a man bequeaths to another what already belongs to him the legacy is of no effect, and the position is the same although the legatee has alienated the thing after the bequest. If a testator bequeaths what is his own believing that it is the property of another the bequest is good, and the same is true if the testator mistakenly believes that the thing already belongs to the legatee. If a testator bequeaths his own property, and afterwards alienates it, Celus holds that the thing becomes due to the legatee unless the testator disposed of it with an intention to oust him. The emperors Severus and Antoninus shared this view and also declared that whoever bequeaths a legacy, and afterwards pawns or mortgages it, shall not be deemed to have retracted it; in this case the legatee may bring an action against the heir and compel him to redeem. If a testator alienates a part of the thing bequeathed, the part which remains is still due, but the part alienated is only due if it was not alienated by the testator with the intention of retracting the legacy.

A man may effectually bequeath a discharge to his debtor, and the debtor can sue the heir to compel him to discharge the debt. A man may also by testament direct his heir not to sue a debtor within a specified time. On the other hand, if a debtor bequeaths to his creditor the money which he owes him and no more, the legacy is of no effect. But if a debtor bequeaths to his creditor a sum of money which was payable on a certain date or was owed subject to some condition, the legacy is effective because it is due immediately. Papinian is right when he says that if the day of payment should come, or the event of the condition happen, during the testator's lifetime, the legacy remains effectual because it was once good.

If a man gives back to his wife by legacy her marriage portion the legacy is valid, as the legacy is more beneficial to her than the action for the recovery of her portion. However, the emperors Severus and Antonius have declared that if a husband bequeaths to his wife her marriage portion which he has never actually received, the legacy is void; but if a certain sum or thing is specified, or reference is made to the instruments in which the exact value of the portion is mentioned, the legacy is valid.

If a thing bequeathed perishes before delivery otherwise than by the act or fault of the heir, the loss falls on the legatee. If the slave of another, who is bequeathed, is manumitted without the act of the heir, the heir is not liable to the legatee. However, if a testator bequeaths the slave of his heir, who afterwards manumits that slave, Julian says that the heir is answerable, whether or not he knew of the legacy. Again, if the heir makes a present of a slave bequeathed, and the donee manumits him, the heir is liable to an action although he was ignorant of the bequest.

Where a testator bequeaths his female slaves and their offspring, although the slaves die their issue pass to the legatee; the same applies where head slaves are bequeathed with their assistants. However, if a slave is bequeathed with his peculium, and afterwards dies, is manumitted or alienated, the legacy of the peculium fails to take effect. Similarly, where land is bequeathed with instruments of husbandry and the testator alienates the land, the legacy of the instruments is extinguished.

If a flock is bequeathed, and afterwards reduced to a single sheep, that sheep may be claimed. If the flock increases after it has been bequeathed, according to Julian the flock and the increase pass to the legatee. When a house is bequeathed, marble and pillars added after the bequest pass under the legacy.

When a slave's peculium is bequeathed any increase or decrease of it in the testator's lifetime is the loss or gain of the legatee. If a slave's peculium is left to him, together with his freedom, and the slave adds to his peculium after the testator's death and before the inheritance is entered upon, Julian says that whatever is acquired during this period passes to the slave as legatee. However, if a slave's peculium is bequeathed to a stranger, any increase during this period does not pass under the legacy unless made by something appertaining to the peculium. The emperors Severus and Antoninus have declared that when a peculium is bequeathed to a slave, it does not follow that the slave can claim whatever he may have expended on his master's account. The same emperors have said that a slave is entitled to his peculium if he is left his freedom on condition that he makes up his accounts and meets any deficiency out of his peculium.

Things incorporeal may be bequeathed as well as things corporeal: therefore a debt due to the testator may be left as a legacy, and the heir obliged to transfer his right of action to the legatee, unless the testator in his lifetime received the money due to him, in which case the legacy would be extinguished. These legacies are valid: 'I command my heir to rebuild the house of Titius' or 'to free him from his debts'.

If a testator bequeaths a slave, or any particular thing generally, the power of election is in the legatee, unless the testator has declared otherwise. The legacy of an option is made when a testator commands his legatee to choose any one of his slaves, or any thing from a certain class of things. Formerly, the legatee was required to make his election during his lifetime, but by our constitution we permit the heir of the legatee to make his option although the legatee in his lifetime neglected to do it. Further, if several legatees, or the heirs of one legatee, differ in their choice, the dissension between the legatees or heirs is decided by lot and the option of him to whom the lot falls prevails.

A legacy can only be left to those who have the capacity of taking by testament. Formerly, not even soldiers could bequeath legacies or gifts in trust to uncertain persons, eg, 'Whoever shall give his daughter in marriage to my son'. Likewise freedom could not be conferred upon an uncertain person as it was necessary that all slaves should be freed by name. However, a legacy might have been given to an uncertain person if he was one of a number of persons certain, eg, 'I command Titius my heir to give such a particular thing to any one of my present collateral relations, who shall think proper to take my daughter in marriage'. If a legacy or gift in trust had been paid to uncertain persons by mistake, the constitutions provided that such persons could not be compelled to refund. Formerly, a legacy could not have been given to a posthumous stranger, ie, a person who, had he been born before the testator's death, could not have been numbered among his proper heirs.

Such was the state of the ancient law and we have amended it with regard not only to inheritances but also to legacies and gifts in trust. However, the constitution does not allow the appointment of uncertain tutors.

A posthumous stranger could and may still be appointed an heir unless he was conceived by a woman who could not have been legally married to his father. Although a testator has mistaken the legatee's name, if his person is certain the legacy is good. The same rule applies to heirs. Similarly, a legacy is not rendered void by a false description; thus if the bequest is 'I give Stichus my slave, who was born in my family' and Stichus was in fact bought, if it is clear to which slave the legacy refers the legacy is valid. Much less is a legacy rendered invalid because a false reason is given for bequeathing it. For example, if a testator says 'I give my slave Stichus to Titius, because he took care of my affairs in my absence' and Titius had never taken care of the deceased's affairs, nevertheless the legacy is good. However, the law is different if the bequest is conditional, eg, 'I give Titius such a piece of ground, if it shall appear that he has taken a proper care of my affairs'.

An unconditional legacy given to the slave of the testator's heir is void, even though the slave is afterwards freed from the power of the heir in the testator's lifetime. However, a testator may effectively give a conditional legacy to the slave of his instituted heir if the slave is not under the power of the heir when the condition is fulfilled. On the other hand, it is beyond doubt that a slave may be appointed an heir and that his then master may take even an unconditional legacy by the same testament. But if a slave remains in the same state and enters upon the inheritance by order of his master, who is the legatee, the legacy, as such, becomes extinct.

Formerly, it was necessary for the institution of the heir to precede the giving of a legacy because the foundation of a testament is the institution of the heir. Similarly, it was necessary for the institution of an heir to come before a grant of freedom, but by our constitution we have provided that a legacy and, much more, a grant of freedom may be bequeathed before the institution of an heir, or where there are several heirs, before or between their institution. It is absurd that a strict regard should be paid to the mere order of writing as opposed to a testator's express intention.

A bequest made to take place after the death of an heir or legatee was also of no effect, but we have given such legacies the same validity as is given to gifts in trust.

Again, if a testator gave, revoked or transferred a legacy by way of penalty, eg, 'If my heir does not give his daughter in marriage to Titius, let him pay ten aurei to Seius', the legacy was void. This rule applied even to the testament of a soldier, to prevent the emperor from receiving a legacy bequeathed by way of penalty, to a gift of freedom and to the addition of another heir. However, we have ordained that legacies left, revoked or transferred by way of penalty should not differ from other legacies, except where the performance of the condition is impossible, prohibited by law or contrary to good morals.

Title XXI: Of the ademption and transfer of legacies

An ademption (revocation) of a legacy is valid, although inserted in the same testament or codicil as the legacy. Any form of words may be used. Similarly, a legacy may be transferred from one person to another, expressly or by implication. Thus a testator may direct 'I give to Seius my slave Stichus, whom I have bequeathed to Titius', and he may do this in the same testament or codicil in which the legacy was first given.

Title XXII: Of the Falcidian law

By the law of the Twelve Tables a testator was permitted to dispose of his whole patrimony in legacies but, following the introduction of two inadequate laws, the Falcidian law was enacted whereby a testator is prohibited from giving in legacies more than three-fourths of all his effects. In other words, there must remain to the heir or heirs an entire fourth part of the whole. When two heirs are instituted, say Titius and Seius, and Titius's share of the inheritance is wholly exhausted or heavily burdened by legacies which he is expressly ordered to pay, while Seius's share is either not encumbered, or is charged with legacies which amount only to a part of his share, Titius may make a stoppage out of the legacies with which he is charged so as to retain a fourth part of his own share, for the law Falcidia is applied to each heir separately.

The law Falcidia has regard only to the value of the estate at the time of the testator's death; increases in the testator's estate after his death and before the inheritance is entered upon, eg, by the acquisition of slaves or the product of cattle, are ignored for this purpose. On the other hand, legatees do not suffer if the estate decreases after the testator's death because of fire, shipwreck or loss of slaves, but at the time of death at least a fourth part of the whole remains to the heir. As the heir may elect whether to accept or refuse the inheritance, in such a case the legatees should come to terms with the heir as to the part that he is to retain lest he abandon the inheritance and in consequence they lose their legacies altogether.

The Falcidian portion is not taken by the heir until debts, funeral expenses and the price of manumission of slaves have been deducted; after such deductions have been made the fourth part of the remainder belongs to the heir and the other three parts are divided amongst the legatees in rateable proportion.

Title XXIII: Of inheritances bequeathed in trust

Let us now proceed to trusts, and first we will speak of inheritances bequeathed in trust.

Originally, trusts were not legally binding, so that testators who wished to give an inheritance or legacy to persons to whom they could directly bequeath committed neither the inheritance nor legacy in trust to those who were capable of taking. Such commitments were called bequests in trust, because the performance of the trust could not be legally enforced, but rested on the honour of the trustee. However, the emperor Augustus commanded the consuls to interpose their authority so as to give such bequests legal effect. This was a popular command, and trusts became so common that a praetor (the praetor fideicommissarius, or praetor for bequests in trust) was appointed to give judgment in these cases. While it is absolutely necessary to appoint an heir in direct terms in every testament, he may be requested to restore the inheritance to any other person. A testator may request his heir to restore a part of the inheritance only, and he may make him a trustee upon condition, or from a certain time.

After an heir has restored an inheritance in obedience to the trust, he nevertheless remains heir; the person who received the inheritance was sometimes regarded as heir, sometimes as legatee. In the reign of Nero, when Trebellius was one of the consuls, it was provided that if an inheritance was restored by reason of a trust, all actions which by the civil law might be brought by or against the heir should be available to and against the person to whom the inheritance was restored. After this decree of the senate the praetor began to give equitable actions to and against the receiver of an inheritance as if he was the heir.

When heirs were requested to restore the whole, or almost the whole, of an inheritance, they often refused to accept it and in consequence trusts were frequently extinguished. However, in the reign of the emperor Vespasian, when Pegasus was a consul, the senate ordained that an heir who was requested to restore an inheritance might retain a fourth, as in the case of legacies by the Falcidian law. The same right of retention is allowed in respect of single things bequeathed in trust. For some time after this decree the heir alone bore the burden of all demands and charges on the inheritance, but later whoever received a share of an inheritance by reason of a bequest in trust was regarded as having a partial legacy (a partition), and the stipulations which were customary between the heir and a legatee in part were interposed so that the heir and the person who benefited under the trust shared the profit and loss between them in due proportion.

Therefore, if an heir had not been requested to surrender more than three-fourths of the inheritance, he was obliged to restore by virtue of the Trebellian senatusconsultum, and all actions relating to the inheritance were brought or sustained by both parties according to their respective shares, in regard to the heir by virtue of the civil law, and in regard to the one to whom the inheritance was made over by virtue of the Trebellian decree. But if the testator requested the heir to restore the whole inheritance, or more than three-fourths, the Pegasian senatusconsultum applied and, once he had taken upon himself the heirship voluntarily, he was obliged to sustain the whole burden of the inheritance, whether or not he retained the fourth to which he was entitled. When an heir retained a fourth part the stipulations partis et pro parte were entered into as between a legatee in part and an heir; when the heir did not retain a fourth the stipulations emptae et venditae haereditatis (analogous to those on the sale and purchase of an inheritance), were interposed. If the heir refused to accept the inheritance, the Pegasian decree provided that the praetor, at the instance of him to whom he had been asked to restore the inheritance, might compel the heir to take upon himself the inheritance, and then restore it, and that afterwards all actions should be brought by or against him who received the inheritance, in accordance with the Trebellian decree. In this case stipulations are not necessary. However, as stipulations were displeasing and simplicity is our aim, we have abrogated the Pegasian decree so that inheritances bequeathed in trust will be restored under the Trebellian decree, whether the heir has been given a fourth part, or more or less than a fourth, or even nothing. When either nothing or less than a fourth part is given to the heir, he is permitted to retain a fourth, by virtue of our authority, or even demand repayment of what he has paid over, and all actions are divided between the heir and the fideicommissary (ie, the recipient of the trust inheritance) in a just proportion, according to the Trebellian decree. The provision of the Pegasian decree by which an heir might be compelled to take upon himself the inheritance and then restore it has been transferred to the Trebellian decree. In such a case the heir neither receives profit nor suffers loss. It makes no difference whether an heir is asked to restore the whole or part only of the inheritance, or the whole of his part, or only a portion of it: the same rules apply.

If an heir is requested to give up an inheritance, after deducting some specific thing, amounting to a fourth, he may be compelled to to give it up by the Trebellian decree in the same way as if he had been asked to restore the remainder after retaining a fourth. In this case all actions are transferred to the fideicommissary and what remains with the heir (ie, the specific thing) is free from incumbrance, as if he had acquired it by way of legacy. In the other case (where the heir retains a fourth) all actions are divided, those relating to the three-fourths being transferred to the fideicommissary, and those relating to the one-fourth remaining with the heir. If the specific thing comprises the largest part of the inheritance, nevertheless all actions are transferred to the fideicommissary, and the law is the same if an heir is allowed to deduct two or more specific things, or a certain sum of money which exceeds in value the greatest part of the inheritance.

Further, even a man who is willing to die intestate may request the person whom he thinks will succeed him to give up the whole inheritance, a part of it or a specific thing. This applies to trusts only, because legacies are not valid without a testament. A fideicommissary may also be requested to hand over to another either the whole or a part of what he receives, or even to give some other thing in lieu of it.

Originally bequests in trust depended on the good faith of the heir; the emperor Augustus made them legally binding and we have enacted by our constitution that if a trust cannot be proved by a written instrument by five witnesses (the number which the law requires), the fideicommissary, having first sworn to his own good faith, may put the heir to his oath and thus compel him either to deny the trust upon oath or to comply with it. The same remedy is available against a legatee or even a fideicommissary to whom a testator has left anything with a request to give it up. If a man admits the trust after denying it, but seeks to shelter behind a subtlety of the law, he will nevertheless be compelled to carry out the trust.

Title XXIV: Of specific things bequeathed by way of trust

A man may also leave specific things in trust, eg, a field, clothes or a certain sum of money, and ask either his heir or a legatee to restore them, although a legatee cannot be charged with a legacy. A testator may leave not only his own property in trust, but also the property of his heir, a legatee, a fideicommissary or any other; however, no man may be requested to give more than he has received by means of the testament, the excess being ineffectually bequeathed. When the property of another is left in trust, the person requested to restore must either obtain from its owner the thing bequeathed, or pay its value.

Freedom may be given to a slave by virtue of a trust, because an heir, a legatee or a fideicommissary may be requested to manumit. If the slave is not the testator's own property, he must be bought and manumitted. If the slave's owner refuses to sell, the bequest is merely deferred until it can be conveniently performed. Even though he was the testator's own slave, if he is manumitted in consequence of a trust he becomes the freedman of the manumitter, not the testator; if he is given his freedom directly by testament he becomes the freedman of the testator. No one can obtain freedom directly by testament (ie, when the testator commands that freedom shall commence instantly by virtue of his testament) unless he was the slave of the testator both at the time at which the testament was made and at which the testator died.

The words generally used for bequests in trust are: 'I ask', 'I beg', 'I wish', 'I entrust', 'I commit to your good faith'. Each is as effective as if all were used together.

Title XXV: Of codicils

Codicils (like bequests in trust) were introduced by Lucius Lentulus. When he was dying in Africa he wrote several codicils, confirmed by his testament, requesting Augustus by way of bequest in trust to perform some act for him. The emperor complied with the request, and others followed the emperor's example. When Labeo, a lawyer of great eminence, disposed of his own property by codicil, the validity of codicils was placed beyond doubt.

Not only may a person who has already made his testament make a codicil; even an intestate may make bequests in trust by means of codicils. Papinian said that a codicil made before a testament must be confirmed by the testament, but the emperors Severus and Antoninus have declared that a thing left in trust in a codicil preceding a testament may be demanded by the fideicommissary if it appears that the testator has not abandoned the intention expressed in the codicil.

An inheritance cannot be given or taken away directly by codicil, although it may be left from the heir in a codicil by means of a trust. No man can impose a condition upon his heir by codicil nor effect a direct substitution.

A man may make many codicils and they require no formalities.

6 The Institutes of Justinian – Book Three

Title I: Of intestate succession

A person dies intestate if he has not made a testament, if he has made a testament but failed to observe the legal formalities, if his testament is either revoked or rendered void or no one will take upon himself the heirship by virtue of the testament. According to the law of the Twelve Tables, inheritances of intestates belong primarily to the sui heredes, ie, the proper or domestic heirs.

As we have seen before (see Book II, Title XIX) proper heirs are those who at the time of the deceased's death were under his power as, eg, a son or daughter, a grandson or granddaughter by a son, a great-grandson or great-granddaughter by a grandson of a son, etc, and it is immaterial whether these children are natural or adopted. In this context natural children include those who, although not born in lawful wedlock, are nevertheless entitled to the rights of proper heirs because they have been admitted into the order of decurions. We must also include those persons who come within our own constitutions by which it is ordained that if any person, without intending marriage, keeps a woman whom he could marry, and has children by her, and afterwards marries her and has other children by her, all such children (ie, those born before as well as after the marriage) are legitimate and in the power of their father. This rule applies although the children born after the marriage are dead or no such children were ever born. However, a grandson or granddaughter, a great-grandson or great-granddaughter, is not a proper heir unless the person preceding them in degree has ceased to be under paternal power by death or some other means, eg, emancipation. Posthumous children who would have been under the power of their father if they had been born in his lifetime are deemed to be proper heirs.

Persons may become proper heirs without their knowledge, and even though they are insane. Note that ownership of an inheritance is continued in the heir from the moment of his ancestor's death; a pupil does not need the authority of a tutor to inherit, nor an insane person the assent of his curator. Sometimes a child becomes a proper heir although he was not under power at the time of his parent's death, eg, when a person returns from captivity after the death of his father. On the other hand, it may happen that a child who, at the time of his parent's death, was under his power, shall not be his proper heir, eg, when a parent, after his decease, is found guilty of treason, by which crime his memory is rendered infamous and his possessions are forfeited to the treasury.

When there is a son or a daughter, and a grandson or granddaughter by another son, they are called equally to the inheritance of their parents; the nearer does not exclude the more remote because it is just that grandchildren should succeed in the place of their father. Similarly, if there is a grandson or granddaughter by a son, and a great-grandson or great-granddaughter by a grandson, they ought all to be called to the inheritance. It follows, therefore, that inheritances are not divided into capita, but into stirpes; thus where there is a son, and grandchildren by another son, the son has half the inheritance and the grandchildren share the other half as representatives of their father. Again, where there are grandchildren by two sons, the grandchildren of one son share one half and the grandchildren of the other son share the other half.

When considering whether a person is a proper heir it must be asked at what time it was certain that the deceased died without a testament, and a man dies without a testament if his testament is relinquished. Thus if a son is disinherited and a stranger is instituted heir, and after the son's death it becomes clear that the stranger was not in fact the heir, because he was unable or unwilling to accept the inheritance, the grandson of the deceased becomes the proper heir as at the time at which it was certain that the deceased died intestate there was no other heir but the grandchild.

A grandchild born after but conceived before the death of his grandfather will, at the death of his father, become his grandfather's proper heir if the grandfather's testament is abandoned by the instituted heir. This would not occur where the grandchild is conceived after the grandfather's death as he whom an emancipated son has adopted is not regarded as a child of the adoptive father's father. It follows that such an adopted child cannot become the proper heir of his father's father nor can he claim possession of goods as next of kin.

By the civil law emancipated children have no right to their parents' inheritances and the law of the Twelve Tables does not allow them to be called to inherit by any other right. However, the praetor, prompted by natural equity, grants them the possession of goods as fully as if they had been under power at their parents' death, and the praetor grants this whether they are the only children or whether there are others who are proper heirs. Thus if there are two sons, one emancipated and the other in power, because of the praetor's indulgence the proper heir will in effect be heir only to one half of their parents' inheritance.

But those who after emancipation have given themselves in adoption are not admitted as children to the possession of the effects of their natural father if at the time of his death they were in the adoptive family. However, if in the lifetime of their natural father they were emancipated by their adopted father, the praetor allows them to take the goods of their natural father as if they had been emancipated by him; it follows that they are regarded as strangers to their adoptive father. Those who are emancipated by their adoptive father after the death of their natural father are nevertheless strangers to their adoptive father and they do not rank as children of their natural father in regard to his inheritance. Adopted children, therefore, are in a less favourable position than natural children.

The same rules apply in regard to that possession of goods which the praetor, contrary to the testament of the parent, gives to children who are not mentioned in the testament, ie, those who are neither instituted heirs nor properly disinherited. The praetor calls those who were in power at the death of their parents, and those also who were emancipated, to the same possession of goods, but he repels those who were in an adoptive family at that time. It should be noted, however, that although those who were in an adoptive family and have been emancipated by their adoptive father after the death of their natural father, dying intestate, are not admitted by that part of the edict by which children are called to the possession of goods, yet they are admitted by another part by which the cognates of the deceased are called to the possession of his effects. But cognates are only called when there are no proper heirs, emancipated children, or agnates.

These were the old rules, but we have enacted a constitution by which it is decreed that when a natural father has given his son in adoption, the son retains all his rights as if he had remained in the power of his natural father and there had been no adoption, but the person adopted may succeed to his adopter if his adopter dies intestate. It is also enacted that if the adopter makes a testament and omits the name of his adopted son, such son can by neither the civil nor the praetorian law obtain any part of the inheritance whether he claims possession of the effects contrary to the letter of the testament or complains that the testament is inofficious. An adopter is under no obligation either to institute or disinherit his adopted son. We have further decreed that no adopted person shall receive any benefit from the Sabinian senatusconsultum by being one of three sons; he shall not obtain a fourth part of his adoptive father's effects, nor have any action upon that account. However, those who are adopted by their natural parents – by a grandfather or great-grandfather, etc – are excepted in our constitution; in such cases we have retained the old law in the same way as when the father of a family has given himself in adrogation.

The old law gave preference to descendants from males and called to the succession as proper heirs only those grandchildren who were so descended. Grandchildren born of daughters and the great-grandchildren of granddaughters were reputed to be cognates and were prohibited from succeeding to their grandfather or great-grandfather, maternal or paternal, until after the line of agnates was exhausted. The emperors Valentinian, Theodosius and Arcadius granted an equal right of succession to descendants from males and descendants from females, but thought it right that the portions of grandchildren, great-grandchildren and other lineal descendants of a female should be one-third less than their mother or grandmother, or father or grandfather, would have received at the decease of a female. Although there were only grandchildren by a female to take an inheritance the emperors did not call agnates to the succession. And as upon the decease of a son the law of the Twelve Tables calls the grandchildren and great-grandchildren, male and female, to represent their father in respect to the succession of their grandfather, so the imperial ordinance calls them to succession in the place of their mother or grandmother, with the reduction of one-third referred to above. However, we have excluded this constitution from our code and enacted that agnates shall not be entitled to any part of the goods of the deceased whilst grandchildren born of a daughter, or great-grandchildren born of a granddaugther, or any other descendants from a female in the right line are living, so that collateral relations may not be preferred to lineal descendants. As in the old law, division of the inheritance is to be in stirpes between sons and grandsons by a daughter and descendants in a right line: each line takes half of the inheritance.

Title II: Of succession by the law of agnates

When there are no proper heirs to succeed the deceased, nor any persons whom the praetor or the constitutions would call to inherit with proper heirs, the inheritance, by a law of the Twelve Tables, belongs to the nearest agnate.

Agnates are those who are related by males: thus brothers who are sons of the same father are agnates although they do not have the same mother. They are also called consanguinei, being of the same blood. An uncle is also agnated to his brother's son, and vice versa, and the children of brothers are also agnates. There are many degrees of agnation – even those born after the death of their parents are admitted – but the law grants the right of inheritance only to those who are in the nearest degree when it is established that the deceased died intestate.

The right of agnation arises also through adoption, although adopted sons are not properly called consanguinei. Again, if a brother, a paternal uncle or any other who is agnated to you in a more remote degree should adopt any person into his family, such person is included in your agnates.

Succession among males proceeds according to the right of agnation, however remote. The ancient lawyers held that females should only inherit by consanguinity if they are sisters, and not in a more remote degree, though males might be admitted in the most distant degree to inherit from females. Thus the inheritance of your brother's daughter or of the daughter of your paternal uncle or aunt would belong to you, but your inheritance would not belong to her. However, the praetor admitted her to the possession of goods (unde cognati), provided there was no agnate or nearer cognate. The law of the Twelve Tables did not make these distinctions, but called the agnates of either sex, or any degree, to succession in the same way as it admitted proper heirs. We have followed the law of the Twelve Tables and by our constitution provided that all descendants from males, whether male or female, shall be equally called to the rights of succession on intestacy according to their degree; thus females are not excluded because they are not sisters.

We have also provided that not only the son or daughter of a brother shall be called to the succession of his or her paternal uncle, but the son or daughter of a sister, who is either by the same mother or father, may also be admitted with agnates to the succession of his or her maternal uncle, although the descendants of the son or daughter of a sister are not admitted. Thus on the death of a person who is both a paternal and maternal uncle who has nephews and nieces living, both by a brother and by a sister, such children succeed as if they were all descendants from males when the deceased leaves no brother or sister, and they take the inheritance per capita: if there are brothers or sisters, and they accept the inheritance, more remote degrees are excluded.

When there are many degrees of agnates, the law of the Twelve Tables calls those who are in the nearest degree; if there are many in the same degree, all are admitted. If there is but one degree of agnates, the inheritance belongs to those who are in that degree. When a man dies and leaves no testament, the nearest agnate is he who was nearest at the time of death; when he leaves a testament, it is he who was nearest when it became certain that the testamentary heir had declined the inheritance because until that time the deceased cannot be said to have died intestate.

It was the law that there was no succession among agnates so that if the nearest agnate failed to enter upon an inheritance remoter agnates were not admitted to succeed him. However, the praetors allowed them to be called to the inheritance as cognates and we have ordained by our constitution that succession should not be denied to agnates in the inheritance of agnates, especially because the burden of tutelage passed to remoter agnates upon failure of the nearest degree.

Under the old law a parent who had emancipated a son or a daughter or any other of his lineal descendants under a trust contract was admitted to his or her succession. By our constitution it is enacted that every emancipation shall be deemed to have been made under such a contract.

Title III: Of the senatusconsultum Tertullianum

The law of the Twelve Tables preferred the issue of males and excluded those who were related by the female line so that there was no right of reciprocal succession between a mother and her son or daughter. The praetors admitted to the succession those who were related by the female line, giving them the possession of goods called unde cognati. However, the emperor Claudius allowed a mother a statutory succession to her children and, later, the senatusconsultum Tertullianum, which was passed in the reign of the emperor Hadrian, ensured that the succession of children should pass to their mother, though not to their grandmother. However, by this senatusconsultum such succession passed only if a mother, who was freeborn, had three children or, in the case of a mother who was a freedwoman, four children. It made no difference that the mother was under the power of a parent, but if she was under power she could not enter upon the inheritance without the authority of him in whose power she was.

Nevertheless, children of a deceased son who are proper heirs, or in the place of proper heirs, either in the first or an inferior degree, are preferred to the mother of such deceased son, and the son or daughter of a deceased daughter is also preferred to his or her grandmother. The father of a son or daughter is preferred to the mother, but a grandfather or great-grandfather is not preferred to the mother when the question of inheritance is only between him and the mother. Again, the consanguine brother either of a son or daughter excluded the mother, although a consanguine sister was admitted equally with the mother. But if there had been a brother and a sister of the same blood with the deceased, the brother excluded the mother, although she had the qualifying number of children, and the inheritance was divided in equal parts between the brother and sister.

However, by our constitution we have disregarded any fixed number of children and given a full right to every mother, whether freeborn or a freedwoman, of being called to the statutory succession of her child or children deceased, whether male or female. Nevertheless, we call all brothers and sisters, whether or not they are agnates, to the inheritance together with the mother, but if only the sisters and mother survive, the mother has one-half and the sisters the other. If a mother survives, and also a brother or brothers, or brothers and sisters, the inheritance of the intestate son or daughter is distributed in capita, ie, in equal shares. Mothers must show concern for the welfare of their children: if a mother fails, within a year, to demand a tutor for her children, or to require a new tutor in the place of one who has been removed or excused, she will be barred from the succession of such children if they die within puberty.

Although a son or daughter is illegitimate, by the senatusconsultum Tertullianum the mother may be admitted to succeed to their goods.

Title IV: Of the senatusconsultum Orfitianum

Reciprocally, children are admitted to the goods of their intestate mothers by the senatusconsultum Orfitianum, which was enacted in the reign of the emperor Marcus Antoninus. This decree gave statutory succession both to sons and daughters, although they are under power, and they are also preferred to consanguine brothers and to the agnates of their deceased mother. Later, by imperial constitutions, grandsons and granddaughters were also called to inherit as well as sons and daughters.

Successions proceeding from the senatusconsulta Tertullianum and Orfitianum are not extinguished by change of status; change of status affects only those inheritances which proceed from the law of the Twelve Tables. Even illegitimate children are admitted by the senatusconsultum Orfitianum to the inheritance of their mother.

When some of the statutory heirs renounce the inheritance, or are prevented from entering upon it by death or any other cause, their shares fall to those who have accepted, or to their heirs, even if they die before the refusal or failure of their co-heirs.

Title V: Of the succession of cognates

After the proper heirs, and those whom the praetor and the constitutions call to inherit with the proper heirs, and after the statutory heirs – among whom are agnates and those whom the above mentioned senatusconsulta and our constitution have placed amongst them – the praetor calls the nearest cognates. By the law of the Twelve Tables, neither agnates who have suffered change of status nor their issue are regarded as statutory heirs, but they are called by the praetor in the third order of succession. However, the constitution of the emperor Anastasius calls an emancipated brother or sister to the succession of a brother or sister along with those who have not been emancipated, although he or she is called subject to a certain deduction. This constitution prefers an emancipated brother or sister to other agnates of an inferior degree, although unemancipated, and consequently to all cognates.

Collaterals related by the female line are called by the praetor in the third order of succession according to their proximity. Children in an adoptive family are likewise called in the third order of succession to the inheritance of their natural parents. Children born of an uncertain father have no agnates and are regarded as having no father. Similarly, consanguinity cannot be said to exist between them because consanguinity is a kind of agnation. Therefore, they can only be allied to each other by cognation, ie, from the mother, and it is for this reason that they are called by the praetor according to their proximity.

It should be noted that any person may by the right of agnation be admitted to inherit, even though he is in, eg, the tenth degree, but the praetor promises the possession of goods to cognates only as far as the sixth degree of cognation, and in the seventh degree to cognates who are children of a second cousin.

Title VI: Of the degrees of relationship

It is necessary to show how the degrees of cognation are computed, and first it must be said that there is one species of cognation relating to ascendants, another to descendants and a third to collaterals. The first or superior cognation is that relation which a man bears to his parents; the second or inferior is that which he bears to his children; the third is that which he bears to his brothers and sisters and their issue, and also to his paternal or maternal uncles and aunts. The superior and inferior cognation commence at the first degree; but the transverse or collateral cognation commences at the second.

A father or a mother is in the first degree in the right line ascending; a son or a daughter is in the first degree in the right line descending. A grandmother or grandfather is in the second degree in the right line ascending; a grandson or granddaughter is in the second degree in the right line descending; a brother or a sister is also in the second degree in the collateral line. A great-grandfather or a great-grandmother is in the third degree in the right line ascending; a great-grandson or great-granddaughter is in the third degree in the right line descending: the son or daughter of a brother or sister is also in the third degree in the collateral line and a paternal or maternal uncle or aunt is also in the third degree, and so on.

It will be seen that a generation always adds one degree and it is much easier to determine in what degree any person is related to another than to denote such person by a proper term of cognation. The degrees of agnation are computed in the same way as the degrees of cognation.

That part of the edict in which the possession of goods is promised according to the right of proximity does not apply to servile cognation, neither has such cognation been regarded by any ancient law. However, by constitution concerning the right of patronage we have ordained that if a slave has a child or children by a freewoman or a slave (or a slave has a child or children by a freeman or a slave), and such father and mother attain their freedom, the children succeed to their father or mother and no regard is paid to the right of patronage. Such children also succeed to each other, whether or not they are by the same father and mother. In brief, children born in slavery, and afterwards manumitted, succeed in the same way as those who are the issue of parents legally married.

It will have been observed that those who are in an equal degree of cognation are not always called equally to the succession and, further, that the nearest cognate is not always preferred. As the first place is given to proper heirs and those who are numbered with them, a great-grandson is preferred to the brother, or even the father or mother, of the deceased; it makes no difference that the great-grandson was or was not under the power of the deceased at the time of his death or that he was descended by the female line. However, when there are no proper heirs or persons who are numbered with them, an agnate, possessing the full right of agnation, although he is in the most distant degree, is generally preferred to a cognate in a nearer degree; thus the great-grandson of a paternal uncle is preferred to an uncle or aunt who is maternal. When there are no proper heirs or persons who are numbered with them, nor any who are preferred by the right of agnation, the nearest cognate is called to the succession and, if there are many in the same degree of cognation, they are called equally. But a brother and sister, although emancipated, are called to the succession of their brothers and sisters as they are preferred to agnates of a more remote degree.

Title VII: Of the succession of freedmen

A freedman could formerly omit from his testament any mention of his patron; the law of the Twelve Tables called the patron to the inheritance only where the freedman died intestate and without proper heirs. The law was amended by the edict of the praetor so that every freedman who made a testament was commanded to leave half of his property to his patron; if he failed to do so possession of half was given contrary to the testament. However, the patron was excluded by natural and lawful children of a freedman, whether under his power or emancipated or given in adoption, provided they had been appointed heirs for any part of his estate or had claimed possession contrary to the testament by virtue of the praetorian edict.

The Papinian law increased the rights of patrons by providing that a patron should take an equal share of his freedman's estate, whether he died testate or intestate, provided he left 100,000 sestertii and fewer than three children. Thus if such a freedman left only one child, the patron took a half; if he left two, a third; if he left three, the patron was wholly excluded.

By our imperial constitution we have ordained that if a freedman or freedwoman leaves less than 100 aurei (the equivalent to one hundred thousand sestertii) the patron shall not be entitled to any share in the succession where there is a testament. If a freedman or freedwoman dies intestate and without children, the right of patronage is preserved entire, as it was under the law of the Twelve Tables. If a freed person leaves more than 100 aurei and leaves a child or children of either sex or any degree as the heirs and possessors of his goods, such child or children succeed their parent to the entire exclusion of the patron and his heirs; if any freed persons died without children and intestate, we have called their patrons or patronesses to their whole inheritances. If any freed person worth more than 100 aurei has made a testament, omitted his patron and left no children, or has disinherited them, or if a mother or maternal grandfather, being freed persons, omitted their children in their testaments, so that such testaments cannot be proved to be inofficious, then, by virtue of our constitution, the patron succeeds to a third part of the deceased's estate by the possession of goods contrary to the testament, free of the burden of trusts or legacies, even for the benefit of the deceased's children. If such freed persons leave less than a third to their patrons, the deficiency is to be made up; the burden of legacies and trusts is borne by the patron's co-heirs. Our constitution provides that patrons and patronesses, their children and collateral relations, as far as the fifth degree, might be called to the succession of their freedmen and freedwomen. If there are many children of one patron or patroness, or of two or more patrons or patronesses, he who is nearest in degree is called to the succession of his freedman or freedwoman; when there are many in equal degree the estate is divided in capita, and the same order applies among the collaterals of patrons and patronesses as we have made the laws of succession almost the same in regard to freeborn and freed persons.

What we have said relates to the freed persons of today, all of whom are citizens of Rome; other classes of freedmen – dedititii (surrendered persons) and Latini (Latins) – have been abolished. Latini never enjoyed any right of succession, their possessions being detained by their manumitter by virtue of the law Junia Norbana. With some additions, the method of conferring the freedom of Latini has become the method of conferring the freedom of Rome.

Title VIII: Of the assignment of freedmen

Although the goods of freedmen belong equally to all the children of the patron who are in the same degree, a parent may assign a freedman to any one of his children so that after the parent's death that child alone is the freedman's patron and the other children are wholly excluded. If the assignee dies without issue the excluded children regain their former right. Every freed person is assignable, man or woman, and an assignment may be made to a daughter or granddaughter as well as to a son or grandson. The power of assigning is enjoyed by him who has two or more children under his power; if a father assigns a freedman to his son and then emancipates the son, the assignment is void. Assignments may be made by testament or even by word of mouth.

Title IX: Of the possession of goods

The right of succeeding by the possession of goods was introduced by the praetor to amend the ancient law not only in regard to the inheritances of intestates but in regard also to the inheritances of those who die testate; for if a posthumous stranger (ie, a stranger born after the date of the testament) was instituted an heir, although he could not enter upon the inheritance by the civil law because his institution as heir would not be valid, by the praetorian or honorary law he might be made the possessor of the goods. By virtue of our constitution such a stranger may now be legally instituted an heir. But the praetor sometimes gives the possession of goods, not to impugn or amend the old law, but rather to confirm it; for he gives the possession of goods in accordance with the testament to those who are appointed the deceased's heirs by a valid testament. He also calls proper heirs and agnates to the possession of the goods of intestates, although the inheritance would be theirs by the civil law. But those whom the praetor calls to an inheritance do not become legal heirs, for the praetor cannot make an heir: heirs are made only by a lex, or what has the effect of a lex, eg, a decree of the senate or an imperial constitution. When the praetor gives any persons the possession of goods, they stand in the place of heirs, and are called the possessors of the goods. But the praetor has devised many other orders of persons to whom the possession of goods can be granted so that no man may die without a successor, and by the rules of justice and equity he has greatly enlarged the right of taking inheritances, which was bound within the most narrow limits by the law of the Twelve Tables.

The kinds of the possessions of goods when there is a testament are, firstly, that possession which is given to children of whom no mention is made in the testament (ie, possession contrary to the testament) and, secondly, that which the praetor gives to all duly instituted heirs (ie, possession in accordance with the testament). The praetor gives possession of goods in regard to intestates, firstly, to the proper heirs or to those whom by the praetorian edict are numbered amongst the proper heirs; secondly, to the statutory heirs; thirdly, to the ten persons whom he preferred to a stranger manumitter, ie, to a father, a mother, or a grandfather or grandmother, paternal or maternal, to a son, a daughter, or to a grandson or granddaughter, by a son or by a daughter, to a brother or sister, either consanguine or uterine (issue of the father or of the mother); fourthly, to the nearest cognates; fifthly, to the nearest member of the patron's family; sixthly, to the patron or patroness, and to their children, and their parents; seventhly, to a husband and wife; eighthly, to the cognates of a manumitter or patron.

By our constitutions we have admitted the possession of goods contrary to the testament and in accordance with the testament as necessary, and also the possessions of goods given on intestacy considered first, second, fourth and seventh; the third, fifth, sixth and eighth possessions of goods on intestacy are now unnecessary and have been abrogated.

However, another possession has been added by the praetors by which possession of goods is promised to all those to whom it is appointed to be given by any law, senatusconsultum or constitution; this is the last and extraordinary resource of those who are called to the successions of testates or intestates by any particular law, decree of the senate or new constitution.

The praetor has seen fit to limit the time for demanding the possession of goods as follows: parents and children, natural or adopted, have one year in which to accept or refuse the possession of goods; all others, agnates or cognates, have only one hundred days. If any person entitled does not claim within the time limited, his right of possession accrues first to those in the same degree with himself; in the absence of such persons, the praetor bestows the possession of goods upon those in the next degree. If the possession of goods is refused it is not necessary to wait till the time limit expires, but those next in succession are admitted immediately. In calculating the time, only dies utiles (days on which a claim could be legally made) are taken into account. A formal claim is not required; any act which clearly shows that a man has consented to accept the praetorian succession within the prescribed time is sufficient.

Title X: Of acquisition by adrogation

There is also universal succession arising from general consent and usage. For example, if the father of a family gave himself in adrogation, all things which belonged to him, and whatever was due to him (with the exception of those things which perished on diminution or change of status, eg, rights of agnation), formerly passed to the adrogator. Use and usufruct were also excepted, but our constitution provides that they are not to be destroyed by the least diminution.

But we have now limited the acquisitions gained by adrogation, in a similar way to gains by natural parents; for nothing is now acquired by either natural or adoptive parents except the bare usufruct of those things which their children possess from an extraneous source, the ownership remaining in the children. But if an adrogated son dies under the power of his adrogator, the ownership of the goods of such son passes to the adrogator, unless there are persons whom we have by our constitution preferred to the father in the succession of those things which could not be acquired for him.

On the other hand, an adrogator is not bound at law to satisfy the debts of his adopted son, but he may be sued in his son's name and if he refuses to defend his son the creditors may, by order of the magistrates, seize and sell those goods of which the usufruct, as well as the ownership, would have been in the debtor had he not made himself subject to the power of another.

Title XI: Of him to whom property is assigned to preserve gifts of freedom

A new kind of succession has arisen from the constitution of the emperor Marcus Aurelius whereby slaves to whom freedom has been bequeathed, in order to obtain their freedom, may ask that the inheritance be assigned to them if it has not been accepted by the instituted heir. A rescript of the emperor to Pompilius Rufus was to the same effect and also provided that when goods are assigned to a particular man for the preservation of liberty, they cannot be sold by creditors.

This rescript applies wherever freedom is conferred by testament. What happens when a master dies intestate, having bequeathed freedom to his slaves by codicil, and his inheritance is not entered upon? We answer that the rescript extends to this case; certainly, if a master dies testate, and by codicil bequeaths freedom, the rescript has full force. The constitution is effective only when it is certain that no one will enter upon the inheritance. Once freedom has been obtained it cannot afterwards be revoked, eg, where the heir is restored in integrum.

This constitution was made for the protection of liberty; if there is no gift of freedom it has no effect. However, although the constitution does not say so, if a master gives freedom to his slaves, either inter vivos or mortis causa, we would allow the slaves to petition that the estate of the deceased be assigned to them in order to prevent the creditors from complaining that freedom was given to defraud them. The rescript was deficient in many ways and we have enacted a constitution explaining the rights of succession in the fullest detail.

Title XII: Of successions now obsolete resulting from the sale of the property and under the senatusconsultum Claudianum

There were many other kinds of universal successions, eg, the bonorum emptio (sale of the property) which was introduced in order that the estates of debtors might be sold. The sale of the property disappeared with the introduction of the extraordinary procedure; creditors can now possess and dispose of the goods of their debtors by order of a judge.

By virtue of the senatusconsultum Claudianum there was another form of universal acquisition called miserabilis; thus if a freewoman cohabited with a slave she lost her freedom and, with her freedom, her property. We have not allowed this to be inserted in our Digest.

Title XIII: Of obligations

Let us now pass to obligations. An obligation is a legal tie by which we are necessarily bound to make some payment in accordance with the laws of our country. Obligations are either civil (ie, constituted by statute, or approved by the civil law) or praetorian or honorary (ie, created by the praetor in exercise of his jurisdiction).

The next division of obligations is into four kinds, ie, those arising from contract, quasi-contract, malfeasance (delict or tort) and quasi-malfeasance. Obligations arising from contract are of four kinds, ie, obligations contracted by the thing itself, by word of mouth, by writing and by the mere consent of the parties.

Title XIV: Of the way in which obligations are contracted by the thing itself

An obligation is contracted by the thing itself, ie, by the delivery of it, as a loan or mutuum : anything which consists of weight, number or measure, eg, wine, oil, coin, silver or gold, may be delivered as a mutuum. When so delivered it becomes the absolute property of the receiver, but other things of the same nature and quality must be paid in lieu of them. This contract gives rise to the action certi condictio.

He who has received what was not due to him, as a result of a mistake, is bound by the thing received, and an action of condictio lies against him for its recovery, in the same way as if he had received it as a mutuum. Hence a pupil, when he has received anything not due to him without the authority of his tutor, is not subject to the action because he is not subject to an action on account of the delivery of the thing as a mutuum.

He also to whom any particular thing is given in order to be used is bound by the delivery of the thing and subject to an action called commodataria. However, a commodatum (thing lent) is not intended to become the property of the receiver, and he is bound to restore the identical thing which he has received. Again, he who has accepted a mutuum is not freed from his obligation if by accident, eg, the fall of a building, fire, shipwreck, thieves or enemies, he loses what he has received; he who has received a commodatum must use the utmost diligence in keeping and preserving it (it is not enough that he has taken the same care as he normally takes of his own property if it appears that a more diligent man might have preserved it), but if the loss was occasioned by a superior force or some extraordinary accident, and not by any fault, he is not obliged to make good the loss. However, if he chooses to travel with what he has received as a commodatum, and loses it by shipwreck or thieves or enemies, he is bound to make restitution, or to pay its value. A commodatum must be gratuitous; if a price is paid the thing is let or hired.

Any person who is entrusted with a deposit is bound by the delivery of the thing, and is subject to an action of deposit, because he is under an obligation to make restitution of the very thing which he received. However, a depositary is only answerable on account of fraud, not fault, such as negligence; thus he is not liable if the thing is stolen from him, even if he was careless in the way he kept it.

A creditor who has received a pledge is bound by the delivery of it, because by the action called pigneratitia he is obliged to restore the very thing which he has received. The creditor is required to use the utmost diligence in keeping the thing pledged; if he does this, and the pledge is lost by mere accident, he is safe and may still sue to recover the debt.

Title XV: Of verbal obligations

A verbal obligation is made by question and answer, when we stipulate that anything shall be given or done; two actions arise, viz, the action called condictio certi (when the stipulation is certain) and condictio ex stipulatu (when the stipulation is uncertain). The following expressions were probably used in all verbal obligations:

Spondes (do you bind yourself)? Spondeo (I do bind myself).

Promittis (do you promise)? Promitto (I do promise).

Fide-promittis (do you become an additional debtor)? Fide-promitto (I do so become).

Fide-jubes (do you become a surety)? Fide-jubeo (I do so become).

Dabis (will you give)? Dabo (I will give).

Facies (will you do)? Faciam (I will do).

The stipulation may be expressed in Latin, Greek or any other language, provided the parties to the stipulation understand it. Indeed, it is not necessary for both parties to use the same language, and two Greeks may contract in Latin. Formerly it was necessary to use the expressions set out above, but the constitution of the emperor Leo removed this formality and required only that the parties should understand each other and agree, using any form of words.

Stipulations may be absolute, have to be performed by a certain day, or conditional. A stipulation is absolute when a man says 'Do you promise to pay me five aurei ?'; in this case the money may be demanded immediately. It has to be performed by a certain day when a man says 'Do you promise to pay me ten aurei on the 1st of March?'; here the money is immediately due, but cannot be demanded or sued for before the day comes. The whole day, in this example 1st March, is allowed for payment. But if a man stipulates 'Do you promise to give me ten aurei a year as long as I live?' the obligation is absolute and perpetual and binding on the heirs of the obliger, although if the heir of the stipulator demands payment, he may be met by a plea founded on the agreement.

A stipulation is conditional when an obligation is referred to some event and takes effect upon something being done or not being done, happening or not happening, eg, 'Do you promise to pay me five aurei if Titius is made a consul?', or 'Do you promise to pay me five aurei if I do not ascend the Capitol?'; the second example is in effect a stipulation that five aurei should be paid to him at the time of his death. In every conditional stipulation there is merely a hope that the thing stipulated will become due, and this hope a man transmits to his heirs if he dies before the fulfilment of the condition. Even places are inserted in a stipulation, eg, 'Do you promise to give me such a particular thing at Carthage?': this stipulation, although it appears to be absolute, involves the period of time which would enable the obligor to pay the thing promised at Carthage. If a man at Rome stipulated 'Do you promise to pay me a sum of money this day at Carthage?' the stipulation is void because its performance is impossible.

Conditions which relate to the time present or past either instantly annul an obligation, or instantly enforce it; thus if a man stipulates 'Do you promise me the payment of a sum of money if Titius has ever been a consul?' or 'If Maevius is now living?' the stipulation is void if Titius has never been a consul or Maevius is not now living. On the other hand, if Titius has been a consul, or Maevius is now living, the stipulation is good and may be enforced.

Not only things, eg, a field, a slave or a book, but also acts may be the subject of stipulations; thus we may stipulate that something shall or shall not be done, and in these stipulations it is wise to add a penalty clause, lest the value of the stipulation should be uncertain and the demandant compelled to prove the amount of his interest.

Title XVI: Of joint stipulators and joint obligors

Two or more persons may stipulate, and two or more persons may become obligors. They are joint stipulators when, after all questions have been asked, the obligor answers

'I promise to pay each of you'. If he first promises Titius and then promises another who questions him, there will be two obligations and not two stipulators to one obligation. Two or more become joint obligors, if, after being questioned, eg, 'Maevius, do you promise to pay ten aurei ?' and 'Serius, do you promise to pay the same ten aurei?', they each of them answer separately 'I do promise'.

By joint stipulations and obligations the whole sum stipulated becomes due to every person stipulating, and every obligor is bound for the payment of the whole. It follows that one of the stipulators receiving the debt, or any one of the obligors paying it, discharges the obligation of the rest, and all are free. Where there are two joint obligors, one may bind himself absolutely, the other to make payment on a certain day, or upon condition; neither the certain day nor the condition will prevent the person bound absolutely from being sued for payment of the whole.

Title XVII: Of stipulations by slaves

A slave obtains the power of stipulating from the person of his master, but in many instances the inheritance represents the person of a master deceased; therefore, whatever an hereditary slave (ie, a slave belonging to the inheritance) stipulates for before the inheritance is entered upon, he acquires it for the inheritance and, of course, for him who afterwards becomes the heir.

No matter how he stipulates, whether for himself, a fellow slave or generally without naming any person, a slave always acquires for his master. And the same applies to children who are under the power of their father with regard to those things which they can acquire for him. But when a thing to be done is stipulated, eg, that a slave shall be allowed to pass through a field, it is the slave only, not the master, who is permitted to pass.

If a slave who is owned in common by several masters stipulates, he acquires a share for each master according to the proportion in which they own him. But if he stipulates at the command of a particular master, or in his name, he acquires solely for that master. If a slave owned in common by two masters stipulates for a thing which cannot be acquired for one of them, eg, when the thing already belongs to him, the whole is acquired for the other master.

Title XVIII: Of the classification of stipulations

Some stipulations are judicial, others praetorian, others conventional, and others common, ie, both praetorian and judicial.

Judicial stipulations are those which proceed merely from the office of the judge, eg, when security is ordered to be given against fraud, for pursuing a slave who has fled or for paying his value.

Praetorian stipulations are those which proceed merely from the office of the praetor, eg, when security is ordered to be given on account of damage not yet done, but likely to occur, and for the payment of legacies. Praetorian stipulations include those required by the aediles.

Conventional stipulations are those made by the agreement of both parties without the intervention of a judge or praetor; they depend upon the consent of the persons contracting.

Common stipulations are those which are ordered for the security of a pupil's estate – sometimes a praetor requires them, sometimes a judge if the circumstances so require.

Title XIX: Of useless stipulations

Everything which we can own can be the subject-matter of a stipulation, whether it is moveable or immoveable. But stipulations are useless if they concern:

things which do not or cannot exist, eg, a slave who is dead, though believed to be living;

things sacred, though thought not to be so;

a thing in constant public use, eg, a theatre;

a free person who was believed to be a slave;

something which we already own.

Such stipulations are immediately void and cannot continue in suspense, eg, because a free person may become a slave. On the other hand, although a thing may properly be made the subject-matter of a stipulation, if it afterwards falls under the class of any of the things mentioned above without the fault of the obliger, the stipulation is extinguished. A stipulation such as 'Do you promise to give me Lucius Titius when he shall become a slave?' is never valid.

If a man promises that another shall give or do something, eg, that Titius shall pay five aurei, the promisor is not bound; however, if he promises that he will cause Titius to pay five aurei, his promise is binding. If a man stipulates for any person other than he in whose power he is the stipulation is void; nevertheless, payment of a thing promised may be made to a stranger, eg, when a man stipulates 'Do you promise to make payment to me, or to Seius?'. In such a case the obligation is to the stipulator, but payment may be made to Seius, even against his will. If this happens the obligor is released from his debt, but the stipulator may have an action of mandate against Seius. If a man stipulates that ten aurei shall be paid to him and to another not under his power, the stipulation is good, although in this case the stipulator acquires only a half. But if you stipulate for another who is under your power, you acquire for yourself.

A stipulation is void if the party questioned does not answer in accordance with the demand, eg, when a person stipulates that ten aurei shall be paid to him, and you answer five, or vice versa. A stipulation is also void if a man stipulates absolutely, and you promise conditionally or on a certain day, or vice versa. However, if you answer only 'I promise', you are deemed to have agreed to his day or condition because it is not necessary to repeat every word used by the stipulator.

A stipulation is also void if you stipulate with him who is in your power, or if he stipulates with you. A slave cannot become liable to anyone, although the son of a family can enter into an obligation with any person except his father.

Anyone who is dumb or completely deaf can neither stipulate nor promise, and a madman cannot transact any business because he does not understand what he is doing. A pupil can transact any business if his tutor consents, where his authority is necessary. Such consent is required when the pupil would bind himself, but he can stipulate, or cause others to be bound to him, without his tutor's authority. What we have said of pupils applies to those who have some understanding, ie, to infants and those a little above that age. Persons a little above the age of infancy are allowed the same rights as those who are near the age of puberty, but a son under the age of puberty and in his father's power cannot bind himself, even with his father's consent.

If an impossible condition, ie, one that is impossible in the nature of things, is added to an obligation the stipulation is void. Thus if a man says 'Do you promise me ten aurei if I touch the heavens with my finger?' the condition is deemed impossible; however, if he says 'Do you promise me ten aurei if I do not touch the sky with my finger?' the stipulation causes an absolute obligation the performance of which may be immediately demanded.

A verbal obligation made between absent persons is also void. However, in our constitution addressed as a rescript to the advocates of Caesarea we have decreed that full credit must be given to documents which declare that the contracting parties were present, unless the party who alleges absence establishes, by writing or witnesses, that either of the parties was in some other place during the whole of the day on which the document was made.

A man could not stipulate that a thing should be given him after his own death any more than he could stipulate that a thing should be given him after the death of the obligor. Neither could any person under the power of another stipulate that anything should be given him after his death. Again, a stipulation 'Do you promise to give me five aurei the day before I die, or the day before you die?' was also invalid, but we have amended these rules so that if it is stipulated that a thing shall be given after, or immediately before, the death of the stipulator or the obligor, the stipulation is good.

Again, if a man stipulated 'Do you promise me a sum of money today if a certain ship arrives tomorrow from Asia?' the stipulation would have been invalid because it was preposterously conceived. However, the emperor Leo thought that such stipulations ought not to be rejected when relating to marriage portions, and we have ordained that such stipulations shall be binding when relating not only to marriage portions but also to anything else.

A stipulation 'Do you promise to give me ten aurei when I shall die?' or 'when you shall die?' was good by the ancient law, and is so now. We may also legally stipulate that a thing shall be given after the death of a third person. If a properly attested document states that a man has entered into an obligation by promise, it will be presumed that the promise was in answer to a precedent question, and that everything was done regularly. When many things are included in one stipulation, a man binds himself to give them all if he simply answers 'I promise'. However, if he promises to give only one or some of the things stipulated, he is bound only in accordance with his promise. Strictly, we ought to stipulate for everything severally, and to answer severally.

As has already been said, no man can stipulate on behalf of another; but if a man would effectually contract for another he should stipulate that unless the covenants of his stipulation are performed, the obliger shall be subject to a penalty payable to him who would otherwise receive no advantage from the obligation. Thus a man may stipulate 'Do you promise to give me ten aurei if you do not give the thing stipulated to Titius?' However, a man may stipulate for the benefit of another when he himself also receives an advantage from it. Thus a man may stipulate that a thing shall be given to his proctor or attorney, or to his creditor. On the other hand, he who promises that another shall perform a particular act is not bound unless he makes himself subject to a penalty if the act is not performed by that other.

No man can legally stipulate that a thing shall be given him when it becomes his own. If the stipulator stipulates in regard to one thing, and the obligor promises in relation to another, no obligation is contracted, eg, where a man stipulates that Stichus should be given to him, and the obligor intends to give Pamphilus, believing that Pamphilus is called Stichus.

A promise made for a base purpose, eg, to commit homicide or sacrilege, is not binding. If a stipulation is entered into upon condition, and the stipulator dies pending the event, his heir has an action against the obligor if the event afterwards happens. Similarly, if the obligor dies before the condition happens, his heir may be sued by the stipulator. If a man stipulates that a thing shall be given to him this year or this month, he cannot sue the obligor until the whole year or month has elapsed. Again, if a man stipulates for a piece of land or a slave, he must allow a reasonable time for delivery.

Title XX: Of sureties

It often happens that others bind themselves for him who promises; such persons are called sureties.

Sureties may be received in all obligations, whether contracted by the delivery of the thing itself, by words, by writing, or the mere consent of the parties, and it is immaterial whether the obligation is civil or natural. Thus a man may make himself surety for a slave when the thing due is a natural debt or obligation, and this is so whether the man who accepts the surety is a stranger or the slave's master. A surety's obligation passes to his heir and a surety may be accepted before or after an obligation is entered into.

Where there are several sureties, each is bound for the whole debt and the creditor may choose from whom he will demand it, but by a rescript of the emperor Hadrian a creditor may be obliged to demand separately and pro rata from every surety who is solvent at the time of the suit; if any surety is insolvent, the burden falls upon the rest. If a creditor obtains his whole demand from one surety, the whole loss is his (ie, the surety's) because he could have called in aid the rescript of the emperor Hadrian.

Sureties ought not to be bound in a greater sum than the debtor owes, though they may be bound for less. Again, when the obliger promises absolutely, the surety may promise conditionally, but the surety cannot be bound absolutely when the principal debtor is bound only conditionally. An obligation to give a thing immediately is greater than an obligation to give it after a time.

If a surety has been obliged to pay anything for the principal debtor he has an action of mandate against him for the recovery of the sum paid.

A surety may bind himself even in Greek. If a man admits in writing that he has made himself a surety it is presumed that all the necessary formalities were observed.

Title XXI: Of written obligations

Formerly, written obligations were made by registering the names of the contractors, but these contracts, which were called nomina, are no longer in use. However, if a man admits in writing that he owes what in fact he never received, when sued he cannot maintain that the money was never paid if much time has elapsed since the date of the obligation. Hence, today, a man is bound by his written note if he cannot legally bring an exception, and from such a written contract arises an action called a condiction when no stipulation or verbal obligation can be established. Formerly, a man was allowed not less than five years in which to bring an exception pecuniae non numeratae (ie, an exception of money not paid), but we have ordained that an exception shall not be brought after the expiration of two years.

Title XXII: Of obligations by consent

Obligations are made by consent in buying, selling, letting, hiring, partnerships and mandates; neither writing nor the presence of the parties is absolutely essential and it is not necessary that anything should be given or delivered. Note also that in contracts by consent the parties are bound to each other mutually to do what is just and right; in verbal obligations one party stipulates and the other promises.

Title XXIII: Of buying and selling

A contract of buying and selling is concluded as soon as the price of the thing to be sold is agreed, although the price has not been paid nor even an earnest (which serves only as proof) given. This applies only to purchases and sales which are not in writing, and in these cases we have made no change. However, where there is a written contract, it is not concluded unless the documents of sale have been written by the contracting parties, or at least signed by them. If the documents are drawn by a public notary, the contract is not binding if any formality has been omitted or the documents are incomplete. Nevertheless, if earnest has once been given, whether the contract is written or unwritten, a buyer who refuses to fulfil loses his earnest, and the seller, if he refuses, must pay double the value of the earnest. The price of the thing to be sold must always be fixed; until then there can be no buying and selling.

At one time there was much doubt as to the position, but we have ordained that where it is agreed that a thing shall be sold at a price to be fixed by a third party, there is a valid contract subject to that condition. If the third party refuses, or is unable, to fix the price, the sale is null, and the same applies to contracts of letting and hiring. The price must consist of a sum of money. At one time there was much dispute as to whether the price could consist of anything else, eg, a slave or a piece of land, but the view has prevailed that an exchange is a special kind of contract distinct from sale.

As soon as a contract of sale is concluded, the goods are at the buyer's risk, although they have not been delivered to him. Thus if a slave dies, or a building is destroyed by fire, the loss falls on the buyer and he must pay the agreed price, unless the loss is occasioned by the fraud or neglect of the seller. On the other hand, if after the sale anything is added to lands by alluvion or otherwise, the buyer profits by it. If a slave who is sold either runs away or is stolen without fraud or negligence on the part of the seller, the seller is answerable if he undertook the safe custody of the slave pending delivery; if he did not he is not responsible. The same applies with regard to all other animals and things, but when the loss falls on the buyer the seller must transfer to the buyer all rights of action, whether real or personal, for he who has not delivered the thing sold is still considered the owner of it.

A sale may be contracted conditionally as well as absolutely, eg, 'If within a certain time you shall approve of the slave Stichus, he shall be yours for ten aurei'. Whoever knowingly purchases a sacred, religious or public place, eg, a court of justice, makes a void purchase, but if the seller leads him to believe it to be private property he has an action ex empto against the seller to recover the damage arising from the deceit. The same rule applies where a freeman is bought as a slave.

Title XXIV: Of letting and hiring

Letting and hiring are closely allied to buying and selling and are governed by the same rules; they are contracted when the hire is fixed by the parties. The person who lets has an action called actio locati; the hirer has an action called actio conducti.

What we have said in regard to the sale of a thing when the price is to be fixed by a third person applies also to lettings and hirings. Therefore, if a man sends his clothes to a tailor to be mended, and does not previously agree any price, a contract of letting and hiring has not properly been made, but an action may be brought by either party praescriptis verbis, ie, in words prescribed and adapted to the circumstances of the case.

Again, an exchange of things does not constitute a letting and hiring, but is a distinct kind of contract. Thus if two neighbours each have an ox and they agree to lend each other their ox alternately for ten days, and the ox of one dies while in the possession of the other, he who has lost his ox can neither bring the action locati, nor conducti, nor even commodati, because the loan was not gratuitous; however, he may sue by virtue of an action praescriptis verbis, ie, by an action upon the case.

In some cases it was difficult to distinguish a contract of buying and selling from a letting and hiring, eg, where lands were demised to be enjoyed for ever, upon condition that a certain yearly rent be paid to the owner. However, doubts were removed when the emperor Zeno declared an emphyteusis to be neither a sale nor a hiring, but a special kind of contract supported by its own particular covenants: when there is no covenant which declares upon whom the loss shall fall, eg, in the event of the whole estate being destroyed by an earthquake, the loss falls on the owner; if part only is destroyed, the tenant is the sufferer. This is still the law.

Similar doubts arose where, eg, Titius agreed with a goldsmith to make a certain number of rings of a particular size and weight, for which Titius would pay ten aurei as the value of the workmanship and the gold. Cassius thought that it would be a buying and selling in regard to the material and a letting and hiring in regard to the work, but it is now settled that only a buying and selling would be contracted. However, should Titius give his own gold and agree to pay only for the workmanship, the contract would be a letting and hiring.

The hirer is not only obliged to comply with the terms of the contract of hiring but must also in equity perform whatever has been omitted. A person who gives or promises hire for the use of clothes, silver, horses, etc, must take the same care of them as the most diligent father of a family takes of his own property. If he does this, yet the things hired are lost by accident, he is not answerable for the loss.

If the hirer dies before the period of the hiring expires, his heir is entitled to the thing hired for the remainder of the term.

Title XXV: Of partnership

Persons often enter into a general partnership, ie, a partnership of all their goods, or into a particular partnership, ie, with regard only to one kind of business, such as buying and selling slaves.

If no express agreement is made by the partners concerning their shares of profit and loss, such profit and loss as there may be are equally divided; if an agreement is made it must be observed. Quintus Mutius thought that an agreement where, eg, Titius should receive two parts of the profit and bear but a third of the loss, and Seius receive but a third of the profit and bear two parts of the loss, should not be binding, but Servius Sulpicius thought otherwise and his opinion has prevailed. Again, a partner may by agreement take a share of the profit and not be accountable for any part of the loss, but it must be understood that if profit accrues from one transaction, and loss from another, only the balance is regarded as profit. If partners expressly mention only the division of profit or loss, and make no mention of the other, that which is not mentioned is shared in the same way as that which is mentioned.

A partnership continues as long as the partners continue to wish it to do so; if one of them renounces the partnership is dissolved. If a man renounces with a fraudulent intent his renunciation is of no avail. Thus if a partner renounces as soon as he finds that he has been appointed an heir, he will be compelled to share the inheritance equally with his former partners, but if an inheritance which he did not expect falls to him after renunciation, the whole of that inheritance is his own. Those from whom a partner has separated himself by renunciation keep for themselves whatever they acquire after the renunciation of that partner. A partnership is also dissolved by the death of one of the partners, unless special provision to the contrary was made when the partnership was formed. Again, if a partnership was entered into in respect of some particular business, and that business is completed, the partnership is at an end. A partnership is also dissolved by confiscation of a partner's property, eg, by the fiscus, in which case the partner is deemed to be civilly dead. Again, if a partner, being pressed by his debts, surrenders his goods and they are sold to satisfy his debts, the partnership is dissolved. If the rest of the partners wish to continue in partnership with or without this man a new partnership begins.

Although there was some doubt as to the position, it is now clear that a partner is answerable to his co-partner for his negligence as well as his fraud. However, he is not answerable for negligence if he used the same care and diligence as he usually observed in keeping his own property.

Title XXVI: Of mandate

A mandate is made in five ways: when it is given solely for the benefit of the mandator; or partly for his benefit, and partly for that of the mandatary; or solely for the benefit of some third person; or partly for the benefit of the mandator and partly for the benefit of a third person; or partly for the benefit of the mandatary, and partly for the benefit of a third person. A mandate given solely for the benefit of the mandatary is useless.

A mandate is given solely for the benefit of the mandator when, eg, he requires the mandatary to transact his business, buy lands or become a surety for him.

A mandate is given partly for the benefit of the mandator, and partly for the benefit of the mandatary, when, eg, the mandator requires you (the mandatary) to lend money upon interest to Titius, who would borrow it for the benefit of the mandator.

A mandate is made solely for the benefit of a third person when, eg, the mandator requires the mandatary to manage the affairs of Titius, buy land for Titius, or become surety for Titius.

A mandate is made partly for the benefit of the mandator, and partly for the benefit of a third person, when, eg, the mandator requires you (the mandatary) to transact some business for the joint benefit of both him and Titius.

A mandate is given partly for the benefit of the mandatary, and partly for the benefit of a third person, when, eg, the mandator requires you (the mandatary) to lend money upon interest to Titius. If you are required to lend money without interest the mandate is only for the benefit of him to whom it is lent.

A mandate is given solely for the benefit of the mandatary if, eg, the mandator requires him to invest his money in the purchase of lands, rather than lend it upon interest, or lend it upon interest rather than buy lands. Such a mandate is regarded merely as good advice; it is not obligatory and no action lies if the advice proves to be bad. However, according to Sabinus, a mandate to lend money to a person who is insolvent is obligatory, and this view has prevailed. A mandate contrary to good morals, eg, to commit theft, is not obligatory, and if the mandatary suffers punishment he has no action against the mandator.

A mandatary must not exceed the terms of his mandate, eg, if required to buy lands for one hundred aurei, he should not buy lands at a higher price. If he exceeds his mandate he cannot sue to recover the excess, although the better opinion seems to be that he can recover the amount of the mandate. Certainly he has an action of mandate if he buys lands for less than the mandator allowed.

A mandate is extinguished if it is revoked before anything has been done under it. Again, if either party dies before anything has been done under a mandate, the mandate ceases to exist. However, if a mandator dies and the mandatary, not knowing of his death, afterwards executes the mandate, he may sue the mandator's heirs. Similarly, if the debtors of Titius, whose steward has been manumitted, should pay to him what was due to Titius without knowledge of the manumission, they would be cleared from their debt, although strictly this would not be so.

A man may refuse a mandate, but if he once accepts, it must be performed or renounced as soon as possible. If a renunciation is so late that the mandator can have no opportunity of transacting his business properly, an action lies against the mandatary unless he can show just cause for the delay. A mandate may be contracted to transact a particular business at a certain time, or upon condition.

If a mandate is not gratuitous it becomes another kind of contract – if a price is agreed upon it becomes letting and hiring. If you give your clothes to a tailor to be mended, and no renumeration is fixed or promised, an action of mandate will lie.

Title XXVII: Of obligations arising from quasi-contracts

We will now consider those obligations which cannot be said properly to arise from a contract yet, because they do not take their origin from wrongs, seem to arise from an implied or quasi-contract.

For example, when one person carries on the business of another in his absence, they reciprocally obtain a right to certain actions called actiones negotiorum gestorum, ie, actions on account of business done; such actions do not arise from a proper or regular contract because the one managed the other's affairs without a mandate and, perhaps, even without his knowing it. The one who managed the other's affairs may hold him liable and, in turn, he is bound to render an account of his management. In the management of the other's affairs he must use the most exact diligence, not merely the care which he usually takes of his own affairs.

Again, although a tutor is subject to an action of tutelage, he is not bound by contract because there is no contract between a tutor and his pupil. However, because tutors are not subject to an action of malfeasance, they are understood to be bound by an implied or quasi-contract, and both tutors and pupils may bring actions reciprocally. The pupil may bring a direct action of tutelage and the tutor, if he has spent his own money on his pupil's behalf, or become bound for him, or mortgaged his own possessions to the pupil's creditors, is entitled to the action called contraria tutelae.

Again, if a thing is owned in common by persons who have never entered into partnership, eg, when a field is devised to two persons jointly, the one may be called to account to the other by the action communi dividundo, eg, because he has taken all the produce or because the other has maintained it at his own expense. There is no contract between them but such persons may be said to be bound to each other by quasi-contract. The same is true where a person is bound to his co-heir and is liable to an action familiae erciscundae for the division of the inheritance. Similarly, an heir cannot properly be said to be bound by contract to a legatee because the legatee did not enter into a contract with the heir or the deceased. However, the heir is presumed to be indebted to the legatee by quasi-contract.

A person who, by mistake, has been paid what was not due appears to be liable by quasi-contract. He who has received the money is bound to repay it as if he had received a loan, and is liable to an action of condiction. In some cases money paid by mistake, when not due, cannot be recovered. Ancient lawyers applied this rule to certain legacies and to those cases where denial of a debt gave rise to an action for double the value, eg, by the law Aquilia. However, by our constitution the privilege of not refunding what is paid by mistake is granted only to churches and other sacred places.

Title XXVIII: Of persons through whom we can acquire obligations

We acquire obligations not only by ourselves, but also by those who are under our power, eg, our slaves and children. Whatever is acquired by our slaves is wholly our own; that which is acquired by our children under our power, by virtue of their contracts, is divided according to our constitution which gives the father the usufruct of the thing gained but the ownership of it to the son.

We may also acquire things by means of freemen, and the slaves of others, whom we possess bona fide, but only where they have gained a thing by their labour or by means of something which belongs to us. In these two cases we also acquire by means of slaves of whom we have only the usufruct or use.

A slave who is owned in common acquires for his masters in proportion to the property which each of them has in him, unless he stipulates or receives something in the name of one of them only. It is now settled that a slave may stipulate for the sole benefit of one of his masters and he acquires for him only who has ordered the stipulation.

Title XXIX: Of the ways in which obligations are dissolved

An obligation is dissolved by the payment of what is due, or by the payment of one thing for another, if the creditor consents. It is immaterial who makes the payment – it may be paid by the debtor himself, or by another, with or without the debtor's knowledge, or even against the debtor's will. When a principal debtor pays, his surety is freed from his obligation; if the surety pays, the principal debtor is also cleared from his debt.

An obligation is also dissolved by acceptilatio, ie, an imaginary payment. Thus if Titius is willing to remit what is due to him by virtue of a verbal contract, it may be done if the debtor says 'Do you regard what I promised you as accepted and received?' and Titius answers 'I do'. An acceptilatio may also be made in Greek if the words used follow the Latin form. Only verbal contracts may be dissolved by an acceptilatio, although any contract may be cast in the form of a stipulation and dissolved in this way. A debt may be paid partly in money and partly by an acceptilatio. The Aquilian stipulation has the effect of reducing every other kind of obligation to a stipulation so that it may be dissolved by acceptilatio. This arose when Aulus Agerius said to Numerius Nigidius 'Do you promise to pay me a sum of money, in lieu of what you were, or shall be, obliged to give me or to perform for my benefit, either absolutely, at a day to come, or upon condition; and in lieu of those things which, being my property, you have, detain or possess; or of which you have fraudulently ceased to possess; and for which I may, or shall be, entitled to any kind of action, plaint or prosecution?' Numerius Nigidius answered 'I do' and then asked Aulus Agerius if he regarded the money, which he Numerius had promised, as accepted and received. Aulus Agerius replied that he did regard it as accepted and received.

An obligation is also dissolved by novation, eg, when you stipulate with Titius to receive from him what is due to you from Seius. By the intervention of a new debtor a fresh obligation arises by which the prior obligation is discharged, and transferred to him. Sometimes a prior contract is discharged by novation although the latter stipulation is of no force, eg, if Titius stipulates to receive from a pupil a debt which I owe him without the tutor's authority. In such a case the debt is lost because the first debtor is freed from his debt, and the second obligation is null. It is otherwise if a man stipulates from a slave with the intent of making a novation; here the first debtor remains bound as if there had been no second stipulation. If you stipulate from the same person a second time, a novation arises if anything new is promised in the latter stipulation, eg, when a condition, a day, or a surety is added or taken away. When only a condition is added, novation does not take place until the occurrence of the event. It was a rule amongst ancient lawyers that novation arose when the judges found that the second contract had been entered into with an intent to dissolve the former. In order to remove the uncertainty of this rule our constitution provides that a novation of a former contract shall only take place when it is expressed by the contracting parties that they promised with an intent to make a novation; if this is not expressed, the prior contract remains valid, and the second is added to it, so that an obligation exists by virtue of both contracts.

Obligations contracted by consent may be dissolved by dissent. Thus if Titius and Seius enter into a contract and, before it is executed, the parties agree that it shall be annulled, they are mutually discharged from it. This applies to all contracts which arise from consent, eg, buying and selling, and letting and hiring.

7 The Institutes of Justinian - Book Four

Title I: Of obligations arising from wrongs

Having discussed the nature of obligations which arise from contracts and quasi-contracts, we here consider those which arise from wrongs. The latter arise from the act itself, eg, from theft, robbery, damage or injury.

Theft is a fraudulent dealing with the thing itself or with the use or possession of it. It is prohibited by the law of nature. Theft is either manifest or not manifest. A manifest thief is he who is taken in the act of thieving, or in the place where he committed it, eg, a man who has stolen grapes and is taken in the vineyard. Further, a thief seen or apprehended by the owner or a stranger in a public or private place whilst in possession of the thing which has been stolen, before he has arrived at the place to which he proposed to carry it, is guilty of manifest theft. But if he actually arrives, before apprehension, at the place proposed, although the thing which has been stolen is found upon him, he is not a manifest thief. The meaning of theft not manifest is clear from what has been said.

A theft is called conceptum (ie, found) when the thing which has been stolen has been searched for and found in the possession of some person in the presence of witnesses, and a special action called actio concepti lies against such possessor, although he did not commit the theft. A theft is called oblatum (ie, offered) when a thing which has been stolen is offered, eg, to Titius, and found upon him, it having been given to him by Seius to the intent that it might rather be found upon Titius than upon himself. In this case a special action, called actio oblati, may be brought by Titius against Seius, although Seius was not guilty of the theft. There is also an action called prohibiti furti which lies against him who hinders another in searching for stolen goods in the presence of witnesses. Further, under the edict of the praetor, a penalty could be recovered by the action furti non exhibiti from any man who failed to produce things which had been stolen which, upon a search, were found in his possession. These four actions are now obsolete; those who knowingly receive and conceal a thing which has been stolen are subject to the penalty of the theft not manifest.

The penalty for committing a manifest theft is quadruple the value, whether the thief is a slave or a freeman. The penalty for theft not manifest is double the value of the thing stolen.

Theft is committed not only when one man takes the property of another for the sake of appropriating it to himself but also in a more general sense when one man uses the property of another against the owner's will, eg, when a creditor makes use of a pledge, or a man who has the use of a thing for a certain purpose puts it to other uses. However, in the latter case, theft is not committed unless the borrower knew that he used the thing contrary to the owner's will and that the owner would not have permitted such use had he been made aware of it. Further, the borrower is not guilty of theft if he thought that the owner would have given his consent. Theft can never be committed unless there was a design and intention of stealing.

If a man believes that he uses a borrowed thing in a way contrary to the owner's will, but in fact the owner consents that it shall be so used, theft is not committed. What is the position if Titius solicits the slave of Maevius to steal from his master and Maevius, having been told of the plot by his slave, allows the slave to take the things to Titius in order that he might catch Titius in the act? Is Titius liable in an action of theft, or in an action for the corruption of the slave, or in neither? By our constitution we have decreed that both actions lie; a party soliciting is in the same position as if he had actually succeeded in corrupting the slave.

A theft may be committed even of free persons, eg, when children under our power are carried off. A man may also commit theft of his own property, eg, when a debtor takes away a thing pledged with his creditor. An action of theft may lie against persons who did not actually commit the theft, eg, against persons by whose aid and advice a theft is committed. Thus it lies against those who knock money out of your hand with the intent that another may pick it up, or against a person who obstructs you to give his accomplice the opportunity of taking your goods. The ancient lawyers also included him who frightened away a herd from its pasture with a red cloth, but if a man does any of these things mischievously, without an intention of committing theft, an action lies only in factum, ie, upon the case, or the fact done. When Titius commits theft by the aid of

Maevius both are liable to an action of theft, eg, when Maevius puts a ladder to a window with the intent that Titius may commit theft, or lends him an iron bar knowing the purpose for which it is borrowed, but he who merely advises, and does not give actual assistance, is not liable to an action of theft.

When persons under the power of parents or masters steal from them, a theft is committed, the thing is regarded as stolen property and no one can acquire it by use until it has returned into the power of its owner. However, the action of theft does not lie between parents and their children or masters and their slaves, although if the theft was committed with the aid and advice of another, the action of theft lies against that other.

An action of theft may be brought by any man who has an interest in the safety of the thing stolen, although he is not the owner; the owner himself cannot bring the action unless he has an interest. Thus a creditor may bring an action of theft in respect of a stolen pledge, although his debtor is solvent, and he may bring the action against the debtor if the debtor is the taker of the pledge. If a fuller receives clothes to clean and they are stolen from him, the fuller may bring an action of theft, but not the owner, because the owner is said to have no interest in their safety. But if a thing is stolen from a bona fide purchaser, he is entitled, like a creditor, to an action of theft, although he is not the owner. However, the fuller (or any tradesman in a similar position) cannot bring an action of theft unless he is solvent, ie, able to pay the owner the full value of the thing lost; if he is insolvent, ie, unable to pay the full value, the owner is allowed to bring the action because he then has an interest in the thing being safe.

The ancients thought that what we have said of the fuller applied equally to a person to whom something was lent, but we have amended the law so that the owner may now bring an action of theft against the thief, or an action on account of the thing lent against the borrower. Having elected to sue one he cannot afterwards sue the other. However, if the borrower is sued, he may bring an action of theft against the thief, but only if the owner knew that the thing had been stolen. If the owner, being ignorant of or doubting the theft, brings an action of loan against the borrower, and afterwards, on ascertaining the facts, wishes to withdraw and bring an action of theft against the thief, he may do so provided the borrower has not satisfied his demand; if the borrower has satisfied his demand, the thief is freed from an action of theft by the owner, but he may be sued by the borrower. If the owner, not knowing the thing to have been stolen, sues the borrower and then, upon receipt of better information, sues the thief, the borrower is released from liability, whatever the outcome of the action against the thief. Similarly, if the owner, knowing of the theft, sues the borrower, the thief is released from liability even where the borrower is unable to meet the owner's claim in full.

A depositary is not answerable for the safe custody of the thing deposited unless he is guilty of fraud; thus if the thing is stolen he cannot bring an action of theft as he has no interest in the thing's preservation, although the action may be brought by the owner. As theft implies a fraudulent intent, a person within puberty is liable for theft only if he is near the age of puberty and it is proved that he knew that what he did was wrong.

An action of theft can only be brought for the appropriate penalty, but the owner of the thing stolen may also recover the thing itself, either by vindication or condiction. An action of vindication lies against the possessor, whether the thief or anyone else; condiction lies only against the thief or his heir, whether or not he is in possession of the thing which has been stolen.

Title II: Of robbery with violence

He who takes the property of another by force is liable to an action of theft, but the praetor has introduced a special action (vi bonorum raptorum) for this kind of wrong which, if brought within a year, leads to the payment of four times the value of the thing taken. If the action is brought after the expiration of a year, only the value of the thing is recoverable. However, where this action is brought within a year the thing itself is included so that, unlike an action of manifest theft, strictly, the penalty is only three-fold.

This special action only lies where there is a fraudulent intent as well as force: a person who mistakenly believing a thing to be his own, and unmindful of the law, takes it away by force thinking that the law allows him to do it is not liable to this action, or to an action of theft. But the imperial constitutions provide that no man is at liberty to take by force any moveable thing or living creature out of the possession of another, although he believes it to be his own: he who thus forcibly seizes his property forfeits it; he who thus takes the property of another, believing it to be his own, must restore the property and pay its value as a penalty. The emperors have applied this rule to invasions or forcible entries upon immoveables, eg, lands and houses.

In this special action it is now asked whether the thing taken by force is or is not the complainant's property; it is sufficient that he has an interest in it, eg, where it has been let, lent or pledged to him, or where he was a bona fide possessor or entitled to the usufruct. In general terms it may be said that causes which entitle a man to bring an action of theft if a thing is taken secretly will also entitle him to bring the action vi bonorum raptorum when force has been used.

Title III: Of the law Aquilia

The action for wrongful or injurious damage is given by the first chapter of the law Aquilia which provides that if any man wrongfully kills the slave or cattle of another, he is to be condemned to pay the owner the highest price for which the slave or beast might have been sold during the preceding year. 'Cattle' does not include wild beasts or dogs, but is confined to animals which feed in herds, eg, horses, sheep, oxen, goats, swine, etc.

A man kills wrongfully if he kills without having a right or authority to do so; thus a man is not liable if he kills a robber when there was no other way of avoiding the danger. Again, a man is not subject to the Aquilian law if he kills by accident, provided there was no negligence; the law applies to negligence as well as to intentional acts. If a man throws a javelin and kills a slave who happens to be passing, he is deemed to be guilty of negligence unless the thrower was a soldier exercising in a place appointed for that purpose. If a man lops a tree, and kills a passing slave, he is guilty if he was working near a public road or a path leading to a village and did not shout a warning: if he did shout, and the slave failed to take care of himself, he is not liable. If a surgeon operates on your slave, fails to attend to his cure and, in consequence, your slave dies, the surgeon is guilty of negligence. Want of skill in a profession also renders a man liable, eg, when a slave dies because a physician gave him the wrong medicine. Lack of strength or skill on the part of a mule-driver or the rider of a horse is also a fault; thus if a mule-driver has not the strength to control his mules and they run over a slave, the mule-driver is guilty of negligence if a stronger man could have controlled the animals.

From the provision of the law Aquilia relating to the highest price for which the slave or beast might have been sold during the preceding twelve months, it follows that the person who kills the slave must pay the slave's highest market value within that year, not his value at the date of death. Thus if the slave was maimed within the year the sum recoverable is his highest market value within the year and before he was maimed. The action upon the law Aquilia is regarded as penal because a person is often required to pay more than the value of the damage for which he is responsible; consequently, the action does not lie against the wrongdoer's heir.

It has been decided that not only the value of the slave is to be calculated, but also such further damage as is occasioned by the death; thus where a slave was instituted an heir, but had not entered upon the inheritance at the command of his master, the loss of the inheritance is taken into account. Again, if the death of a horse breaks a pair, or the slave who was killed was one of a company of comedians, account is taken not merely of the value of the actual horse or slave but also of the diminution of the value of those which remain.

The master of a slave who is killed may sue for damages by a civil action founded on the law Aquilia and at the same time prosecute the wrongdoer for the capital offence.

The third chapter of the law Aquilia gives a remedy for every other kind of damage: therefore, if a man wounds a slave or four-footed animal (whether or not that animal comes within the definition of 'cattle') an action lies against him under this chapter. A remedy is also given under this chapter in respect of injury to all other animals, and to things inanimate, and for the recovery of the value of whatever is burned, spoiled or broken. In fact whenever a thing is made worse it is said to be ruptum (broken). Again, where a man damages the oil or wine of another by mixing anything with it, an action lies under this chapter. In the case of an action brought under the third chapter the person who caused the damage is required to pay the value of the thing damaged at any time within the preceding 30 days; Sabinus held that this means the highest value.

Where a man has with his own hand or body done damage to another, an action lies by virtue of this law; where damage is done by other means, eg, imprisoning a slave till he starves to death, or chasing cattle till they leap down a precipice, or persuading a slave to climb a tree or go down a well, as a result of which he is killed or maimed, the action called utilis is given. If a man throws another's slave into the water and the slave drowns he obviously caused the damage with his own hand. Where neither of these actions applies an action upon the case or fact will lie against the causer of the damage; thus if a man, impelled by compassion, unchains another's slave and thereby enables him to escape, damages may be obtained against him by an action upon the fact.

Title IV: Of injuries

The word injuria, in a general sense, means anything done contrary to law; in a special sense it may mean outrage or insult, or it may signify a fault, as in the law Aquilia where reference is made to wrongful or injurious damage, or it may denote iniquity or injustice, eg, where the praetor pronounces sentence unjustly against a man, the man is said to have suffered an injury.

An injury (in the special sense meaning an outrage) may be committed not only by beating and wounding, but also by raising an outcry against a man, or by seizing his goods as if he were a debtor, the person seizing them well knowing that nothing is due to him. Again, an injury is committed by the writing of a defamatory libel, or by maliciously causing another to write one, or by persistently soliciting the chastity of a boy or girl or respectable woman, and in many other ways.

A man may suffer an injury not only in his own person but also in the person of children under his power and in the person of his wife; thus if a married daughter is injured, not only can an action be brought in the name of the daughter but also in the name of her father and husband. However, if a husband is injured, the wife cannot bring an action. A father-in-law may bring an action in the name of his son's wife, provided her husband is under his father's power. An injury is never understood to be done to a slave, but is reputed to be done to the master, through the person of his slave; in this case, however, some atrocious or grave damage must be done to the slave, and it must openly affect his master. Thus an action lies at the suit of the master if the slave is cruelly beaten or scourged, but not if he is merely abused or struck with a fist. If injury is done to a slave owned in common, the various masters recover according to their rank or personal status, not the proportions in which they own the slave. Injury to a slave is regarded as injury to the person who owns him rather than the person who has the usufruct. If a free person is in another's service the servant must bring an action in his own name; if he was injured principally to affront his master, the master also may bring an action. The same rule applies where another person's slave is in your service: if the injury was inflicted with a view to affronting you, you may yourself bring an action.

The Twelve Tables provided that injury was to be punished as follows: the maiming of a limb, retaliation; if only a bone was broken, the punishment was pecuniary. The praetors afterwards allowed the injured party to fix the amount that was to be paid, but this served only as a guide to the judge who was at liberty to award a lesser amount at his discretion. In course of time the praetors introduced the present method of assessing the amount to be paid, ie, according to the status and reputation of the person who has suffered injury. This is known as the praetorian or honorary penalty: the amount awarded in respect of injury to a slave is determined according to the position which the slave holds in his master's service.

The law Cornelia also deals with injuries and provides an action where a man complains that he has been struck or beaten, or that a person has forcibly entered his house, whether he owns the house, hires or borrows it, or is merely a guest.

An injury is regarded as atrocious sometimes from the nature of the act, eg, where a person has been wounded or beaten with a club; sometimes from the place, eg, in a theatre or market, or in the presence of the praetor; sometimes by reason of rank, eg, when a magistrate or a senator is injured by a person of low condition, or when a parent is injured by his child, or a patron by his freedman; in these cases a heavier punishment is awarded. Again, the part of the body wounded may make the injury atrocious, as where a man is wounded in the eye; in such a case it makes no difference whether the injury is to the father of a family or to a son in power.

Finally, it should be noted that the person injured may sue the offending party either criminally or civilly. If he sues civilly, the damage is assessed and the penalty imposed as described above; if he sues criminally, the judge must inflict an extraordinary punishment upon the offender, observing the constitution of Zeno by which those of illustrious rank or above may bring or defend criminal proceedings for injury by their proctors.

An action of injury lies not only against the one who actually inflicted the injury, but also against him who by craft and persuasion caused it to be done.

A right of action may be lost by dissimulation; thus if a man takes no notice of an injury at the time at which it is inflicted he cannot afterwards sue on account of that injury.

Title V: Of obligations arising from quasi-wrongs

If a judge makes a suit his own, by giving an unjust judgment, an action for wrong does not properly lie against him but, even though he is not subject to an action for wrong, or of contract, and he has erred unintentionally, he may be sued by an action of quasi-wrong and suffer such penalty as a superior judge sees fit to impose. Again, if a person occupies an upper room (it matters not whether he owns it, pays rent for it or occupies it gratuitously) from which something is thrown or spilt so as to cause damage to another person, he is liable to an action of quasi-wrong; an action of wrong is inappropriate because it is normally someone else, eg, a slave or a child, who is actually at fault. The same action lies where a man has hung or placed anything in a public road so that in the event of it falling it might cause damage; in this case the penalty is ten aurei. Where anything is thrown or spilt double the amount of damage is recoverable; if a freeman is killed, the penalty is 50 aurei; if a freeman only receives injuries, the amount of damages is assessed by the judge taking into account medical and other expenses and loss of business, actual or prospective.

If the son of a family lives apart from his father, and anything is thrown or spilt from his room, or hung or placed so that it might do damage, it is Julian's view that the son, but not the father, can be sued. The same applies where the son has acted as a judge and given an unjust judgment.

The master of a ship, tavern or inn may be sued for a quasi-wrong in respect of every damage or theft committed in any of these places by his servants, although no action for wrong or contract lies against him. In all these cases the action given is an action upon the fact, which may be brought by an heir, but not against an heir.

Title VI: Of actions

We must now deal with actions. An action is nothing more than the right which every man has of taking legal proceedings for whatever is due to him.

The principal division of actions is into two kinds, real and personal. An action is personal if based on contract or wrong, for the plaintiff alleges that the defendant must give or do something, as the occasion requires. An action is real where there is no obligation, but concerns a certain thing, eg, an action to determine the ownership of property. Again, actions by which a person alleges that he has the right to the usufruct of a field, or the right of drawing water in his neighbour's field, are real actions, as are actions relating to urban servitudes, eg, a right of view, of raising the height of his house, of making a projection over his neighbour's land or of resting beams on his neighbour's walls. There are also contrary actions to these, eg, when the plaintiff alleges that the defendant has not the right to the usufruct of a field; these actions are also real, though negative in character, and cannot, therefore, be brought in respect of corporeal things as the plaintiff would be the possessor and, as a general rule, the possessor cannot bring an action to confirm that the things are not the claimant's.

The actions mentioned above, and all actions of a similar character, are derived from the civil law, but the praetor has introduced other actions, both real and personal; thus he often allows a real action to be brought, either by allowing the plaintiff to allege that he has acquired by use something which he has not so acquired, or, on the contrary, by allowing a former possessor to allege that another has not acquired by use something which he has so acquired. If a thing belonging to one man is delivered in trust to another on some lawful ground, eg, by reason of a purchase, a gift, a marriage or a bequest, and the trustee loses possession of the thing before he has become its owner, he would have no direct action for its recovery as real actions are given by the civil law only to claim ownership. However, the praetor allows the trustee to aver that he has acquired the thing by use, and by this means he may recover possession. This is called the actio Publiciana. On the other hand, if any man whilst abroad in the service of his country, or a prisoner in the hands of the enemy, acquires by use a thing which belongs to another who was not abroad, the former owner may within a year of the possessor's return bring an action against him, alleging that the thing has not been acquired by use, and therefore that the thing is his.

If a debtor disposes of a thing in order to defraud his creditors, notwithstanding the delivery of the thing the creditors may bring an action for its recovery if they have obtained an order of the magistrate putting themselves into possession; in other words they are allowed to plead that the thing was not delivered and that it continues to be part of the debtor's goods.

The actions Serviana and quasi-Serviana (the latter is called hypothecary) also arise from the praetor's jurisdiction. By the action Serviana a suit may be commenced for a tenant farmer's stock and cattle which he pledges to secure the payment of his rent. The action quasi-Serviana allows a creditor to sue for a thing pledged or mortgaged to him; in regard to this action there is no difference between a pledge and a mortgage – a pledge is actually delivered to a creditor, whereas with a mortgage there is no delivery.

The praetors have also introduced personal actions, eg, the action de pecunia constituta and the action concerning the peculium of slaves and sons in power. The former action lies against a person who has engaged to pay money either for himself or another, without stipulation; actions de peculio lie against fathers and masters and render them liable in respect of the contracts of their children or slaves to the extent of a peculium, ie, a child's or a slave's separate estate.

Again, if a man at the request of a creditor makes oath that the debt for which he sues is due and unpaid, the praetor allows the creditor an action upon the fact in which it is simply asked whether the oath was taken, not whether the debt is due.

The praetors have also introduced many penal actions, eg, against a person who wilfully damages or erases an edict; against an emancipated son or a freedman who commences an action against his parent or patron without first obtaining the magistrate's consent; or against a person who by force or fraud has prevented a person duly summoned from appearing in court.

Prejudicial actions, eg, those by which it is inquired whether a man is born free or made free, or whether he is a slave or a bastard, are also real, but only that by which it is inquired whether a man is free born proceeds from the civil law; the rest arise from the jurisdiction of the praetor.

As actions are divided into real and personal it is clear that a man cannot sue for his own property by a personal action in the following form, viz, 'If it appears that the defendant ought to give it to me', for the act of giving implies the conferring of property, and that which is the property of the plaintiff can never be understood to be given to him, or to become more his own than it already is. However, besides the double and quadruple penalty to which they are liable, thieves and robbers may be sued by a personal action for the thing taken in the very form recited above, although a real action would also lie against them in which a person claims the thing taken as his own.

Real actions are called vindications; personal actions are called condictions. Actions are further divided into those which are given for the purpose of recovering the very thing, those for recovering a penalty, and mixed actions which are given for the recovery both of the thing, and the penalty. All real actions are given for the recovery of the thing as are almost all the personal actions which arise from a contract, eg, the action for a mutuum, a commodatum, or on account of a stipulation, and also actions on account of a deposit, a mandate, a partnership, buying and selling, letting and hiring. When the action is for a thing deposited by reason of a riot, a fire, or any other calamity, the praetor gives an action for a double penalty, besides the thing deposited, if the suit is brought against the depositary, or against his heir, for fraud, and in this case the action is mixed.

In cases of wrong some actions lie for the penalty only while some are mixed, ie, both for the thing and the penalty. In an action of theft a person sues only for the appropriate penalty, and the owner may recover the thing by a separate action against the thief or any other person who is in possession of his property. The thief may also be sued by a personal action for the recovery of the thing stolen. An action for goods taken by force is a mixed action because the value of whatever is taken is included in the quadruple value. The action introduced by the law Aquilia for wrongful damage is also a mixed action, not only when it is given for double value against a man denying the fact but sometimes when the action is only for single value, eg, when a slave at the date of his death was lame, or blind in one eye, and during the previous year had been sound and of greater value. A mixed action is also brought against those who have delayed the delivery of a legacy or bequest in trust in favour of a church or other holy place until they have been summoned before a magistrate; in this case they are compelled to deliver the thing, or pay the money bequeathed, and an equal amount by way of penalty – in other words, they must pay double the amount that was due.

There are also some actions which are mixed in character as they are, in effect, both real and personal, eg, the action familiae erciscundae, which may be brought by co-heirs for the division of their inheritance, the action de communi dividundo, which lies for the division of property held in common, apart from an inheritance, and the action finium regundorum, which lies between persons whose lands are contiguous. In these cases the judge may give a portion of the property to one party and, if such portion is in excess of his share, require him to pay to the other a certain sum of money.

All actions are for the single, double, triple or quadruple value of the thing in litigation; no action extends beyond this. The action is for the single value, eg, upon a stipulation, a loan, a mandate, the contract of buying and selling, letting and hiring. The double value is sued for, eg, in actions for theft not manifest, of injury, under the law Aquilia, and sometimes in an action of deposit; also, where a slave has been corrupted, against the one who by his advice has caused the slave to flee from his master, or to become insolent to him, or to become in any other way less valuable, and account is also taken of anything which the slave stole from his master when he fled. A suit may be brought for triple value when a person inserts in his statement of claim a greater sum than is due to the intent that the court officers may exact a larger fee from the defendant; in such a case the defendant may obtain from the plaintiff triple the amount of the additional fee, but he must include in this sum the additional amount that he has been required to pay. Quadruple value is recoverable in actions for manifest theft, for putting a man in fear and for money given to induce a person to bring, or desist from, a suit against a third person. A condiction ex lege for the quadruple value arises from our constitution against court officers who demand anything unlawfully from a defendant.

However, actions of theft not manifest and on account of the corruption of a slave are different from the other actions of which we have spoken because they are always brought for double the value; in actions under the law Aquilia for wrongful damage, and sometimes in actions of deposit, double value is recoverable only if liability is denied. If liability is admitted the single value is all that can be recovered. In the case of actions in respect of bequests to sacred places, the penalty is doubled if liability is denied or payment delayed until the defendant is summoned before a magistrate; if liability is admitted and payment made before the defendant is summoned, the single value must suffice. The action for putting a man in fear differs from other actions for quadruple value because in this case alone it is tacitly implied that the party who has obeyed the order of the judge and restored the thing taken is absolved from liability; in other cases the condemnation is always for the quadruple, as in actions of manifest theft.

The fourth division of actions is into those of good faith and those of strict right. The following are actions of good faith: buying and selling, letting and hiring, carrying on another's business, mandate, deposit, tutelage, partnership, loan, mortgage, division of an inheritance, division of things owned in common, and actions in prescribed words, which either arise out of a commission for sale at a fixed price, or on an exchange. It is now settled that the action by which we claim an inheritance is also an action of good faith. The action called rei uxoriae, which was given for the recovery of a marriage portion, was an action of good faith, but we have merged this action, with many additions, in the action of stipulation given on account of marriage portions. This action of stipulation is an action of good faith and we have added to it, by implication, the full powers of an action of hypothec giving wives, whenever they sue for marriage portions, preference over all other creditors by mortgage.

In all actions of good faith the judge calculates according to the rules of justice and equity how much the plaintiff is entitled to recover, taking into account anything that the plaintiff is found to owe the defendant. Even in actions of strict right the emperor Marcus allowed a counter-claim by a defendant by a plea of fraud, but we allow all counter-claims founded on a clear right whether the action is real, personal or of any other kind. The only exception to this is an action of deposit, as to allow a defendant to bring a counter-claim in this case may result in the plaintiff being unable to recover the property which he deposited.

Some actions are called arbitrary because they depend entirely upon the arbitration or discretion of the judge; in these, if the defendant fails to obey the court's order, eg, to restore a thing or give up a slave, he is immediately condemned. Some arbitrary actions are real, eg, the actions Publiciana, Serviana and quasi-Serviana; others are personal, eg, those where a suit is commenced on account of something done by force, fear or fraud, on account of something which was promised to be paid or restored in a certain place, and the action ad exhibendum which was given for the production of a certain thing. In all these and similar actions the judge determines, according to equity and the nature of the subject-matter of the suit, in what manner and proportion the plaintiff ought to receive satisfaction. Wherever possible the judge ought to award a certain thing or sum of money, even though the claim was for an uncertain amount.

Formerly, if a plaintiff claimed more than was due or belonged to him, he failed in his cause and lost even that which he was entitled to claim; nor was he easily restored to his rights by the praetor, unless he was under the age of 25, or the error was one which even the most cautious or knowledgeable of men might have made, eg, where a legatee demanded his whole legacy, and codicils were afterwards produced by which part of it was revoked. A man may demand more than what is due to him in four ways, viz, in respect of the thing, eg, instead of demanding ten aurei which are due to him, by demanding twenty; in respect of time, eg, by making his demand before the day of payment; in respect of place, eg, by requiring that which was stipulated to be given at Ephesus to be given to him at Rome (in this case the plaintiff is given an arbitrary action so that the judge can take into account the advantage which the defendant would have gained by giving delivery at Ephesus); and in respect of cause, eg, if a person stipulates for the giving either of a certain slave or ten aurei, and demands one or other of the alternatives (in this case he ought to have made his demand in accordance with the stipulation and claimed either the slave or the money). Again, if a man stipulates in general terms that a slave should be given, and then sues for a particular slave, he demands more than his due. As has been said, according to the ancient practice if a man over-demanded he lost even that which was really due to him. However, this law has been altered by the constitution of the emperor Zeno and by our own: if more than is due is demanded in regard to time, the constitution of Zeno applies; if more is demanded in any other way, the plaintiff must pay the defendant triple the amount which he has lost as a result of the overclaim, as mentioned above in relation to the fees of court officers.

If a plaintiff sues for less than he is entitled to claim, eg, only for five aurei when ten are due, he is quite safe because, in accordance with Zeno's constitution, the judge may condemn the defendant to pay or deliver everything which is due to the plaintiff. Again, if a plaintiff demands one thing instead of another, eg, the slave Erotes instead of the slave Stichus, he runs no risk because he is allowed to correct his mistake in the same proceedings. There are some actions in which we may or may not recover all that is due to us; thus in a suit against the peculium of a son or a slave, if the peculium is sufficient to answer the demand, the father or master must pay the whole debt, but if the peculium is insufficient, the father or master can be condemned to pay only to the extent of its value. Similarly, if a woman sues for the recovery of her marriage portion, the man will be condemned to pay either the whole or a part, according to his ability to pay. In this case the husband is entitled to deduct anything which he has necessarily expended upon the estate given as a marriage portion. Again, if a person sues his parent, patron or partner he cannot recover more than the defendant is able to pay, and the same applies where a donor is sued on his promise to give.

When a counter-claim or set-off is made by the defendant, the plaintiff normally recovers less than he claims, but this has already been explained. Creditors to whom a debtor has surrendered his goods may commence fresh proceedings if the debtor subsequently acquires property, but the debtor will be condemned only to the extent that he is able to pay.

Title VII: Of actions in respect of transactions with a person in the power of another

We have already referred to the action which may be brought against the peculium or separate estate of a son or slave, but we must now speak of this more fully and also of some other actions which are given on account of children and slaves against their parents and masters. The law is much the same whether the transaction is with a slave or with a person under the power of his parent. We will speak only of slaves and their masters and, unless we indicate to the contrary, the same applies to parents and children under their power.

If any business is transacted by a slave acting under the orders of his master, the praetor gives an action against the master for the whole value of the transaction. In similar circumstances the praetor gives two other actions for the whole amount, viz, the action exercitoria and the action institoria. The former lies when a master has made a slave captain of a vessel and a contract is entered into with him in that capacity; the latter lies when a master has made a slave manager of a shop or any particular business and someone is thereby induced to enter into a contract with the slave. These two actions also lie where a man has employed a free person, or another's slave, to captain his ship, manage his shop, or deal with any particular business.

The praetor has also introduced the action tributoria, for if a slave, without the command but with the knowledge of his master trades with his peculium, and persons are induced to contract with him, whatever results from these transactions is distributed between the master, if anything is due to him, and the rest of the creditors, in proportion to their claims. The master himself makes the distribution, and if any creditor complains that the share which he is given is too small the praetor allows him the action tributoria.

The action concerning a peculium, and things converted to the master's benefit, has also been introduced by the praetor; for although a slave has made a contract without his master's consent, where money arising from it is converted to the master's benefit, the master ought to be answerable for its performance; where no benefit accrues to the master, he is liable to the extent of the slave's peculium. A thing or money is deemed to be converted to a master's benefit whenever it is necessarily used or expended by a slave upon his master's affairs, eg, where a slave who has borrowed money pays his master's debts, repairs his buildings or buys any thing which is of use to him. It follows that if a slave borrows ten aurei, pays five to his master's creditors and squanders the rest, the master is liable for the whole of the five and as much of the rest as is covered by his peculium. In actions of this kind the judge first considers whether the whole, or a part, has been converted to the master's benefit, and then proceeds to value the peculium, deducting whatever the slave owes to the master or to any person under the master's power. However, there are occasions on which what one slave owes to another under the power of the same master is not deducted, eg, where the creditor slave is part of the debtor slave's peculium.

Nevertheless, he who has made a contract with a slave at the command of the master of that slave, and is entitled to the action institoria or exercitoria, is also entitled to the action de peculio and de in rem verso described above, although he is wise to take advantage of the actions institoria or exercitoria if he can. A person to whom the action tributoria is given is also entitled to the action de peculio and de in rem verso, but it is often more expedient to use the former as no deduction is made of what is due to the master. A person should select the action which may be most beneficial to him, but if he can prove a conversion to the master's benefit, he ought to commence his suit by the action de in rem verso.

Although what has been said with regard to slaves and their masters applies equally to children under power and their parents, the Macedonian decree of the senate places children in a special position in so far as it prohibits the lending of money to them while they are under the power of their parents; creditors cannot sue the children or their parents, either before or after the children are emancipated.

Finally, it should be noted that whatever has been contracted for by order of a parent or master and converted to his benefit may be recovered by a direct action against him if the contract had been made with him in the first place. Again, anyone who is liable to the action institoria or exhibitoria may also be sued by a direct action as the contract is presumed to have been made by his order.

Title VIII: Of noxal actions

Noxal actions are given on account of the wrongful acts of slaves, as when a slave commits a theft or robbery, or does any other damage or injury. When a master is condemned on this account he may at his option either pay the value of the damage, or deliver up his slave as a recompense. 'Noxa' means the slave by whom the wrong was committed; 'noxia' denotes the wrongful act itself.

When a noxal action is given against a master and he elects to deliver up his slave to the plaintiff, if the slave can pay the value of the damage to his new master, with the assistance of the praetor he may be manumitted even against his new master's will.

Noxal actions arise either from the laws or from the edict of the praetor; those on account of theft come from the law of the Twelve Tables, those on account of wrongful damage from the law Aquilia, and those on account of injuries and robbery with violence from the edict of the praetor. Every noxal action follows the person of the slave by whom the wrongful act was committed; if he passes under the power of a new master the new master is liable, but if the slave is manumitted he becomes liable to a direct action. On the other hand, an action which was at first direct becomes noxal if the wrongdoer afterwards becomes a slave.

No obligation can arise between a master and his slave; if a slave commits a wrong against his master no action lies, even where the slave passes under the power of a new master or is manumitted. If a slave commits a wrong against Titius, and afterwards becomes Titius' slave, the right of action is lost. Again, if a slave causes damage to his master, and ceases to be under that master's power, no action lies against him. A slave who has been alienated or manumitted cannot sue his former master by whom he has been ill-treated.

The ancients allowed forfeiture of the person in the case of children of both sexes, but this rule has fallen into disuse. Noxal actions now apply only to slaves, and the ancient commentators have often said that sons in power may themselves be sued for their own wrongful acts.

Title IX: Of damage caused by animals

A noxal action is given by the law of the Twelve Tables where damage is caused by playful, frightened or ferocious animals, but if they are delivered up the defendant is discharged from the action. However, a noxal action lies only where an animal acts contrary to its nature; thus if a bear breaks loose from its master and damage results the owner cannot be sued, because he ceased to be the owner when the animal escaped.

However, by the Aedilitian edict we are prohibited from keeping a dog, a boar, a bear or a lion in a public passage or highway, and if this rule is broken, and a freeman is injured, the owner may be condemned in whatever sum the judge thinks just and fair. Where any other damage is suffered, the condemnation is double the loss sustained. The noxal action and the Aedilitian action do not extinguish one another.

Title X: Of those by whom we may sue

A man may sue either in his own name or in that of another, eg, when he sues in the capacity of a proctor, a tutor or a curator; formerly, a person could not sue in the name of another unless the action was brought on behalf of the people, a person claiming freedom, or a pupil. The law Hostilia allowed an action of theft to be brought in the names of persons held captive by the enemy, persons absent on state business, and those who were under the tutelage of such persons. In course of time it became the practice to sue by proctors where a man was unable to attend to his affairs in person, eg, in cases of illness, old age and unavoidable absences.

A proctor is a person employed to sue or to defend for another; no particular form of words is required for his appointment and he need not be appointed in the presence of the opposite party. The appointment of tutors and curators has been explained in the first book.

Title XI: Of taking security

Formerly, if a real action was brought, the defendant, or party in possession, was required to give security so that if he lost the suit, and would neither hand over the thing nor pay its estimated value, the plaintiff might sue either the defendant or his sureties. This form of security is called judicatum solvi; not only was a person who defended his own cause required to give his security, but also a proctor acting on behalf of another. On the other hand, a plaintiff in a real action was not required to give security, although if he sued only as a proctor he was required to give security that his acts would be ratified by his principal. Tutors and curators were compelled to give security in the same way as proctors, although this requirement was sometimes waived when tutors or curators were plaintiffs. The same rule applied in personal actions with regard to the plaintiff, and if a person defended a personal action on behalf of another he was required to give security; however, if he defended his own cause, no security was required.

Now the position is quite different; a person who defends a real or personal action in his own name is not required to give security for the payment of the estimated value of the subject-matter of the action, but only for his own person, ie, that he will remain in attendance until the case is decided. This security may be given by sureties, by a promise on oath or by a promise without an oath, according to the defendant's rank. Where a person sues by a proctor, if the proctor does not enrol in court a mandate of appointment to act, or cause his client to appear in court to nominate him, the proctor must give security that his principal will ratify his acts. The same applies where a tutor, curator or other person to whom the management of the affairs of others is entrusted commences a suit by a proctor. Where a person is sued, and wishes to appoint a proctor, he may appear in court and confirm the nomination by giving the security judicatum solvi, or give security out of court that his proctor will satisfy the judgment. Whether the security is given in court or out of court, the defendant must give a hypothec of his property so that his heirs as well as himself become liable. Further, he must give security that he will either appear in person when judgment is given or that his sureties will satisfy the judgment, unless there is an appeal.

When a defendant fails to appear, any other person may act for him in either a real or a personal action, provided the security judicatum solvi is entered into for the payment of the estimated value of the subject-matter of the action.

These rules apply not only in Constantinople, but also in all our other provinces.

Title XII: Of perpetual and temporary actions and those available for and against heirs

Actions which arose from a law, a decree of the senate or the constitutions were formerly regarded as perpetual, ie, available at any time, but later emperors have fixed certain limits to both real and personal actions. Actions given by virtue of the praetor's authority are generally limited to one year, although sometimes they are made perpetual, ie, extended to the limits introduced by the constitutions: such are those given by the praetor to the possessor of goods, and to those who stand in the place of heirs. The action of manifest theft is also perpetual, although it arises from the authority of the praetor.

Not all actions, whether given by the law or the praetor, also lie against heirs; penal actions arising from a wrong, eg, actions of theft, robbery, injury and wrongful damage, do not lie against the wrongdoer's heir. However, with the exception of actions for injury and others of a similar nature, these actions pass to heirs. There are times when even an action arising from contract does not lie against an heir, eg, when a testator acted fraudulently and nothing came to the heir by reason of the fraud. If penal actions are once contested by the principal parties concerned, they will afterwards pass both to and against the heirs of such parties.

If before judgment the defendant gives full satisfaction to the plaintiff, the judge must dismiss the defendant although he deserved to be condemned.

Title XIII: Of exceptions

Exceptions have been introduced as a means of defence for the person against whom the action is brought; the suit itself may be just, but it may be unjust with regard to a particular defendant.

For example, if a man is compelled by fear, or induced by fraud or mistake, to make a promise to Titius by stipulation, he is bound by the civil law and Titius has an action, but the man may plead an exception of fear or fraud, or as the case may be. These are called exceptions in factum compositae, ie, exceptions on the fact. Again, if Sempronius causes Titius to stipulate to repay him money which Titius has never received Sempronius may bring an action, but Titius may defend himself by an exception pecuniae non numeratae, ie, on account of money not paid. Further, if a debtor has agreed with his creditor that no claim will be made against him, the debtor remains bound and an action in the form 'if it appears that he ought to give' would lie against him, but the debtor may plead an exception of the agreement. If at the instance of his creditor a debtor swears that nothing is due from him, in law he remains bound but may defend himself by pleading his own oath by way of exception. Exceptions of this kind are equally necessary in real actions, eg, where a possessor, at the request of the claimant, swears that the thing in dispute is his own, and the claimant (who may be the true owner) proceeds with his action, it would be unjust for the possessor to be condemned. Let us take another example: if a man has been sued in a real or personal action, nevertheless the obligation remains and in strict law he may be sued again upon the same account; however, in the second suit he may defend himself by the exception that judgment has already been given. These examples in general may suffice; further information is to be found in the Digest.

Some exceptions result from the laws themselves, or enactments having the force of laws; others arise from the authority of the praetor. Some exceptions are called perpetual and peremptory; others are called temporary and dilatory. Perpetual and peremptory exceptions are those which stand in the way of the plaintiff and destroy his cause of action, eg, exceptions of fraud, of fear and of agreement when it is agreed that the money shall not be sued for. Temporary and dilatory exceptions are those which operate for a time, and create delay, eg, an exception of agreement when it is agreed that the money will not be sued for within, say, five years, but at the expiration of this time the creditor may proceed. Formerly, if the creditor sued within the agreed time, and an exception was pleaded, he lost his right of action altogether, but we have decreed that he shall be subject to the constitution of Zeno concerning those who claim more than their due, and the debtor is allowed twice the time previously agreed. Even when that time has expired the debtor cannot be compelled to appear until he has been paid all his costs of the former action. Dilatory exceptions may also arise in respect of the person who brings the action, such as those which are made against proctors; soldiers and women cannot act as proctors, although soldiers may act in their own affairs if they can do so without any breach of military discipline. Exceptions of infamy against proctors or persons appointing them have been abolished.

Title XIV: Of replications

An exception which at first sight appears to be valid may not be so; the plaintiff may make an additional allegation, known as a replication, destroying the force of the exception. For example, if a creditor agrees with his debtor that no claim will be made against him, and they afterwards agree that the creditor may sue and in consequence of such agreement the creditor sues, the debtor may plead an exception of the agreement not to sue, but it would be unjust that the creditor should be defeated by this exception, and he may make a replication by setting up the subsequent agreement.

It sometimes happens that a replication which at first sight appears to be valid may be unfairly prejudicial to the defendant. In such a case the defendant may make another allegation known as a duplication, and this the plaintiff may answer by an allegation called a triplication. Further information with regard to exceptions may be found in the Digest.

The exceptions by which a debtor may defend himself are generally available to his sureties; thus if a creditor has agreed not to sue his debtor, the debtor's surety may take advantage of an exception of the agreement as if the promise had been made expressly to him. However, although a debtor who has surrendered his goods may defend himself by the exception 'unless he has surrendered his property', this exception is not available to the debtor's surety because the purpose of demanding a surety is that he may be sued in the event of the debtor's insolvency.

Title XV: Of interdicts

We now speak of interdicts or of the actions which have taken their place. Interdicts were certain forms of words by which the praetor either commanded something to be done or prohibited something from being done. They were mainly used when a dispute arose concerning possession or quasi-possession.

The main division of interdicts is into prohibitory, restoratory and exhibitory interdicts. Prohibitory interdicts are those by which the praetor prohibits something from being done, eg, forbids force to be used against a lawful possessor, or a building to be erected in a sacred place. Restoratory interdicts are those by which the praetor orders something to be restored, eg, orders possessions to be restored to a person who has been forcibly ejected. Exhibitory interdicts are those by which the praetor orders production, eg, the production of a slave concerning whose liberty a suit is pending.

The next division of interdicts is into those which are given for the acquisition, retention or recovery of possession. An interdict for the acquisition of possession is given to him whom the praetor appoints to be the possessor of the goods of a deceased person; this interdict is called quorum bonorum and it is given against heirs or possessors. A person possesses as heir who thinks he is an heir; a person possesses as possessor if, without legal right, he retains a part or the whole of an inheritance knowing that it does not belong to him. This interdict is not available to a person who has once acquired possession, and afterwards lost it. The Salvian interdict is also available for the acquisition of possession, and is used by owners of farms in order to acquire goods which their tenants have pledged as security for the payment of rent.

The interdicts uti possidetis and utrubi are available for the retention of possession: when there is a dispute as to ownership it must first be asked which of the parties is in possession, and the party found to be in possession is the defendant, the other the plaintiff. It is advantageous to be the defendant because if the plaintiff fails to prove that the thing is his, or the rights of the parties are not clear, judgment is always given in favour of the defendant whether or not he is the owner. The interdict uti possidetis is used in disputes about land or buildings, while the interdict utrubi is used when the possession of moveables is in question. In the case of the former interdict the party in possession at the time of the interdict prevailed unless he had obtained possession against his opponent by force, secretly or by permission; how he had obtained possession from any other person was immaterial. In the case of the interdict utrubi the party prevailed who had been in possession for the greatest part of the year preceding, provided he had not obtained that possession by force, secretly or by permission. Now, in the case of both interdicts, the party prevails who was in possession at the time of the suit unless it appears that he gained such possession by force, secretly or by permission.

A man is regarded as a possessor, not only when he is himself in possession, but also when another (who need not be in his power) is in possession in his name, eg, a tenant, or a person who has received a thing by way of deposit or loan. Possession may be retained by the mere intention to possess, eg, where a person gives up possession of lands, with the intention of returning. However, a mere intention is not sufficient for the acquisition of possession.

The interdict for the recovery of possession is generally used when a person has been forcibly ejected from the possession of his house or land; such person is entitled to the interdict unde vi by which the ejector is compelled to restore possession although the person ejected was in possession by force, secretly or by permission. As has already been stated, imperial constitutions provide that if a man seizes a thing by force, if it is his own, he loses his ownership of it; if it belongs to another, he must restore the thing and pay to his victim its full value. Moreover, whoever dispossesses another by force is liable under the Julian law relating to private and public violence; if he seized or intruded with the use of arms it is private violence, if he used arms (ie, clubs and stones as well as shields and swords) it is public violence.

The third division of interdicts is into simple and double interdicts; simple interdicts are those where there is both a plaintiff and a defendant, and restoratory and exhibitory interdicts are all of this kind. Prohibitory interdicts may be either simple or double: they are simple when the praetor forbids something to be done in a sacred place, on a public river or on its banks. The interdicts uti possidetis and utrubi are examples of double interdicts; here the condition of each litigant is equal, the one not being understood to be more particularly the plaintiff or the defendant than the other, each fulfilling the part of both.

It is now superfluous to speak of the mode in former times of using, and the consequences of, interdicts, for now that proceedings are extraordinary interdicts are unnecessary; judgments are delivered without interdicts in the same manner as if an equitable action had been given in consequence of an interdict.

Title XVI: Of the penalties for rash litigation

The rashness of plaintiffs and of defendants is restrained by pecuniary punishments, the coercion of an oath, and the fear of infamy.

By one of our constitutions a defendant is not allowed to plead until he has sworn that he firmly believes that his defence is sound, and an action for double or triple value might lie against a defendant who denies liability, eg, in an action for wrongful damage, or for a legacy left to a church. Of course, in some cases the action is, from the beginning, for more than the simple value, eg, actions of theft manifest. By our constitution the plaintiff is required to swear that he commences the suit with an honest intention, and the advocates on both sides are required to take a similar oath. This procedure has replaced the action of calumny by which the plaintiff could be compelled to pay one-tenth of his claim as a punishment. Now we use the oath, and every rash or dishonest litigant must bear the other party's loss and expenses of the suit.

In some actions those who are condemned become infamous, ie, in actions of theft, robbery, injury or fraud and, where the action is direct, in actions of tutelage, mandate or deposit. An action of partnership, which is always direct, is the same: any partner who is condemned is branded with infamy. In actions of theft, robbery, injury or fraud those who have bargained to prevent a criminal prosecution are also rendered infamous.

In accordance with the praetor's edict all actions begin with a summons calling the other party before the judge who is to decide the case. However, parents and patrons, and the children and parents of patrons, cannot be summoned by their children or freedmen unless a successful application has been made for the praetor's leave; if any man sues without first obtaining such leave he is liable to a penalty of 50 solidi.

Title XVII: Of the office of a judge

A judge should never give a decision otherwise than in accordance with the laws, the constitutions or the customs and usages. Therefore, in a noxal action, if the defendant is to be condemned, the judge must use the words 'I condemn Publius Maevius to pay Lucius Titius ten aurei, or to deliver up the slave who did the damage'. In a real action, if the judge decides against the plaintiff, he must absolve the possessor; if against the possessor, he must order him to restore the thing, together with its produce or fruits. If the possessor says that he is unable to make immediate restitution, and in good faith asks for time, his request should be granted provided he gives security for the payment of the value of the thing and costs if he fails to make restitution within the time appointed. Where an inheritance is sued for, the rule as to produce or fruits is the same as where a particular thing is claimed: in the case of a possessor in mala fide the rule is much the same in both actions whether the produce was taken by the possessor or, through negligence, was not taken by him; if the defendant was a possessor bona fide no account is taken of fruits before the commencement of proceedings, but he must account for fruits after this time whether he gathered and used them or, through his negligence, they were left ungathered.

In an action ad exhibendum, the defendant must not merely produce the thing but also account for all profits accruing from it so that the plaintiff will be in the same position as if his property had been restored to him at the time at which he commenced his action. If, owing to his delay in surrendering the thing, the possessor acquires it by use, it must nevertheless be restored because he cannot take advantage of his own delay. The judge must also take into account profits accruing between the commencement of the suit and the giving of judgment. If in good faith the defendant asks for time to produce, his request should be granted upon his giving security for restitution. If he fails to give immediate production, or to give security for production at a future time, he must be ordered to pay the full amount of damages which the plaintiff has sustained by not having the thing restored to him at the commencement of the suit.

In an action familiae erciscundae for the partition of an inheritance the judge must decree to each heir his respective portion; if the partition is more advantageous to one than to the other, he must order the one who has received too much to make a money payment to the other. Every heir who has taken the profits of an inheritance to his sole use and consumed them may be required to compensate his co-heir. These rules apply where there are two heirs or more than two.

The same law applies in an action communi dividundo for the division of a number of things held in common. If the action concerns only one thing, eg, a field, if it can be conveniently divided the judge ought to award to each party his specific share, making such monetary adjustment as may be necessary. If the thing cannot be divided, eg, a slave, it must be given entirely to one who will be ordered to compensate the other by a money payment.

When an action finium regundorum is brought for the determination of boundaries, the judge must first consider whether an adjudication is necessary, as it always is where it is desirable that land should be divided by more conspicuous boundaries than was formerly the case; for part of one man's land must be awarded to the other, and that other must compensate him for his loss. By this action a man may be prosecuted for any fraud in relation to boundaries, eg, by removing stones, and he may be condemned for contumacy (contempt of court) if he refused to allow his lands to be measured in accordance with the judge's order.

It should be noted that whatever is adjudged to a person in any of these actions immediately becomes his property.

Title XVIII: Of public proceedings

Public proceedings are not conducted like actions, nor are they similar to the other proceedings which we have considered. They also differ from one another in the manner of institution and prosecution.

These proceedings are called public because they may be sued to execution by any of the people; some are capital, others are not. Capital proceedings are those by which a criminal is prohibited from fire and water, sentenced to death, to deportation, or to the mines. Other proceedings, by which persons are fined and rendered infamous, are public but not capital.

The following are examples of public proceedings:

By the law Julia majestatis those who undertake any enterprise against the emperor or the state may be sentenced to death, and even the memory of the offender becomes infamous.

The law Julia de adulteriis punishes with death those who commit adultery and those who commit lewd acts with persons of their own sex. The same law also makes it an offence (stuprum) to debauch a virgin or a widow of upright character without using force; in this case the punishment is confiscation of half of the offender's possessions, but if the offender is of low degree he is subjected to corporal punishment and relegation.

The law Cornelia de sicariis punishes with death those who commit murder or carry weapons (tela) with intent to kill. The term telum formerly signified an arrow, but now denotes anything that is thrown from the hand, eg, a club, a stone or a piece of iron. The same law also inflicts capital punishment upon those who by poison or magical charms cause death, and also upon those who sell pernicious drugs.

The law Pompeia de parricidiis inflicts a new punishment upon those who commit parricide, ie, publicly or privately hasten the death of a parent or a child, or any other relation to whose death the term parricide applies or, though a stranger to the family, advises or is privy to such a crime. A person guilty of parricide is sewn up in a sack with a dog, a cock, a viper and an ape and then thrown into a river or the sea. A man who murders any other person related to him by cognation or affinity is subject to the punishment of the law Cornelia de sicariis.

The law Cornelia de falsis, which is also called testamentaria, punishes any man who knowingly and with fraudulent intent writes, signs, dictates or produces a false will or other instrument, or who makes, engraves or impresses the seal of another. In this case slaves are punished with death and free persons are deported.

The law Julia de vi publica seu privata punishes all who use violence: if armed violence, the punishment is deportation; if unarmed violence, one-third of the offender's goods are confiscated. Under our constitution a person who commits rape of a virgin, a widow, a nun or any other woman is subject to capital punishment and his accomplice is dealt with in the same way.

The law Julia de peculatu punishes those who have stolen public money or anything which is sacred; if judges commit this crime during their term of office their punishment is capital, as is the punishment of those who assist them or knowingly receive the proceeds. Other persons are deported.

The law Fabia de plagiariis also gives rise to public proceedings for kidnapping, and under the imperial constitutions offenders may be punished with death or something less severe.

There are also other public proceedings, eg, the Julian laws de ambitu, repetundarum, de annona and de residuis, which result in punishments other than death; a fuller knowledge of public proceedings may be gained from the Digest.

(For the circumstances of the publication of the Institutes, see Historical Background, p27.)

Glossary

(References to 'INSTITUTES' are to the Institutes of Justinian, p44 et seq: other words printed in capital letters have such an entry elsewhere in the glossary.)

Acceptilatio. See CONTRACTS; INSTITUTES, BOOK III, TITLE XXIX.

Accessio. Accession. This occurred when one person's property became intermixed with the property of another so that it could not be separated at all, or could not be separated without inflicting damage out of proportion to the gain. The owner of the principal became the owner of the accessory, eg, the owner of land became the owner of alluvial deposits (alluvion). However, if it was possible to detach the accessory so that it recovered its individual character, it reverted to its former owner. See also INSTITUTES, BOOK II, TITLE I.

Acquisition by use. See USUSCAPIO

Actio praescriptis verbis. An action which was available whenever there was an agreement for reciprocal performances which was not referable to one of the recognised types of consensual contracts (see CONSENSUAL CONTRACTS), and one party had performed his part, and the other had not. Transactions of this kind are referred to as innominate real contracts. For example, if a man gave his clothes to a fuller to clean, and no price was fixed at the time, the transaction would give rise to an actio praescriptis verbis. See also INSTITUTES, BOOK III, TITLE XXIV.

Actions. An action was nothing more than the right which every man had of taking legal proceedings for whatever was due to him. Actions were principally classified as follows:

i)   In rem (for a thing); in personam (against a person).

ii)   Civil (evolved by civil law or created by statute); praetorian (introduced by the praetor's edict, either a new action or an adaptation of a civil law action).

iii)   In jus concepta (the formula referred to the existence of civil law rights, eg, 'owning'); in factum concepta (no reference was made to a civil law right – the judge was told to condemn if he found certain facts stated in the intentio (see FORMULA) to be true, if not to absolve).

iv)   Directa (an existing action, usually civil but sometimes praetorian); utilis (an action founded on utility, an adaptation or extension of an existing action through the intervention of the praetor).

v)   Stricti juris (of strict law or right – equitable defences were required to be pleaded expressly by way of an exceptio: see FORMULA); bonae fidei (of good faith – the judge was given unrestricted power to decide the fairness or equity of the case).

vi)   Rei persequendae gratia (for the recovery of compensation); poenae persequendae gratia (for punishment and, perhaps, compensation).

vii)   Temporal (actions which had to be brought within a limited time); perpetual (actions which could be brought at any time).

viii)   Transmissible (actions which passed to heirs); not transmissible (actions which did not pass to heirs).

ix)   Judicia legitima (statutory proceedings); judicia imperio continentia (proceedings which depended on the jurisdiction of the praetor).

x)   Actio popularis (an action in which it was in the public interest that a person should be allowed to sue for a penalty); actio privata (an action in which only the plaintiff's interest was involved).
See also INSTITUTES, BOOK IV, TITLE VI.

Adjudicatio. An award of property by a judge, eg, in an action where the court was required to determine a boundary (actio finium regundorum). Such a judgment was recognised as a mode of acquisition. See also FORMULA.

Adoptio. Adoption. The oldest form of adoption was adrogatio, ie, the adoption of a person SUI JURIS, and at first it was brought about by a legislative act of the COMITIA CURIATA or CALATA. By JUSTINIAN's time adrogation was by imperial rescript, ie, by the emperor's authority.

In early times the adoption of a person ALIENI JURIS was achieved by three sales and manumissions, which broke the PATRIA POTESTAS, followed by a fictitious action (IN JURE CESSIO) in which the magistrate declared the child to be the child of the adopting father. Justinian substituted adoption by means of a declaration before the magistrate followed by a magisterial order and registration in court. He also distinguished between adoptio plena (adoption by a natural ascendent whereby the child passed into the power of the adopter) and adoptio minus plena where there was no change of patria potestas, the child merely acquiring a right of intestate succession to the adopter. See also INSTITUTES, BOOK I, TITLE XI.

Adrogatio. See ADOPTIO

Aediles plebeii. Two plebeian officers appointed by the CONCILIUM PLEBIS about 489BC to control the detailed work of police administration. They also acted as judges in cases referred to them by the tribunes, whom they assisted in other spheres. Caesar instituted two plebeian aediles cereales to supervise the supply of corn. Early in the empire this duty was passed to a special imperial prefect (praefectus annonae: see PREFECTS) and police work in Rome was undertaken by the prefect of the city (praefectus urbi). See also CURULE AEDILES.

Aerarium. The state treasury. Controlled by the CONSULS and supervised by the QUAESTORS, the censors alone were entitled to draw upon its funds, eg, for public works, but only to the extent allowed by the consuls. Resolutions of the SENATE (SENATUSCONSULTA) were reduced to writing and deposited in the aerarium for safe keeping.

The importance of the aerarium diminished with the establishment during the empire of the fiscus, a new imperial treasury which received taxes from all parts of the empire.

Agency. In early law a person incurred no rights and duties under a contract entered into by his agent with a third party, but in certain cases (in all of them the agent was a member of the principal's family or household) the praetor allowed an action against the principal as well as the agent; these actions are normally called actiones adjecticae qualitatis. For example, the actio quod jussu lay against a master on a contract which his slave had entered into with his authority.

Later, as a result of the work of jurists, a principal was made liable for contracts entered into by his agent in his (the principal's) name within the scope of the agent's authority, but the agent was also liable. Apart from a few special cases (eg, the owners of a vessel engaged in the import of grain could sue their captain's debtors), the principal could only sue upon a contract entered into by his agent if the agent gave the principal a mandate to sue, and this the agent could be compelled to do by an actio mandati.

Alieni juris. A person subject to anyone's potestas (power), MANUS or MANCIPIUM. See also PATRIA POTESTAS.

Alluvion. See ACCESSIO

Augurs. Religious officials and members of a priestly college, they gave warnings of the result of contemplated enterprises by observing (according to Festus) lightning, birds, the sacred chickens, four-footed animals and portents. The taking of auspices by a magistrate possessing IMPERIUM preceded every important act of state, whether civil or military. In 300BC the number of augurs was increased to nine, and it was provided that five of them should always be PLEBEIANS.

Augurs were required to be present in the COMITIA CURIATA, and they were generally members of the senate. Cicero thought that augurs possessed the 'highest and most important authority in the state' because they could adjourn the assembly and cause any business to be abandoned by declaring 'On another day'.

Bonitary (praetorian) ownership. Effective ownership protected by praetorian remedies but devoid of civil law title, eg, if A transferred a res mancipi (see MANCIPATIO) to B by simply handing it over, B became bonitary owner of the thing and A remained quiritary owner until B acquired it by USUCAPIO, at which stage B became also quiritary owner as if the thing had been transferred by MANCIPATIO, or IN JURE CESSIO. The distinction between bonitary ownership and quiritary ownership was abolished by Justinian. See also DOMINIUM EX JURE QUIRITIUM.

Bonorum possessio. Although the PRAETOR could not make an heir, he could grant bonorum possessio, ie, give to persons of his choice the right to use certain remedies to obtain possession of a deceased's goods. See INSTITUTES, BOOK III, TITLE IX.

Capitis deminutio (diminutio). Change of status, which was either:
i)   capitis deminutio maxima (the greatest diminution);
ii)   capitis deminutio minor (the less or mesne diminution); or
iii) capitis deminutio minima (the least diminution).
A change of social standing, eg, removal from the senate, did not involve capitis deminutio. See also INSTITUTES, BOOK I, TITLE XVI.

Capito. Regarded as a rival of his contemporary LABEO, he is believed to have founded the Sabinian school of jurists. He loved wealth and power and hated change; he held the office of CONSUL in AD5.

Censors. The office of censor was instituted in 443BC. Two in number, the censors were elected every five years by the COMITIA CENTURIATA from the members of the SENATE, but no senator could be elected for a second period of office. Originally the office was held for five years, but in 434BC the term was reduced to eighteen months so that in each period of five years there were three and a half years when there were no censors. During this period urgent business was transacted by other magistrates. In 351BC the first plebeian censor was elected, and the leges Publiliae (339BC) provided that one censor should always be a PLEBEIAN.

At first the censors' main duty was the keeping of the roll of citizens (the census) to enable them to be placed in the appropriate century or tribe. Although they did not have IMPERIUM, their responsibilities increased; they became the guardians of public and private morals and concerned with the proper administration of the state's domestic affairs. By 350BC they nominated members of, and for serious misconduct expelled members from, the senate. In making their choice of senators they were required to give preference to former magistrates (CONSULS, PRAETORS and CURULE AEDILES) and subsequently former AEDILES PLEBEII, TRIBUNES and QUAESTORS had the right to be chosen. In course of time the censors also assessed for purposes of taxation, placed government contracts (eg, leased public land and contracted for the erection and maintenance of public buildings) and invested surplus revenue. They were sometimes called the 'budget-makers' and they could also impose fines of a small amount.

Eventually, the office of censor became of such importance that it was normally held by a consul and no separate appointment as censor was made after 22BC. From this date the censors' functions were carried out by the emperor and other officers, although the title was allowed to lapse towards the end of the first century AD.

Centumviral court. By 241BC this court normally comprised three members from each of the thirty-five TRIBES, although its numerical strength was later increased to 180. Its jurisdiction was limited to Rome, perhaps to Italy, and extended to actions in rem in the widest sense of the meaning of that term. Thus the court dealt with matters relating to inheritance, especially cases of QUERELA INOFFICIOSI TESTAMENTI, and the more important vindicationes, ie, real actions.

During the empire the court was divided into several parts or senates which sometimes sat alone, sometimes together. The court probably disappeared about AD200, possibly a little later.

Cessio in jure. See IN JURE CESSIO

Clientelae. Probably immigrants (PLEBEIANS) or freed slaves and their issue; in ancient Rome they were persons whose status was between that of the PATRICIANS and other plebeians. From the free choice of the parties clients were attached to the patrician houses by bonds of clientage and each had his patron who was under a general obligation to protect his client's interests. Under the law of the

Twelve Tables a patron who defrauded his client was liable to be outlawed and to have his property confiscated. It was the duty of the client to ransom his patron or patron's son from captivity, and to provide marriage portions for his daughter. The client was also expected to pay certain public charges, eg, fines and expenses connected with magisterial offices. Neither the patron nor his client could render assistance to the enemy of the other: thus a client could not be a witness against his patron, or vice versa.

Later, when a FREEDMAN remained in the service of his master and enjoyed his protection, the master became his patron from the moment that the slave was manumitted. A freedman owed respect to his patron (obsequium) and could not sue him without the leave of a magistrate, but the patron was bound to support him in case of need. The patron could require the performance of service (operae) and in certain circumstances was entitled to a share of his freedman's estate (bona). JUSTINIAN made all freedmen of equal standing with those of free birth except that operae and bona were retained unless expressly renounced; a freedman could not be released from the duty of obsequium.

Codex Repetitae Praelectionis. A second edition of the Codex Vetus (Code of Justinian: see CODEX VETUS) issued in AD534. The work was entrusted to Tribonian, Dorotheus and three advocates: it embodies recent decisions and constitutions and also made certain changes which had been found to be necessary when compiling the Digest (see DIGEST (PANDECTS)). The Codex Repetitae Praelectionis replaced Justinian's first code and may be said to have completed the work of consolidating the law.

Codex Theodosianus. An official collection of all the imperial constitutions (see CONSTITUTIONES PRINCIPUM) prepared with the sanction of the emperor Theodosius II. The work was entrusted to two commissions of eight (AD429) and sixteen (AD435) members respectively, both of which were under the direction of Antiochus. It brought up to date the Gregorian and Hermogenian codes (these codes were probably compiled between AD312 and AD429 as a result of the private labours of Hermogenianus and Gregorianus, but may have been published in the reign of Diocletian (AD284–305)) and when it was published in AD438 it was declared to be the sole source of imperial law. Valentinian III, the emperor of the west, published the code in the same year as the imperial law of his people. See also NOVELLAE.

Codex Vetus. Initiated by JUSTINIAN in AD528, a collection in twelve books of the imperial enactments then in force. The ten compilers, who worked under the direction of TRIBONIAN (Tribunian), were instructed to suppress preambles, repetitions, contradictory or disused clauses, and to collect and classify the laws under proper titles, adding, cutting down, modifying, compressing, as occasion should require, several constitutions into a single enactment. The work was published on 13th April AD529 and came into force on 16th May in the same year. Justinian decreed that these constitutions, together with the works of the ancient interpreters of the law, must suffice to decide all suits. See also CODEX REPETITAE PRAELECTIONIS.

Codicilli. Codicils: informal written directions to an heir, frequently made by letter. A TESTAMENT (will) was an instrument for the appointment of an heir; a codicil had no validity unless an heir was in possession, either under a will or on intestacy. No one could make a codicil who could not make a will. See also INSTITUTES, Book II, Title XXV.

Coemptio. See MANUS

College of Pontiffs. College of the priesthood of which originally the king was chief (PONTIFEX MAXIMUS: chief pontiff). At first there were four pontiffs (pontifices – their name was derived from their duty to repair wooden bridges); they may be regarded as the earliest of the Roman jurists and they were not liable to prosecution or punishment. By the Ogulnian law 300BC the number of pontiffs was increased to eight, in addition to the pontifex maximus, and it was laid down that four of them should be plebeians. Sulla increased their number to fifteen and Caesar added one more. In 253BC Coruncanius became the first PLEBEIAN to be appointed to the office of pontifex maximus.

In addition to their religious duties and jurisdiction, the pontiffs controlled proceedings in the COMITIA CURIATA for the giving of formal sanction to adrogations (see ADOPTIO) and wills. For about one hundred years after the enactment of the law of the Twelve Tables (452BC) their interpretation was the prerogative of the pontiffs, and they advised magistrates as to the law. This right enabled them to develop new legal institutions, and they played an important part in developing the LEGIS ACTIO PROCEDURE by formulating the words required to bring an action before the court. Cicero said that the pontiffs should inflict capital punishment on persons guilty of incest.

Comita Calata. See COMITIA CURIATA

Comitia Centuriata. Servius Tullius (578–535BC) taxed the people (PLEBEIANS as well as PATRICIANS) according to their means and arranged them in five classes according to their wealth, originally land, later money, finally wealth in any form. For the purpose of voting he is said to have divided the classes into centuries and these centuries comprised the comitia centuriata (assembly of the centuries). In the first and wealthiest class there were eighty centuries, in the second, third and fourth twenty centuries, and in the fifth thirty centuries. Above all were eighteen centuries of equites (cavalry) and there were also four centuries of artificers and buglers and one of those (proletarii) who could not even qualify for the lowest class. Thus there was a total of 193 centuries, and as each century had one vote the wealthiest class (80) and the equites (18) could outvote the remainder. Subsequent reorganisation of the centuries may have removed this overall majority of the wealthy, but their power was temporarily restored by Sulla in 88BC.

Voting normally took place in the Field of Mars and it continued until an overall majority was obtained; it was therefore unusual for the lower classes to vote at all. Apart from its right to cast one vote, each century may have had certain commitments to make provision in men or equipment for the Roman army.

The comitia centuriata was additional to, not in substitution for, the COMITIA CURIATA, although in the early republic it was the legislative assembly. Meetings of the comitia centuriata were summoned by a CONSUL who would submit proposals for legislation. The comitia centuriata also elected the consuls, PRAETORS and CENSORS, decided constitutional questions including those affecting peace and war, and heard appeals in criminal cases, especially where a capital sentence had been passed upon a citizen. The law of the Twelve Tables provided that only the comitia centuriata had the right of legislating so as to inflict a punishment on a citizen involving his life, liberty or civic rights, but all its enactments required the approval of the senate before they became law.

Although the comitia centuriata continued to exercise certain of its traditional functions, eg, the election of consuls, praetors and censors, by the third century BC the COMITIA TRIBUTA had become the most important legislative body.

Comitia Curiata. The oldest of the legislative assemblies; during the early period of the monarchy it was a meeting of the thirty curiae held in the centre of the city at a place called the comitium. There were ten curiae in each of the three ancient tribes, and each curia had one vote which was cast according to the wish of the majority of its members. Convoked by the KING or by patrician magistrates acting under the direction of the SENATE and presided over by the king or CONSUL, its duties included the election of the king and the highest sacerdotal, civil and military officers and the enacting of the law of investiture (lex curiata) by which the IMPERIUM or right to command was conferred. It also determined the composition of families and regulated testamentary succession, but the comitia curiata could deal only with the particular matter for which it had been convoked and it was essential that the AUGURS should be present at its meetings. With the exception of the lex curiata no decree of the comitia curiata was law until confirmed by the senate.

The comitia curiata became less important as the legislative powers of the COMITIA CENTURIATA increased, but it retained the right to give formal authority to the higher magistrates at the commencement of their term of office by enacting the law of investiture. In addition, until the reign of Diocletian (AD284–305), under the name of the comitia calata, it continued to sanction or witness wills, confirm adrogations (see ADOPTIO) and deal with matters concerning religion. For these purposes it met twice a year and was probably presided over by the PONTIFEX MAXIMUS: proceedings were controlled by the college of pontiffs and the curiae were represented by thirty LICTORS.

Comitia Tributa. This assembly of the people first met in 489BC when, with the concurrence of the senate, it was convened to try the patrician Coriolanus. It was composed of PATRICIANS and PLEBEIANS and organised on the basis of TRIBES or local divisions. Originally four in number, by 240 BC there were thirty-five tribes, each of which had one vote which was cast according to the wish of the majority of its members. AUGURS were not required to be present at the meeting of this assembly.

The comitia tributa came to BE convoked by a CONSUL or PRAETOR who could submit proposed legislation to it for approval: by the third century BC it had become the most important legislative body. It also elected the CURULE AEDILES and several minor magistrates and, later, the quaestors and some of the military tribunes (tribuni militares). The comitia tributa disappeared during the early empire.

Comitium. See COMITIA CURIATA

Commixtio. The mixing of solids. See also ACCESSIO and INSTITUTES, BOOK II, TITLE I.

Commodatum. See REAL CONTRACTS and INSTITUTES, BOOK III, TITLE XIV.

Concilium Plebis. Closely allied to but distinct from the COMITIA TRIBUTA, an assembly comprised exclusively of PLEBEIANS organised on the basis of TRIBES. Its functions included the election of the TRIBUNES and their assistants, the AEDILES PLEBEII, and its resolutions (PLEBISCITA) were originally binding only on plebians. However, when the lex Hortensia (287 BC) confirmed that plebiscita should be binding on all equally, plebiscita obtained equal force with LEGES. In the later republic it became the normal vehicle of legislation and the term 'leges' was often used in reference to its enactments. Theoretically, at least, the COMITIA CENTURIATA and the comitia tributa retained the right to pass general legislation, but by this time PATRICIANS were numerically an insignificant minority so that the membership of these assemblies was almost the same as that of the concilium plebis.

The concilium plebis was convoked and presided over by a tribune who also submitted proposals for legislation. It disappeared during the early empire.

Concubinatus. Concubinage; a relation of the sexes which did not satisfy the requirements of legal marriage (see JUSTAE NUPTIAE). The relation failed to give the potestas over the children born of the concubine, but they could be legitimated. By law no man could have a wife and a concubine.

Condictio. An action for the recovery of a determinate sum of money, later extended to the recovery of every determinate thing. See also LEGIS ACTIO PROCEDURE and INSTITUTES, BOOK II, TITLE I, and BOOK III, TITLE XIV.

Confarreatio. See MANUS

Confusio. The mixing of liquids. See also ACCESSIO, CONTRACTS and INSTITUTES, BOOK II, TITLE I.

Consensual contracts. Contracts by consent: writing or acts or special forms were not required. The presence of the parties was not essential. Consensual contracts were bilateral and bonae fidei and persons seeking to enforce them could not succeed unless they showed that they had performed or were ready and willing to perform their part. There were four kinds of consensual contracts, viz.:

i) Emptio venditio (sale) where one person (the seller) promised to deliver a thing to another (the buyer) who in turn promised to pay a price. The duties of the seller could be enforced by the actio empti, the actio redhibitoria (to cancel a sale in consequence of faults in the thing sold) or the actio aestimatoria seu quanti minoris (to reduce the price, although the judge could, at his discretion, cancel the sale). The duties of the buyer could be enforced by the actio venditi.

ii) Locatio conductio (hire) where one person (the lessor) agreed to give another (the hirer) the use of something, or to do some work, in return for a fixed sum. The actio locati was available to the lessor, the actio conducti to the hirer.

iii) Societas (partnership) where two or more persons combined their property, or one contributed property and another labour, with a view to sharing amongst themselves the profits. A partnership could exist where one party was to share in the profit, but not in the loss, but there could be no partnership where one of the parties was to share in the loss only, and not in the profit. The rights of the partners could be enforced by the actio pro socia and they could usually take advantage of the actio communi dividundo for the division of common property and adjudication.

(iv) Mandatum (mandate) where one person promised to do or to give something, without remuneration, at the request of another who, for his part, undertook to save him harmless from all loss. If a payment was agreed upon, the contract was one of hire. The mandator (the person making the request) could enforce his rights by an actio mandati directa while the mandatarius had the actio mandati contraria. See also INSTITUTES, Book III, Titles XXII et seq.

Constitutiones principum. Decrees, edicts and letters or rescripts of the emperor. A constitutio principis (constitution) had the force of a lex because, it was said, it was by a lex that the emperor was invested with the IMPERIUM. Ulpian thought that 'everything which the emperor decides has the force of statute, since by the royal law passed concerning his imperium the people gave to him and put into his hands all its own imperium and power'. It is probable that constitutions were introduced by Octavianus (Augustus) at the beginning of the first century AD, but he and his immediate successors generally obtained the sanction of the people or the SENATE to their decrees.

Constitutions were either personal or general; personal constitutions extended only to a particular person, *eg*, by awarding an extraordinary punishment or granting some unprecedented indulgence, while general constitutions were binding on all people. At various times constitutions were referred to as decreta (decisions given by the emperor on a question brought before him judicially: such decisions were recognised as binding for future cases), rescripta (written answers to questions submitted to the emperor in writing), mandata (instructions to officials, eg, provincial governors) and edicta (orders issued by the emperor in his capacity of chief magistrate). Rescripta were either epistolae (answers to magistrates sent by post) or subscriptiones (answers given to private citizens, the emperor's finding being written at the foot of the petition).

When there was more than one emperor, constitutions were issued in the name of both and were binding throughout the empire. However, in AD429 Theodosius II decreed that constitutions of one emperor should not have effect in the territory of the other until they had been submitted to and approved by him. See also INSTITUTES, BOOK I, TITLE II.

Consuls. In early times higher magistrates in rank next to the KING, the chief magistrate. After 509BC all the king's powers (with the exception of his pontifical duties) were vested in two magistrates known as consuls (at first they were called 'praetors') who were elected to this office in the COMITIA CENTURIATA for a period of one year. They held the fasces, a bundle of rods which was the emblem of IMPERIUM, for a month at a time; they did not themselves carry the fasces; it was borne before them by 12 LICTORS. During the republic the office of consul was the highest in the state and, subject to the exception noted above and to specific statutory provisions to the contrary (eg, the CENSORS' right to nominate members of the SENATE), consular imperium or power was unlimited in both the civil and military spheres. It was also enacted that consuls could not inflict capital punishment on a Roman citizen without the consent of the people. It should be noted, however, that their civil jurisdiction was passed to the PRAETORS, while the QUAESTORS exercised their criminal jurisdiction on their behalf. By virtue of the leges Liciniae Sextiae (367BC) one consul was required to be a PLEBEIAN and plebeians were admitted to the priestly colleges.

The consuls enjoyed equal powers and one consul could veto the act of the other (intercessio). They could convene the senate, initiate legislation in the comitia centuriata and in times of crisis either consul could appoint a DICTATOR for not more than six months, although the dictator could be re-appointed at the expiration of this period. At first they also appointed the military tribunes (TRIBUNI MILITARES).

During the empire consuls were appointed by the emperor, although the emperor himself frequently held the office. When there were emperors for both east and west each emperor normally appointed one of the consuls, usually himself. At this time the consuls had no real powers and the office was finally abolished by JUSTINIAN in AD541.

Contracts. A contract existed when one person voluntarily undertook a duty with the intention of thereby creating in favour of another a right in personam. Contracts were actionable only if they came within one of the following categories:

i)   re (real): see REAL CONTRACTS;
ii)   verbis (words): see VERBAL CONTRACTS;
iii)   literis (writing): see LITERAL CONTRACTS;
iv)   consensu (consent): see CONSENSUAL CONTRACTS.

Contracts were further distinguished as:

i)   unilateral, ie, consisting wholly of promises by one person, eg, a loan; or
ii)   bilateral, ie, consisting of promises made by two persons, one promise being the consideration for the other, eg, sale.

Unilateral contracts were stricti juris (of strict law or right); bilateral contracts were bonae fidei (of good faith). See also ACTIONS.

Formal contracts were those where the validity of the contract depended upon the observance of certain formalities, eg, stipulatio; informal contracts depended on the intention of the parties, eg, sale.

The ways in which contracts could be discharged included:

i)   solutio (performance), ie, the discharge of what is due or, if the creditor consents, of something else in its place, by the debtor or someone else for him;
ii)   acceptilatio (release), ie, crediting the debtor with payment (this was available principally in the case of verbal contracts, and the creditor was estopped from alleging that there had been no payment);
iii)   novatio (novation), ie, the substitution of a new obligation for an old;
iv)   interitus rei (impossibility of performance), eg, where a thing perished;
v)   confusio, ie, where the character of the creditor and debtor met in the same person, eg, when a creditor became heir to a debtor, or vice versa;
vi)   lapse of time (the time varied according to the nature of the action);
vii)   where the contractual obligation was personal, by the death of either party;
viii) litis contestatio (taking a debtor into court): this extinguished the debt and gave the creditor a new claim.

See also INSTITUTES, BOOK III, TITLE XXIX.

Corpus Juris Civilis. The term used to describe the Institutes, Digest and Code of JUSTINIAN, and the NOVELLAE. These works subsisted entire until the final dissolution of the empire in AD1453.

Culpa. Failure to exercise the required degree of diligence. It was usual to classify diligence as:

i)   diligentia exacta, ie, the degree of care habitually exhibited by a good father of a family in his own affairs; or
ii)   diligentia quam suis rebus, ie, the degree of care exhibited by the person in question in his own affairs.

Culpa lata was gross negligence and occurred, eg, when a person with whom a testament had been deposited for safe custody read it aloud to his neighbours. If he acted maliciously this was DOLUS.

Cura. Curatorship. A curator was appointed to a person above the age of puberty to manage his affairs, when from any cause he was unfit to manage them himself. Thus curators were appointed for minors, madmen, lunatics, persons who were deaf or dumb and spendthrifts. See also TWELVE TABLES, TABLE V and INSTITUTES, BOOK I, TITLE XXI et seq.

Curule aedile. Minor magistrates elected by the COMITIA TRIBUTA. The office was created about 366BC and was at first open only to PATRICIANS. Originally two in number, they were responsible for the oversight and control of the slave and cattle markets, with jurisdiction in questions arising out of market transactions. They also exercised a general police function, were responsible for (and after 264BC had themselves to meet the cost of) the festal games, and controlled public works, *eg,* repair of roadways and maintenance of the city's water supply. Although they exercised a minor criminal jurisdiction, they did not have IMPERIUM and could only convene the assembly for the purpose of reviewing their sentences when they imposed a fine above a certain amount. They published edicts (the law contained therein was part of the JUS HONORARIUM) and these edicts, which were consolidated by Hadrian about AD130, played an important part in the development of the law of sale. However, in the days of the empire their powers and influence gradually declined.

Cicero referred to aediles who were 'caretakers of the city, of the markets, and of the traditional games' and it would seem that he included both the curule aediles and the AEDILES PLEBEII and that they thenceforth had similar duties. Caesar made all aediles responsible for the repair and paving of public roads within, or within one mile of, the city of Rome. See also EDICTA MAGISTRATUUM.

Custom. Roman law originated in custom; indeed, the law of the TWELVE TABLES was based upon the customs of the day. Local as well as general customs were recognised, but its importance as a source of law gradually diminished. Justinian referred to custom as jus non scriptum, ie, unwritten law. See also INSTITUTES BOOK I, TITLE II.

Damnum injuria. See DELICTS (WRONGS) and INSTITUTES, BOOK IV, TITLE III.

Decemvirs. The ten magistrates, all of whom were patricians, who drew up ten tables of laws which in 451BC were submitted to and approved by the senate and the COMITIA CENTURIATA. During this year all other magistrates resigned their offices and their powers were vested in the decemvirs (decemviri). In the following year a new commission of ten, including in its ranks some plebeians, added two tables which, together with the first ten, became the law of the TWELVE TABLES. The second commission abused, and refused to lay down, its powers and in 449BC its members were overthrown, imprisoned or exiled and their estates were confiscated. As a result of this uprising the former offices were re-established. It should be noted that the PLEBEIAN members of the second commission were the first plebeian magistrates of the Roman people.

Delicts (wrongs). Public delicts were crimes; private delicts were torts. There were many delicts, but the principal ones included:
i) furtum (theft), ie, a fraudulent dealing with a thing itself or with the use or possession of it; theft was either manifest or not manifest;
ii) rapina (robbery), ie, the taking of the property of another by force; this was first distinguished from theft in 78BC;
iii) damnum injuria (wrongful or injurious damage): the actio damni injuriae was established by the law Aquilia, 287BC;
iv) injuria (injury), ie, in the special sense of an outrage or an insult.
See also INSTITUTES, BOOK IV, TITLE I et seq. and TWELVE TABLES, TABLE VIII.

Depositum. See REAL CONTRACTS and INSTITUTES, BOOK III, TITLE XIV.

Dictator. During the republic in times of crisis either CONSUL could appoint a dictator to exercise his powers for a period not exceeding six months, although re-appointment was possible at the expiration of this period. The appointment was normally made by the consul who at that time held the fasces (the emblem of power), but when the power of the SENATE was at its height the authority of that body was required.

The dictator was superior to all magistrates and had jurisdiction over both PATRICIANS and PLEBEIANS. His IMPERIUM had to be confirmed by a lex curiata, but he always appointed an assistant (magister equitum) on whom the dictator himself could confer imperium. After 356BC the office of dictator was open to plebeians as well as patricians, and a dictator had the right to be attended by 24 LICTORS who would carry the fasces bearing an axe even within the city. The axe was the symbol of unrestricted authority normally reserved for a consul in the provinces. Originally, at least, dictators were not subject to an appeal against a capital sentence (provocatio) or the veto of the tribunes (intercessio).

Although others, eg, Sulla and Caesar, continued to use the title, as a result of the growth of the senate's power no temporary and constitutional dictator was appointed after 202BC. Caesar was, in fact, the last Roman to use the title, it being abolished by Mark Antony in the last years of the republic.

Dictio dotis. See VERBAL CONTRACTS

151

Digest (Pandects). In AD531 JUSTINIAN instructed TRIBONIAN 'to make a complete revision of the whole civil law, and of all Roman jurisprudence, by collecting together in a single code the dispersed volumes of so many jurists'. Tribonian was entrusted to choose the most skilful professors and the greatest advocates to perform the work, but it was to be carried out under his (Tribonian's) direction. The work was to consist of fifty volumes and to be based on the writings of those jurists whom the emperors had authorised to interpret the laws, and equal authority was to be given to all of them. However, where there was a conflict amongst the jurists the compilers were empowered to follow and adopt what seemed to them to be the better view. The decisions of the authors quoted in the Digest were to have authority as if they had emanated from the imperial constitutions, and nothing in ancient manuscripts was to cast doubt on what they wrote. Jurists were forbidden to add commentaries to the Digest, except a summary under each article indicating its contents. Everything, said Justinian, was to be ruled by the Digest and the code of the constitutions (see CODEX VETUS) and the INSTITUTES, if and when they were produced.

The Digest was published on 16th December AD533 (in the event, shortly after the Institutes) and given the force of law from the 30th of that month.

Divorce. A marriage could be dissolved by the wife's father if she remained in his potestas (ie, had not passed into the MANUS of her husband), although Antoninus Pius prohibited a father from disturbing a harmonious union.

Divorce by mutual consent (divortium bona gratia) was also possible, but JUSTINIAN at first restricted it to certain cases (ie, where the husband was impotent, or either party wished to enter a monastery or was held in captivity for a certain length of time) and later provided that it should involve forfeiture of all their property.

One party could divorce the other without that other's consent, but the lex Julia de adulteriis 18BC required a written bill of divorce (libellus repudii) to be given in the presence of seven witnesses. Over the years legislation imposed restraints of various kinds, and Justinian repealed the former constitutions and resettled the grounds on which marriages could be validly dissolved without the consent of the other party. See also DOS.

Dolus. In the law of contract dolus came to mean every act or default which did not satisfy the requirements of good faith. In particular, it occurred where a person represented as a fact something that he did not believe to be a fact (suggestio falsi) or concealed a fact having knowledge or belief of the fact (suppressio veri). Simple damages only were recoverable. A contract which provided that a person was not to be answerable for dolus was of no effect.

Dominium. Property, or ownership; an aggregate of the right of possession and enjoyment, and the right of alienation. See also INSTITUTES, BOOK II, TITLE I.

Dominium ex jure quiritium. Ownership by quiritary title, *ie,* ownership by a Roman citizen of a Roman thing acquired by Roman process. Quiritary title should be distinguished from bonitary ownership (see BONITARY OWNERSHIP).

Donatio. Donation; gift. Gifts were either:
i)   Donationes inter vivos (gifts between living persons). By the lex Cincia 204BC gifts beyond a certain amount, except in favour of certain relatives, were prohibited. JUSTINIAN enacted that gifts of more than 500 solidi should be registered in court. Originally gifts between husband and wife were prohibited, but in AD206 Antonius allowed them to become valid if the donee survived the donor, the parties had not been divorced and, at the time of the death, the donor still wished the gift to be effective. Until Justinian's time gifts by PATRONS to FREEDMEN could always be revoked, but he provided that such gifts were only revocable in the event of the subsequent birth of issue to the donor if he was childless at the time of making the gift.
ii)   Donationes mortis causa (gifts on account, or in contemplation, of death). Such gifts did not take effect if the donor survived the donee, but they were effective if they died simultaneously. They could be revoked inter vivos or by will. Septimius Severus extended the lex Falcidia (see LEGACIES) to donationes mortis causa and in AD530 Justinian provided that donationes mortis

causa made in the presence of five witnesses did not require registration.

iii) Donationes propter nuptias (gifts on account of marriage): gifts, usually contracts to make gifts, made by husbands to provide for their wives in the event of their predeceasing them or being divorced through no fault of their own. Justinian allowed such gifts to be made before or after marriage; previously they had been made before (donationes ante nuptias).

See also INSTITUTES, BOOK II, TITLE VII.

Dos. Dowry: the property contributed by a wife, or by someone else on her behalf, to her husband, as her contribution towards the expenses of the marriage. If given by the wife's father or paternal ancestor it was known as dos profecticia, if by anyone else (including the wife) dos adventicia, but if it was given on condition that it should revert to the donor on dissolution of the marriage it was called dos recepticia. A dos could either be given (dotis datio), declared (dotis dictio) or promised (dotis promissio), the normal means of constituting a dos.

With the exception of dos recepticia, in early law once the dos was vested in the husband it was his for all purposes and for all time. In the later republic a wife could recover her dos, or at least a part of it, in the event of a divorce or the death of her husband; if the wife predeceased the husband, if the wife's father was alive he could reclaim dos profecticia. Where a wife was entitled to recover the dos the husband could retain his necessary expenses (propter impensas), where the marriage was dissolved without the fault of the husband, one-sixth for each child but never more than half (propter liberos), and one-sixth if the wife had committed adultery or one-eighth for a lesser offence (propter mores).

The lex Julia de fundo dotali (18BC) provided that immoveables in Italy forming part of the dos could not be sold without the wife's consent and prohibited their hypothecation. In AD531 JUSTINIAN prohibited the alienation or hypothecation of dotal immoveables, wherever situated, and provided that the dos should revert to the donor unless the wife was divorced for a permitted cause or had divorced the husband for a cause which was not permitted. The husband continued to be entitled to retain his necessary expenses. See also INSTITUTES, BOOK IV, TITLE VI.

Edicta magistratuum. Declarations of law (edicta) issued by the praetor urbanus, the praetor peregrinus (see PRAETORS) and the CURULE AEDILES in Rome and the provincial governors and QUAESTORS which together were known as the jus honorarium (honorary law) because they were sanctioned by those who bore honour in the state. All the higher magistrates were entitled to issue edicts, but only the edicts of those whose duties included jurisdiction comprised the jus honorarium. Such persons were said to have the jus edicendi, and their work mitigated the effect of many rules of the jus civile arising from statute and interpretation which were found to be inequitable. In the words of Papinian, the jus honorarium could 'aid, supplement or correct' the civil law.

Edicts of the jurisdictional magistrates gradually became less important as a source of law and were in fact consolidated and systematically arranged during the reign of the emperor Hadrian (AD131). This work was carried out by the jurist Salvius Julianus and confirmed by a senatusconsultum passed at the emperor's wish. From this point in time edicts ceased to be a source of new law, although praetors continued the formality of publishing an edict at the beginning of their year of office.

The term edicta was also applied to orders issued by the emperor in his capacity of chief magistrate. Unlike the edicts of other magistrates, the edicts of the emperor probably did not lose their validity when his term of office expired, ie, upon his death. See also CONSTITUTIONES PRINCIPUM and INSTITUTES, BOOK I, TITLE II.

Emancipatio. Emancipation: a means by which children were released from the potestas (power) of their parents, originally accomplished by triple sales by mancipatio, after the first two of which the child was manumitted by vindicta and so returned to his father's power, and by the third of which he was released from his father's power. Anastasius (AD503) allowed emancipation by imperial rescript and registration in court. For JUSTINIAN, the acquiescence of the child, a declaration before the magistrate and registration in court was sufficient. See also TWELVE TABLES, TABLE IV and INSTITUTES, BOOK I, TITLE XIII.

Emphyteusis. A grant (lease) of land or houses in perpetuity, or for a long period, on the condition that an annual sum be paid to the owner or his successors. The emphyteuta (lessee) was also bound to manage the property so as not to seriously reduce its value, and he could be ejected for a breach of either of these duties. However, Justinian provided that the emphyteuta could not be ejected for non-payment of rent unless the rent was three years in arrears. See also SUPERFICIES and INSTITUTES, BOOK III, TITLE XXV.

Emptio Venditio. See CONSENSUAL CONTRACTS and INSTITUTES, BOOK III, TITLE XXII.

Equites. Originally the providers of cavalry for the army, by the end of the republic they were a distinct social class comprising, in the main, merchants, bankers and moneylenders.

Exceptio. See FORMULA

Exceptio doli. An equitable defence, introduced by the PRAETOR, which was available in cases of violence (vis) and intimidation (metus). See also METUS.

Extraordinarium judicium. Extraordinary procedure. In AD342 the emperors Constans and Constantius finally abolished the FORMULARY PROCEDURE. Suitors were relieved from the technical snares of the formula and after AD428 the court issued and served a libellus conventionis, ie, a written summons which informed the defendant of the nature of the complaint made against him. However, as early as AD294 the emperor Diocletian had enacted that all causes should be heard entirely by the magistrates, a constitution which may be said to have marked the beginning of extraordinary procedure. From this point in time it was the exception rather than the rule for proceedings to be conducted in two stages.

In the first days of the extraordinary procedure, when the parties came to court the plaintiff stated his complaint and demand and the defendant pleaded such defences as the law allowed him. No written formula was prepared, but the substance of the discussion – which ended with the settlement of the issue to be tried – was recorded by clerks of the court. After this preliminary discussion witnesses were called and speeches made as formerly in judicio.

In JUSTINIAN'S time the defendant was required to give security for his attendance and, within twenty days, to lodge an answer (libellus contradictionis). At the trial witnesses were called and argument heard, and the court could then order specific performance, enforced by court officers, as well as pecuniary condemnation. As a last resort, specific performance could be enforced by the armed force of the state.

In the case of pecuniary condemnation, execution was levied on the property of the judgment debtor sufficient to satisfy the debt (pignus ex judicati causa captum), execution against the person probably being a thing of the past. Where the judgment debtor was insolvent or there were several judgment creditors the whole estate was liquidated and sold in parts (distractio bonorum).

Fasces. See CONSULS

Feciales. In the days of the monarchy, judges of treaties, truces, embassies and matters of a similar kind; they also declared war and determined questions of international law. If a dispute arose with a foreign state one of the 21 members of the college of feciales would go to that state and demand reparation. If satisfaction was not given within 33 days the matter was referred to the SENATE, and if it was decided to go to war the member returned to the frontier and, thrusting his lance into the soil, made the solemn declaration of war.

Fideicommissum. A trust; a request to an heir to make over the whole or a part of the property or some specific thing to some other person (the fideicommissarius) who was disqualified by civil law from taking it as an heir or legatee. No one could make a fideicommissum unless he had the capacity to make a will. See also LEGACIES and INSTITUTES, BOOK II, TITLES XXIII and XXIV.

Fidejussio. See SURETIES and INSTITUTES, BOOK III, TITLE XXI.

Fiducia. See REAL CONTRACTS

Fiscus. See AERARIUM

Formula. In formulary proceedings (see FORMULARY PROCEDURE) the formula usually comprised:

i) at its head, the name of the judge agreed upon by the parties to the dispute;

ii) the demonstratio (demonstration) pointing out the matter in dispute, eg, 'Whereas Aulus Agerius sold Numerius Negidius a slave';

iii) the intentio (statement of claim) in which the plaintiff defines what he wants, eg, 'If it appears that Numerius Negidius ought to give Aulus Agerius ten thousand sestertii';

vi) the condemnatio (condemnation) in which the judge is empowered to acquit or to condemn, *eg,* 'Judge, condemn Numerius Negidius to pay Aulus Agenius ten thousand sestertii';

v) the adjudicatio (adjudication) in which the judge is empowered to adjudge the thing to one of the parties, eg, in an action between co-heirs familiae erciscundae (for sharing the inheritance), 'As much as ought to be adjudged, Judge, adjudge to Titius or Seius'.

The formula did not necessarily contain all these parts, although an intentio was always required. In special circumstances there was written first before the formula a clause called the praescriptio which limited the scope of the action so that a future claim arising out of the same transaction might not be extinguished by the litis contestatio. For example, the praescriptio might read 'Let that only come into trial whose day of payment is now due'.

The intentio might contain the exceptio (exception: equitable defence) reciting some fact that made it inequitable that the plaintiff should succeed; the defendant did not deny (although he did not admit) the plaintiff's right, but denied his right to enforce it. The most important exception was the exceptio doli which was available as a defence when the transaction was fraudulent or the plaintiff had acted dishonestly in bringing the proceedings. An exception could in turn be challenged by a replication (replicatio) by which the force of the exception might be 'unfolded and destroyed'. See also INSTITUTES, BOOK IV, TITLES XIII and XIV.

Formulary Procedure. In or about the year 177BC the lex Aebutia introduced or extended the formulary system and thereby reduced the importance of the leges actiones (see LEGIS ACTIO PROCEDURE) which were noted for their vigorous formularism. It is probable that the formulary system was first adopted to deal with disputes between foreigners, later between Romans and foreigners and finally between Roman and Roman; the legis actiones were normally available only to Roman citizens.

Although the plaintiff was still required to procure the defendant's presence in court, in practice the defendant normally gave by stipulation, with or without sureties, an undertaking to appear. Under the legis actio procedure the form had been all-important; under the formulary system words were adapted in each case to the particular matter in dispute between the parties. Proceedings remained in the following two stages:

i) In jure (before the PRAETOR) at which the plaintiff gave particulars of his claim and asked for an action which was given or refused at the praetor's discretion. If the action was granted the parties agreed the point in issue and embodied them in a document (the FORMULA) which was probably executed in duplicate and sealed by the parties and by witnesses. One copy was given to the defendant, and the praetor referred the matter to the judge agreed upon by the parties. This point in the proceedings was called the litis contestatio (the commencement of the action).

ii) In judicio (before the judge) at which the plaintiff was required to show that the dispute should be decided in his favour. Argument was heard and witnesses were called and, at the conclusion of the hearing, the judge gave his answer to the question contained in the formula.

Execution was against either the person or the property of the debtor:

i) Execution against the person. The legis actio per manus injectionem was replaced by an action on the judgment (actio judicati). If the debtor wished to defend the action he was required to furnish security and, if the defence failed, he was liable to be condemned to pay double the amount of the original judgment. If the action succeeded the plaintiff was entitled to keep the debtor in bondage until he satisfied the debt or liquidated it by his labour.

ii) Execution against property. This was introduced by the praetor Publius Rutilius not later than 118BC. The creditor made application to the praetor to be put in possession of the debtor's whole estate and it was eventually sold to the highest bidder (venditio bonorum), although this did not release the debtor from liability. In the case of persons of high rank the estate could be sold in parts (distractio bonorum). It was to the insolvent debtor's advantage to give cession of his goods (cessio bonorum) as he was then exempted from imprisonment, was not rendered infamous and could retain such after-acquired property as was necessary for the subsistence of himself and his dependants.

The formulary procedure was finally abolished in AD342 by the emperors Constans and Constantius and was succeded by the extraordinary procedure: see EXTRAORDINARIUM JUDICIUM.

Freedmen. Persons who by manumission (see MANUMISSIO) had been set free from lawful slavery. Such persons were known as libertines (libertini). See also CLIENTELAE and INSTITUTES, BOOK I, TITLE V.

Freeman. A person who was free at the instant of his birth. See also INSTITUTES, BOOK I, TITLE IV.

Fructuum perceptio; fructuum separatio. Perception (gathering) of fruits; separation of fruits. As a general rule an owner in possession of land was entitled to the fruits of the land, but the emphyteuta and the bona fide possessor of land were owners of the fruits only when they became separated from the tree, by the hand of man or otherwise. However, a bona fide possessor of land was accountable for all fruits actually in his possession at the time at which his possession of the land was challenged by the real owner of the land, and a mala fide possessor was accountable for all fruits. A usufructuary became owner of the fruits only when he gathered them, and he became owner even though he gathered the fruits before they were ripe. A lessee (conductor) was in a similar position. See also INSTITUTES, BOOK II, TITLE I.

Furtum. See DELICTS (WRONGS) and INSTITUTES, BOOK IV, TITLE I.

Gaius. Roman jurist and private teacher of law, possibly from Asia Minor, whose works were probably written between AD130 and 180. He was a member of the Sabinian school of jurists, and after his death the authority of his writings was acknowledged in the Law of Citations. His main work, his Institutes, was discovered as recently as 1816 and was probably being written in AD161; he also wrote commentaries on the law of the TWELVE TABLES and the urban and provincial edicts. The INSTITUTES of JUSTINIAN were based largely upon the writings of Gaius, and the DIGEST contains 535 excerpts from his work.

Gens. A group of independent PATRICIAN households, more or less closely related by blood, claiming descent from a common ancestor, called by a common family name and sharing common religious rites. They may be said to have been the most primitive element in Roman society, but they were integral parts of the political community; a combination of gentes formed a curia. See COMITIA CURIATA.

Governors. Governorships of the provinces were normally held by CONSULS or PRAETORS whose year of office had come to an end; such persons were known as proconsuls. At times former magistrates could only be appointed governor five years after the expiration of their term of office in Rome. Governors issued edicts and were always assisted by a QUAESTOR. In the time of GAIUS governors exercised in the provinces the same jurisdiction as the urban and peregrine praetors in Rome but in the later empire governors' responsibilities for civil administration often passed to the praefectus urbi (see PREFECTS) of his province, while the troops of the province were commanded by a dux (duke). In such cases the governor became a civil officer concerned with civil administration and jurisdiction, and appeal lay to the praefectus urbi.

Gregorianus Codex. See CODEX THEODOSIANUS

Habitatio. See SERVITUDES and INSTITUTES, BOOK II, TITLE V.

Heirs. See TESTAMENTARY HEIRS

Hermogenianus Codex. See CODEX THEODOSIANUS

Hypotheca. See REAL SECURITIES

Imperium. Supreme authority: powers given to CONSULS, which were similar to those formerly enjoyed by the KINGS, except that the consuls' powers did not extend to matters concerning religion. Later, imperium was given to a few other magistrates, eg, PRAETORS, and the powers were restricted by statute, eg, the right to inflict capital punishment was withdrawn, and generally by the conventions of the constitution. The COMITIA CURIATA conferred imperium by enacting the law of investiture (lex curiata).

Indebiti. See QUASI-CONTRACTS and INSTITUTES, BOOK III, TITLE XXVII.

Injuria. See DELICTS (WRONGS) and INSTITUTES, BOOK IV, TITLE IV.

In jure cessio. Cession in court; title by a fictitious surrender in court. A civil law mode of acquisition available from an early date which had ceased to be used by the time of JUSTINIAN. It took place before a magistrate of the Roman people, eg, the PRAETOR, and the person to whom cession was to be made (the transferee) declared the thing to be his by QUIRITARY RIGHT. The transferor did not dispute the assertion and the magistrate awarded the thing to the transferee. In the provinces this took place before the governor. In jure cessio was applicable both to res nec mancipi and res mancipi, to corporeal and incorporeal things. See also TWELVE TABLES, TABLE VI.

Institutes. By order of JUSTINIAN a work of this name was compiled by TRIBONIAN and two professors of law (Theophilus of Constantinople and Dorotheus of Berytus) 'to the intent that the rudiments of law might be more effectually learned by the sole means of our imperial authority, and that your minds for the future should not be burdened with obsolete and unprofitable doctrines, but instructed only in those laws, which are allowed of and practised'. The Institutes was divided into four books and designed to give to students a general introduction to the first elements of the science of law, although the work itself had the force of a constitution (see CONSTITUTIONES PRINCIPUM). The sources included the institutes of the ancient law, but the work was based upon the writings of GAIUS. It was published on 21st November, AD533, and came into force on the 30th of that month.

The Institutes of Gaius were written in the second century AD. Other institutiones of this period took the form of text-books for beginners dealing with the JUS CIVILE and JUS HONORARIUM. See THE INSTITUTES OF JUSTINIAN p44 et seq.

Interdict. An order issued by the PRAETOR on the application of a person believing himself to be aggrieved or thinking that a public interest is in danger, requiring a person to do or abstain from doing a certain thing. For example, an interdict could take the form of an order to produce (exhibeas), as in the case of an order for the production to a parent of children in his power. Although absolute in form, the order was, in effect, 'Obey if you ought', and reference to a judge was therefore possible. The interdict procedure had fallen out of use by the time of JUSTINIAN. See also INSTITUTES, BOOK IV, TITLE XV.

Interitus rei. See CONTRACTS

Interpretatio. For about one hundred years after the enacting of the law of the TWELVE TABLES their interpretation was the prerogative of the pontiffs (see COLLEGE OF PONTIFFS). However, about 300BC the rules of practice of the law became available to the public at large, especially as a result of the work of the consul Tiberius Coruncanius, and the jurists of this period (jurisprudentes, later referred to as veteres, or ancients) advised clients, the magistrates and the judges (the giving of such advice was known as respondere), ensured that legal forms were properly used (cavere), drafted legal documents, eg, wills and contract (scribere) and assisted in the conduct of litigation, eg, by drafting the formula (agere). The jurists of this time also wrote legal textbooks and gave instruction by means of consultations, but cases were actually presented in court by orators who were not necessarily legally trained. Opinions given by the early jurists were not binding upon the courts, although they were usually followed. Their weight depended on the reputation of the jurist who gave them. See also RESPONSA PRUDENTIUM and INSTITUTES, BOOK I, TITLE II.

Interrex. A person appointed by the PATRICIAN members of the SENATE when the supreme office of the state (ie, both consulships) became vacant. The interrex held office for five days, then nominated a successor. Such nominations continued until one of the interreges held elections for the appointment of new consuls.

Intestate succession. By the law of the TWELVE TABLES (see TWELVE TABLES, TABLE V) those entitled on intestacy were:

i)   sui heredes (proper heirs), ie, persons who lived under the power (potestas) of the deceased and were by his death released from that power. Those in the first degree of descent, whether male or female, took equally, but those in the second or a more remote degree were entitled per stirpes, ie, the descendants of a deceased child took that child's share equally between them;

ii)   proximus agnatus (nearest agnate). All agnates succeeded (if there were no sui heredes) per capita, *ie,* those of equal degree took equally;

iii) gentiles (the men of the GENS), ie, descendants of the same ancestor, who succeeded if there were no sui heredes or agnates.

These rules remained in operation until late in the Republic when the PRAETOR intervened by giving BONORUM POSSESSIA (equitable or praetorian inheritance), in the case of a freeborn intestate, to the following in this order:

i)   liberi (descendants), ie, in relation to a male ascendant, sui heredes, emancipated sons and daughters and the children of emancipated sons;

ii)   legitimi (statutory heirs), ie, those with a statutory claim, probably only the nearest agnate;

iii) cognati (cognates), ie, the nearest relations of any kind, although the only persons who could claim beyond the sixth degree were children of a second cousin in the seventh degree;

vi)   vir et uxor (husband and wife); this applied only where the marriage was without manus.

As to a mother's right of succession to her children (including rights conferred by the senatusconsultum Tertullianum), see INSTITUTES, BOOK III, TITLE III. As to the rights of children to succeed to their mothers (including rights conferred by the senatusconsultum Orfitianum), see INSTITUTES, BOOK III, TITLE IV.

JUSTINIAN (in his NOVELLAE) introduced the following order of intestate succession:

i)   descendants, the nearer excluding the more remote, children taking per capita, grandchildren per stirpes;

ii)   ascendants, the nearer excluding the more remote, and brothers and sisters of the whole blood;

iii) collaterals (brothers and sisters of the whole blood excluded all other collaterals), preference being given to children of deceased brothers and sisters of the whole blood and brothers and sisters of the half blood (the children of the deceased brothers and sisters of the half blood took their parents' shares) and, in the case of other cognates, the nearer excluding the more remote.

See also INSTITUTES, BOOK III, TITLE I.

Jus capiendi ex testamento. The right of taking under a will. A Junian Latin (Latini Juniani), ie, a person who became a FREEMAN but not a Roman citizen, could not take under a will unless he acquired Roman citizenship within one hundred days of the time at which the inheritance was open to acceptance by him (lex Junia). Males over 25 and under 60 and females over 20 and under 50 who were unmarried lost the whole inheritance, and persons who were married but childless lost half (lex Julia 18BC and the lex Papia Poppaea AD9). However, these disabilities did not apply to near relations and they were abolished by the emperor Constantine in AD320. A person who wrote a benefit for himself in the will of another, even at that other's request, could not take under it; in the case of a slave he was punished with death, a freeman with deportation, if he acted fraudulently (lex Cornelia de falsis): see also INSTITUTES, BOOK IV, TITLE XVIII. An heir could not keep an inheritance if he was found to be unworthy of it, eg, if he caused the testator's death; in such cases the inheritance was normally handed to the treasury.

Jus civile. The civil law or the law of the state which, for Romans, was the whole body of the law of Rome as interpreted by the jurists. It was distinguished from the JUS GENTIUM, ie, those principles which natural reason had taught to all mankind and were equally observed by all, but in course of time the jus gentium became mingled with and much modified the jus civile. It was also distinguished from the JUS NATURALE, ie, rules of conduct which were regarded as being rational and of universal application. For practical purposes there was little difference between the jus gentium and the jus naturale.

In this and similar contexts the word 'jus' meant a body or collection of rules as opposed to 'rights'. At first the jus civile consisted of the customary law as partly embodied in the law of the TWELVE TABLES; later it included LEGES, PLEBISCITA, SENATUSCONSULTA, CONSTITUTIONES PRINCIPUM, EDICTA MAGISTRATUUM and RESPONSA PRUDENTIUM. JUSTINIAN also classified the law as jus scriptum (written law) and jus non scriptum (unwritten law, ie, custom or law which had been approved by usage). See also INSTITUTES, BOOK I, TITLE II.

Jus gentium. For GAIUS, these were those principles which natural reason has taught all mankind, and are equally observed by all. JUSTINIAN distinguished between the particular laws of a state or community (JUS CIVILE) and general laws which are common to all mankind (jus gentium). In course of time the jus gentium became mingled with and much modified the jus civile.

The jus gentium applied equally to Roman citizens and foreigners and it included rules relating to commercial transactions and the transfer of property in moveables by the transfer of possession. Its development was mainly due to the work of the courts, the lay jurists and, to a lesser extent, the edicts of the praetor peregrinus (see PRAETORS). See also INSTITUTES, BOOK I, TITLE II.

Jus honorarium. See EDICTA MAGISTRATUUM

Jusjurandum liberti. See VERBAL CONTRACTS

Jus naturale. ULPIANUS defined it as 'the law which nature has taught all animals', but it is more correct to regard it as consisting of rules of conduct which were regarded as being rational and of universal application, or 'an ideal to which it is desirable that law should conform' (Buckland). JUSTINIAN said that from the jus naturale 'proceeds the conjunction of male and female, which we among our own species style matrimony; from hence arises the procreation of children, and our care in bringing them up'. Such rules, he added, were 'established by nature at the origin of mankind'.

For practical purposes it is difficult to distinguish the jus naturale from the JUS GENTIUM, except in relation to slavery which was permitted by the jus gentium yet repugnant to the jus naturale. GAIUS made no mention of the jus naturale and it may be doubted whether it had any active operation in the sphere of Roman law. See also INSTITUTES, BOOK I, TITLE II.

Justae nuptiae. Civil law marriage, the requirements of which were:
i) connubium, ie, the capacity of marrying;
ii) the male must have been fourteen years of age, the female twelve;
iii) the consent of the parties, and the consent of the PATERFAMILIAS of either party if he or she was in power. The consent of the paterfamilias was not required, eg, if he was insane or held in captivity by the enemy for three years. If his consent was unreasonably withheld a magistrate could compel him to give his consent.
See also INSTITUTES, BOOK I, TITLE X.

Justinian. Believed to have been born in Serbia of a peasant family, he was emperor of the east from AD527 until his death in AD565. Extremely conscientious, he would rise in the middle of the night to work and for this reason he became known as the 'sleepless monarch'. He took a personal interest in legal reform and consolidation, although nominally, at least, the burden of the work fell upon TRIBONIAN. Justinian's Code (see CODEX VETUS), a collection of constitutions (see CONSTITUTIONES PRINCIPUM), came into force in AD529 and the CODEX REPETITAE PRAELECTIONIS (AD534) was a second edition of the earlier code embodying fifty decisions and certain constitutions of date later than AD529. Justinian's DIGEST (PANDECTS), a complete revision of the whole civil law, was published in AD533, shortly after his INSTITUTES which were written 'to the intent that the rudiments of law might be more effectually learned'. Between AD534 and the date of his death (AD565) Justinian published 146 novels (see NOVELLAE) modifying the Code, the Digest and the Institutes, and his laws subsisted in the east until the dissolution of the empire in AD1453 when Constantinople was taken by the Turks. The Institutes, Digest, Code and Novels are together referred to as the corpus juris, or corpus juris civile, to distinguish them from the corpus juris canonici. Justinian sought to simplify the professional work of lawyers, establish complete legal uniformity and protect the interests of the more humble citizens. It was also his hope that he might regain sovereignty over all the territories which the Romans had once subdued, and he succeeded in taking and, for a time, holding Africa and at least some parts of Italy, including Rome.

King. Probably selected by the SENATE (he may have nominated his successor), he was not fully king until sovereign power had been conferred upon him by the lex curiata (lex rege), a decree of the COMITIA CURIATA. Chief priest and supreme commander in war and peace, he called new members to the senate and summoned and presided over both the senate and the comitia curiata. He was also supreme judge in both civil and criminal trials, and when he sat in person he might be advised by senatorial assessors known as a consilium. The king may have submitted proposals as to new laws to the comitia curiata for approval.

The king held office for life. The last king was Tarquinius Superbus (Tarquin the Proud) (534–509BC) and at this time the territory of Rome extended only about fifteen miles.

Labeo. A jurist in the time of the emperor Augustus and author of 400 books including an interpretation of the law of the TWELVE TABLES. He was a PRAETOR and is noted for having made innovations in the existing law; he is also said to have founded the Proculian school of jurists. See also CAPITO.

Latina. Latin; a person other than a Roman citizen who enjoyed the privilege of acquiring property and making contracts (commercium), but was denied the right of contracting a civil law marriage. By Justinian's time the term Latin was rarely used. See also INSTITUTES, BOOK I, TITLE V, and Book III, TITLE VIII, and MANUMISSIO.

Legacies. 'A diminution of the inheritance whereby the testator directs that something which would otherwise form part of the whole estate going to the heir is to go to some other person' – Florentinus. A legatee was not liable for the testator's debts, but he was not entitled to his legacy until all such debts had been paid. During the republic there were four kinds of legacy, viz.:

i)   per vindicationem (by giving a claim to the thing), eg, 'I give the slave Stichus';

ii)   per damnationem (by condemning the heir to pay), eg, 'let my heir give my slave Stichus';

iii)   sinendi modo (by allowing the legatee to take), eg, 'let my heir allow Lucius Titius to take and have for himself the slave Stichus';

iv)   per praeceptionem (by allowing the legatee to pick out first), eg, 'let Lucius Titius pick out first the slave Stichus'.

It should be noted that in the case of a legacy per vindicationem after the inheritance was entered upon the thing at once became the property of the legatee ex jure quiritium: it follows that things could rightly be left per vindicationem only if they were the testator's ex jure quiritium, or, in the case of res fungibiles, if they were the testator's ex jure quiritium at the time of his death. The senatusconsultum Neronianum (in the reign of Nero) provided that a legacy left in appropriate words should take effect as if it had been left in the best way known to the law, ie, per damnationem.

During the Empire fideicommissa (trusts) (see FIDEICOMMISSUM) mitigated the strictness and technicality of the older law, and neither the use of the Latin language nor writing was required. In AD339 it was enacted that no special form of words was required for any legacy.

JUSTINIAN fused fideicommissum and legatum (legacy) and in AD529 and 531 enacted that, according to the circumstances, any legatee could seek a remedy by way of a real, personal or hypothecary action.

Other enactments of importance in relation to legacies included:

i)   the lex Furia testamentaria (between 204 and 169BC) which forbade legacies of more than 1000 asses, except to near relations; there was a fourfold penalty for receiving such a legacy;

ii)   the lex Vocania (168BC) which enacted that, in the case of wills of persons in the first class of the census, no one could take more than the heir or heirs collectively;

iii)   the lex Falcidia (40BC) which provided that, except in the case of military wills, the testator could not dispose of more than three-quarters of his estate by way of legacies; if there were two or more heirs each was entitled to one-quarter of the share in the inheritance to which he was heir. Justinian allowed testators to exclude the lex Falcidia by express provision in their wills.

See also INSTITUTES, BOOK II, TITLE XX.

Leges. Laws ordained and established by the Roman people on the proposition of a senatorial magistrate, eg, a CONSUL. They resembled the statutes of English law and were originally passed by the COMITIA CURIATA, although in the early republic the COMITIA CENTURIATA became the chief legislative assembly. Leges were also passed by the COMITIA TRIBUTA, and the term was often used to describe enactments of the CONCILIUM PLEBIS. The word lex (or the phrase lex publica) was occasionally employed by jurists to denote the law of the TWELVE TABLES. Leges had disappeared as a source of new law by the end of the first century AD. See also INSTITUTES, BOOK I, TITLE II.

Legis actio procedure. The procedure provided, or at least confirmed, by the law of the TWELVE TABLES: it was normally available only to Roman citizens. The plaintiff was required to procure the defendant's attendance in court (both parties were required to be present to perform the ceremonies) and the trial was normally in the following two stages:

i)   in jure (before the magistrate) at which the question to be decided was settled (originally these proceedings were before a consul or military TRIBUNE with consular power; later they were normally before the PRAETOR); and

ii)   in judicio (before the judge) at which the point in issue between the parties was actually decided (the judge was appointed by agreement between the parties, normally but not necessarily from a list of qualified persons kept by the magistrate; originally the list comprised senators only, later senators or EQUITES).

    The principal forms of legis actiones were:

i)   legis actio sacramenti, a name derived from the money staked as a wager (sacramentum); this sum was forfeited by the party who eventually lost the case and at first was devoted to religious purposes, later to the public use. This form was available where no other action was provided by statute whether the claim was in rem or in personam and whether the subject matter of the dispute was a moveable or an immoveable. Interim possession of the thing in dispute was awarded by the magistrate and he then remitted the case to the judge.

ii)   Legis actio per judicis postulationem (by demanding a judge); the plaintiff gave the facts of the dispute and requested the magistrate to appoint a judge. No penalty was involved in these proceedings and statute provided that they were to be taken in certain circumstances, eg, for the division of an inheritance between co-heirs.

iii)   Legis actio per condictionem (by formal notice); the plaintiff said that the defendant ought to pay him a certain amount and, when this was denied, gave the defendant thirty days notice to appear for the appointment of a judge. No penal sum was involved.

iv)   Legis actio per manus injectionem (by laying hands on a man); a mode of execution where the debt was not satisfied within thirty days of the judgment. If the debt was not satisfied within a further 60 days, in early times the debtor was put to death or sold across the Tiber. Later, the debtor could be kept in bondage until he satisfied the debt or liquidated it by his labour.

v)   Legis actio per pignoris captionem (by taking a pledge): a mode of distress against property. A pre-existing judgment was not necessary, but this remedy was available only to certain persons, eg, a soldier in respect of his pay or a person who had hired a beast to another with the intention of spending the hire money on a sacrifice.

    The legis actiones were 'cumbrous, troublesome and dangerous' and were abolished by the lex Aebutia in the second half of the second century BC, although it is probable that the formulary procedure was in use before this time. However, the legis actio system survived for proceedings before the centumviral court and in cases of damnum infectum (threatened damage); technically it also survived in the fictitious

process of manumissio vindicta (see MANUMISSIO) and IN JURE CESSIO.
See also TWELVE TABLES, TABLE I et seq.

Legitim. See QUERELA INOFFICIOSI TESTAMENTI.

Legitimatio. Legitimation: the process by which children born to Roman citizens, not in a regular marriage, were brought under their father's potestas (power). Children could be legitimated:

i) Per subsequens matrimonium (by subsequent marriage); this was first allowed by Constantine (AD335), abolished by Zeno (AD476) and restored by JUSTINIAN (AD529).

ii) Per oblationem curiae (by offering to a local council): this may be said to have originated in an enactment of Theodosius and Valentinian in AD442 and it was confirmed by Justinian.

iii) Per rescriptum principis (by imperial rescript); this was introduced by Justinian who later provided that if a father failed to apply for a rescript, but in his will expressed the desire that his children should become legitimate, the children were able to apply for and obtain the rescript of legitimation. This method of legitimation was especially important where the marriage of the parents was impossible, eg, where the mother was dead.

See also INSTITUTES, BOOK I, TITLE X.

Lex curiata. See COMITIA CURIATA.

Lictors. Public servants who waited upon the magistrates to fulfil their commands. Their name (lictores) was derived from their duty to bind offenders hand and foot in preparation for the punishment of scourging.

When a magistrate of high rank appeared in public the lictors went before him in file to clear the road of the people; in the case of CONSULS they also carried the fasces, the symbol of authority. A consul was accompanied by 12 lictors whereas a PRAETOR, who was subordinate to a consul, could have only six. A DICTATOR, a supreme ruler, was entitled to 24 lictors but his assistant (magister equitum) could have no more than six.

In the days of the republic the lictors represented the curiae in the COMITIA CALATA.

Literal contracts. Originally, an entry in a creditor's ledger in respect of a payment to a debtor, the effect of which was to replace a bonae fidei contract by one stricti juris. For JUSTINIAN, a literal contract was a written acknowledgement of a debt which, according to the circumstances, was evidence of either a mutuum or a stipulatio. The alleged debtor could plead the exceptio doli or the exceptio non numeratae pecuniae. Alternatively, he could bring an action to be released from his engagement and to have the instrument returned to him (condictio sine causa). In either case he was required to show that the money had not been paid, but after the second century AD, if the debtor denied liability by the querela non numeratae pecuniae (complaint that the money had not been paid) the burden of proof rested upon the person who claimed to be his creditor. However, this defence was not available where the instrument was found to constitute a stipulation as he was then liable on a verbal contract. See also INSTITUTES, BOOK III, TITLE XXI.

Litis aestimatio. A civil law mode of acquisition; where, in a real action, a person paid money instead of restoring the property, it became his own. See also INSTITUTES, BOOK IV, TITLE VI.

Litis contestatio. See CONTRACTS

Locatio conductio. See CONSENSUAL CONTRACTS and INSTITUTES, BOOK III, TITLE XXIV

Magister equitum. The master of the horse, he exercised supreme authority over the cavalry and the replacement troops. He was assistant to the DICTATOR and in rank equal to a PRAETOR.

Mancipatio. Mancipation. A civil law mode of acquisition of property which took the form of a fictitious sale before five witnesses. A sixth person (the libripens) held a pair of scales and the transferee took hold of the thing to be transferred and declared it to be his by quiritary right (see DOMINIUM EX JURE QUIRITIUM), at the same time striking the scales with a piece of bronze (copper) which he gave to the transferor as the price. The declaration made by the transferee was called the nuncupatio (declaration). Before the days of bronze coins the libripens actually weighed the correct amount of bronze and the sale was not, therefore, 'fictitious'.

When moveable things, eg, horses, were to be transferred, they were required to be present at the time of the sale, but immoveables, eg, land, could be present symbolically. Only res mancipi could be transferred by mancipatio, and these included land and houses in Italy, slaves and beasts of draft and burden. It was also possible to make a will by mancipatio (see TESTAMENTS) and it was the original method of emancipation (see EMANCIPATIO).

Mancipatio was available from an early date, but had ceased to be used by the time of JUSTINIAN. See also TWELVE TABLES, TABLE VI.

Mancipium. Civil bondage which arose from the mancipation of a free person, *eg,* where a father made a noxal surrender of his son; it continued until the son had made good the injury which he had caused. Although a person in mancipio remained a freeman and a citizen, he acquired for his master and could not be instituted heir by his master unless he was at the same time given his liberty. When released, he was subject to the rights of patronage, but was ingenuus, not libertinus. Mancipium could be terminated by manumission (see MANUMISSIO); it was abolished by JUSTINIAN.

Mandatum. See CONSENSUAL CONTRACTS, SURETIES and INSTITUTES, BOOK III, TITLE XXVI.

Manumissio. Manumission: the liberation of slaves by the voluntary act of their master. Formal manumission released a man from slavery and made him a Roman citizen; it was achieved by one of the following methods:
i)   Vindicta, ie, a fictitious law suit before one of the higher magistrates, eg, a CONSUL or a PRAETOR, in which the plaintiff (the lictor) touched the slave with a rod (vindicta) and, with the consent of the master, alleged that the slave was free; judgment was given in favour of the liberty demanded. In later days this could take place wherever a magistrate could be found.
ii)   Censu, ie, enrolment of the slave on the census. This method was of little practical use as the occasion arose only once in five years; a census was last held in AD249.
iii)   Testamento, ie, by testament or codicil. Testamentary manumission was either directa (direct) or fideicommissum (by way of trust); in the former a slave became free as soon as the heir entered upon the inheritance; in the latter a slave did not obtain his freedom until the person to whom he was committed manumitted him by the vindicta.
iv)   In the church, ie, a declaration of the master, in the presence of the congregation, to the bishop, of his desire that the slave should be free; this method was evolved by Constantine.
v)   By the master appointing a slave to be his heir, adopting him as his son, or appointing him by will to be his son's tutor; these methods were added by JUSTINIAN.

Informal manumission released a man from slavery and made him a Latin: the methods by which it was achieved included the following:
i)   inter amicos (between friends), ie, an oral declaration of freedom in the presence of witnesses;
ii)   per epistolam (by letter), ie, sending a slave a letter telling him of his freedom; and
iii)   convivii adhibitione, ie, asking the slave to sit at table with his master.

Justinian enacted that a slave, whether manumitted formally or informally, should be a citizen.

The lex Aelia Sentia (AD4) stipulated that where the master was under twenty years of age or the slave under thirty manumission was to be by the vindicta. The lex Fusia Caninia (2BC) restricted manumission by will in proportion to the total number of slaves owned and provided that in no case was the number manumitted by this method to exceed one hundred. See also INSTITUTES, BOOK I, TITLE V et seq.

Manus. Marital power: rights that a husband possessed over his wife. A wife in manu ceased to be under the potestas of her father and took the position of a daughter to her husband; she could acquire property only for her husband, although in common with slaves and children she could enjoy the PECULIUM. A woman passed in manum by:
i)   coemptio (purchase), ie, by MANCIPATIO;
ii)   usus (prescription), ie, by living with a man as his wife throughout a whole year;

iii) confarreatio (confarreation), ie, a religious rite, probably confined to PATRICIANS, before the PONTIFEX MAXIMUS and the Priest of Jupiter, normally in the presence of ten witnesses.
Manus was obsolete by the time of JUSTINIAN. See also TWELVE TABLES, TABLE VI.

Metus. Intimidation, ie, the threat of such present immediate evil as would shake the constancy of a man of ordinary firmness. There were three possible remedies, viz., action, restitutio in integrum and exceptio. See also RESTITUTIO IN INTEGRUM and EXCEPTIO DOLI.

Missio in possessionem. A process by which the PRAETOR authorised a person to be placed in possession of another's property, either of his whole estate (eg, in the case of insolvency) or of a particular thing (eg, in the case of damnum infectum: threatened damage). Thus if the owner of a house foresaw damage to his property because of the condition of his neighbour's house, upon complaint to the praetor, if the neighbour declined the stipulation cautio de damno infecto (see PRAETORIAN STIPULATIONS) the praetor would give possession of his property to the complainant. Such de facto possession could be followed by a second decree giving juristic possession which could ripen into ownership by usucapion (see USUCAPIO).

Modestinus. A pupil of ULPIANUS, he may be regarded as the last of the great classical jurists and writers. He is known to have held the office of praefectus vigilum in AD244.

Mortgages. See REAL SECURITIES

Mutuum. See REAL CONTRACTS and INSTITUTES, BOOK III, TITLE XIV.

Negotiorum gestio. See QUASI-CONTRACTS and INSTITUTES, BOOK III, TITLE XXVII.

Nexum. An early transaction by which a debtor (generally a PLEBEIAN) bound himself per aes et libram (by the scales and copper) to his creditor by way of security for the debt. The debtor was almost a slave; he was bound to work for the creditor and the creditor could chastise him. This form of bondage was abolished by a lex Poetelia, probably of 326BC; perhaps it would be more correct to say that the lex Poetelia led to its disuse.

Novatio. See CONTRACTS and INSTITUTES, BOOK III, TITLE XXIX.

Novellae. Modifications of or amendments to the CODEX VETUS, DIGEST and the INSTITUTES. JUSTINIAN recognised that these works, all of which had the force of a constitution, would require amendment and between AD534 and AD565 (the date of Justinian's death) 146 novellae were published. The term novellae was also used to describe all constitutions subsequent to the Theodosian Code: see CODEX THEODOSIANUS.

Noxal actions. Actions for the surrender of slaves or animals which had committed wrongs or caused damage. Originally, children in power were also liable to be surrendered, but they were entitled to be manumitted (see MANUMISSIO) if they compensated for their wrong by their labour. See also INSTITUTES, BOOK IV, TITLE VIII and TWELVE TABLES, TABLE XII.

Obligations. JUSTINIAN defined an obligation as 'a legal tie by which we are necessarily bound to make some payment in accordance with the laws of our country'. An obligation was a RES INCORPOREALIS and it created a right (jus) in personam. GAIUS took the view that the term obligation was confined to rights and duties recognised by the jus civile, but Justinian included some which were praetorian, and classified obligations as follows:
i) civil (ie, those constituted by statute, or approved by the civil law) and praetorian (ie, those created by the PRAETOR in the exercise of his jurisdiction);
ii) ex contractu (from contract): see CONTRACTS;
iii) quasi ex contractu (from quasi-contract): see QUASI-CONTRACTS;
iv) ex delicto (from delict or wrong): see DELICTS (WRONGS);
v) quasi ex delicto (from quasi-delict or wrong): see QUASI-WRONGS (DELICTS).
A distinction was also made between civil and natural obligations. A civil obligation was one protected by law and enforceable by action, whereas a natural obligation was one which could not be

enforced by action, although it was not completely without legal effect. Thus if anything due by a natural obligation was voluntarily paid by the debtor, he could not demand it back by the condictio indebiti (see QUASI-CONTRACTS) on the ground that it was not due. See also INSTITUTES, BOOK III, TITLE XV.

Occupatio. The taking possession of a thing belonging to no one (res nullius), but capable by appropriation of becoming the object of private property, with the intention of becoming its owner. This was a natural law mode of acquisition which applied, eg, to the acquisition of wild birds and animals. See also THESAURUS and INSTITUTES, BOOK II, TITLE I.

Operae servorum. See SERVITUDES

Pacta. Simple agreements: agreements which did not conform to any type of contract. Originally they could not be enforced by action (pacta nuda: nude pacts), although they were recognised as a valid ground of defence. Later, certain pacts (pacta vestita: clothed pacts) were actionable and these were:
i)   pacta adjecta (added pacts), ie, pacts annexed to a principal contract which were intended to modify or form part of it;
ii)   pacta praetoria (praetorian pacts), ie, pacts which were recognised as binding by the PRAETOR, *eg*, constitutum;
iii)   pacta legitima (pacts made actionable by imperial legislation): these included:
    a)   pactum de constituenda dos (an agreement to give a dowry): this was enacted by the emperors Theodosius and Valentinian in AD428;
    b)   pactum donationis (a promise to give): by this enactment JUSTINIAN put a gratuitous promise to give on the same footing as a promise for a price.
See also SURETIES

Pactum de constitutio. See SURETIES

Papinianus. An outstanding jurist, believed to have been a Syrian at birth; his opinion was given a privileged position under the Law of Citations. His offices included praefectus praetorio and he was put to death in AD212 by the emperor Caracalla.

Paterfamilias. A person invested with potestas over another. The term is also used as equivalent to sui juris. See also PATRIA POTESTAS.

Patria potestas. The rights enjoyed by the head of a Roman family (the PATERFAMILIAS) over his legitimate children and their property. Potestas could be enjoyed only by Roman citizens, and loss of citizenship involved the loss of potestas. If a slave was manumitted, became a Roman citizen, and married, he acquired potestas over his children born after the manumission. Potestas included:
i)   the power of life and death (this was formally abolished by Constantine);
ii)   the power of sale into slavery (JUSTINIAN allowed only the sale of newborn children in cases of extreme poverty);
iii)   the right to give children in marriage, to divorce them, to give them in adoption and to emancipate them (later the child's consent was required for adoption and emancipation, while marriage was recognised as being principally the concern of the immediate parties);
iv)   the right to receive whatever property was acquired by members of the family (in practice sons were allowed a PECULIUM and, after Augustus, they were entitled to property which they acquired in military service (peculium castrense); they could also retain earnings in various employments (peculium quasi-castrense). Constantine (AD319) gave the father a usufruct in property coming to the son by way of inheritance from his mother (bona materna), and this was gradually extended to all acquisitions by the son (bona adventicia); such property became the absolute property of the son only on the father's death. The father was entitled to gifts made to the son with the object of conferring a benefit on the father (contemplatione patris).
See also TWELVE TABLES, TABLE IV and INSTITUTES, BOOK I, TITLE IX. BOOK II, TITLE IX, and BOOK III, TITLE XXX.

Patricians. The nobility or privileged citizens who could trace their ancestors through an unbroken line of ingenui. A person was said to be ingenuus if he was born into a GENS (*ie*, one of the artificial families into which patricians were divided) and none of his ancestors had possessed any lower status.

Patrons. See CLIENTELAE

Paulus. A contemporary of ULPIANUS, he held the office of praefectus praetorio (see PREFECTS) under Severus (AD193–211). His writings included a commentary on the edict in eighty volumes.

Peculium. Private savings. See MANUS, PATRIA POTESTAS and SERVI

Perpetua tutela mulierum. Perpetual tutelage of women. It did not apply, eg, to VESTAL VIRGINS, and Augustus exempted married women who acquired the jus liberorum by having three children if the woman was ingenua (freeborn), four if libertina (freed). In AD410 Honorius and Theodosius gave all women the jus liberorum, and in the time of JUSTINIAN the tutela of women was on the same basis as that of men, ie, it was confined to those under the age of puberty. See also TWELVE TABLES, TABLE V.

Pignus. See REAL CONTRACTS, REAL SECURITIES and INSTITUTES, BOOK III, TITLE XIV

Plebeians. Unprivileged citizens who were not members of any patrician GENS; all citizens other than PATRICIANS. The distinction between patricians and PLEBEIANS was made from the earliest times, but it became less important during the days of the republic. The original plebeians were probably foreigners attracted to the new city state of Rome soon after its foundation (753BC), but it is possible that they were merely unprivileged and (with few exceptions) poor citizens.

Although plebeians were members of the popular assembly (at first the COMITIA CURIATA) and fought in the Roman army, they were originally excluded from all high offices, both civil and religious. Such offices were reserved for patricians. During the early republic land acquired by the state as a result of success in battle was never assigned to plebeians, and many plebeians were heavily indebted to patricians and thus subject to their control.

The last traces of plebeian political inferiority were removed in 300BC when the lex Ogulnia stipulated that four of the pontiffs (members of the most important of the priestly colleges: see COLLEGE OF PONTIFFS) and five of the AUGURS (religious officials who gave warnings as to the outcome of contemplated enterprises) should be plebeians. Earlier (337BC) a plebeian had been elected to the office of PRAETOR, and the jus Flavianum (304BC) led to the publication of a collection of the formulae of the legis actiones (statute actions: see LEGIS ACTIO PROCEDURE). Until this time such formulae had been the property of the patricians.

Plebiscita. Laws ordained and established by the PLEBEIANS (ie, by all citizens other than PATRICIANS) on the proposition of a TRIBUNE. In early times the patricians maintained that they were not bound by plebiscita, but the lex Hortensia 287BC finally established that plebiscita were binding on all equally, and in consequence plebiscita became equivalent to leges. In the later republic enactments of the CONCILIUM PLEBIS (ie, plebiscita) became the normal means of legislation, and the term leges was often used to describe laws passed by this assembly. Plebiscita ceased to be a source of law by the end of the first century AD. See also INSTITUTES, BOOK I, TITLE II.

Pontifex Maximus. Head of the college of pontiffs and 'the judge and arbiter of divine and human affairs'. In 253BC Tiberius Coruncanius became the first PLEBEIAN to hold this office. The duties of pontifex maximus included the regulation of the calendar, and it was while Caesar was pontifex maximus that he introduced the calendar which is essentially the calendar of today. Pontiffs were generally members of the SENATE and after Augustus had become pontifex maximus in 12BC the office was always held by the emperor. See also COLLEGE OF PONTIFFS.

Praefectus annonae. See PREFECTS

Praefectus praetorio. See PREFECTS

Praefectus urbi. See PREFECTS

Praefectus vigilum. See PREFECTS

Praetorian stipulations. Stipulations which the PRAETOR required a person to make as an incident of legal proceedings in order to overcome deficiences in the civil law. For example, if a person's house seemed likely to fall and damage his neighbour's property, the latter could insist on the former promising to pay compensation for any damage that might be caused (this was the stipulation cautio de damno infecto); if no such promise was made compensation was recoverable only if the requirements of the law Aquilia were satisfied. See also INSTITUTES, BOOK III, Title XVIII and BOOK IV, TITLE III.

Praetors. Officers elected annually by the COMITIA CENTURIATA; they were minor colleagues of the CONSULS. The office of praetor urbanus (urban praetor) was created in 367BC to administer the law in the city of Rome and to protect the civil rights of citizens; in other words, he was invested with the consuls' civil jurisdiction. In the absence of the consuls he convoked and presided over the SENATE; he could also command armies and initiate legislation in either comitia. By his intercessio a consul could veto the act of a praetor, but consuls were not subject to a praetor's veto.

In 247BC a second praetor, the praetor peregrinus (praetor for aliens) was appointed in Rome to hear cases between foreigners, or between a Roman and a foreigner; previously such cases may have been heard by the praetor urbanus. The appointment of the praetor peregrinus was especially significant because he applied to the cases which came before him the doctrines and principles of the JUS GENTIUM in so far as they were not repugnant to the JUS CIVILE.

As new provinces were acquired, the number of praetors was increased to four (227BC), six (198BC) and eight (81BC) in order that they might be sent into the provinces (only after the expiration of their year of office) or exercise a special jurisdiction in Rome, eg, as praetor fideicommissarius, to whom all matters relating to testamentary trusts were referred, or quaestiones perpetuae, presidents of the criminal courts. Unlike consuls, praetors could normally exercise IMPERIUM only within their allotted sphere (provincia). During the empire the number of praetors occasionally rose to eighteen and they were elected by the senate. Their functions were mainly judicial and some had special tasks, eg, deciding cases between the FISCUS (imperial treasury) and private citizens. The office of praetor peregrinus disappeared in AD212 when Caracalla conferred citizenship on nearly all inhabitants of the empire, and in the later empire the praetor urbanus ceased to have any judicial functions.

Special note must be made of the praetors' edicts. It became the custom, probably only after the passing of the Lex Aebutia (about 175BC), for a praetor urbanus to issue an edict at the beginning of his year of office laying down the rules of legal procedure that he would follow. Such edicts were displayed in the forum and were called the edictum perpetuum or tralaticium (perpetual or traditional edict) because they were intended to be valid throughout the praetor's year of office. In fact such edicts normally followed closely the edict of their predecessors and this part, as opposed to edicts of an occasional nature, became known as the edictum tralaticium. A lex Cornelia of 67BC required a praetor to abide by his perpetual edict during his term of office, and these edicts were consolidated and systematically arranged in AD131: this was known as the edictum perpetuum or Salvianum. Although praetors could not make law by the provisions of their edicts they could bring about changes in the legal system and 'aid, supplement or correct' (Papinianus) the civil law; it is said that they thereby introduced a system of equity which existed side by side with the civil law. They did not, indeed could not, give rights; they did, and could, promise remedies in certain circumstances. Although little is known of its contents, the edict of the praetor peregrinus played some part in the development of the jus gentium. See also EDICTA MAGISTRATUUM.

Prefects. The prefect of the city (praefectus urbi) was originally appointed only in the temporary absence of the emperor, but it soon became a permanent appointment. He was invariably selected from the ranks of the senators, and usually a former CONSUL; his responsibilities included the maintenance of order in the city and the command of the police force; he also heard criminal cases in Rome and within a radius of 100 miles of the city. In the later empire he became the city's chief magistrate, assuming many of the functions of the republican PRAETORS and AEDILES, and trials of senators and serious criminal cases were conducted before him. Appeal from his decisions lay to the emperor. At this time there was also a praefectus urbi for the city of Constantinople who had similar powers and duties in and around that city.

Augustus also appointed the praefectus praetorio who was commander of the emperor's personal body-guard (the praetorian guard); his office came to be considered second to that of the emperor himself, and his duties came to include those of chief adviser and executive officer in both military and civil matters. He also exercised many judicial functions and in course of time the responsibilities of the office were shared by two or three persons. In the later empire four such prefects were appointed, each being responsible for the civil administration of a part of the empire, with the exception of the area controlled by the praefectus urbi and the provinces of Africa and Asia. The praetorian guard was finally disbanded by Constantine.

Other prefects appointed by Augustus were the praefectus annonae and the praefectus vigilum. The former official was responsible for maintaining sufficient provisions for the city, especially the supply of corn, at reasonable prices, and he had both civil and criminal jurisdiction in matters arising out of his work. The praefectus vigilum (sometimes called prefect of the night patrol) was a high-ranking police officer mainly responsible for the fire brigade. He had minor criminal jurisdiction in connection with his duties, eg, he could punish those who were careless in the use of fire. In the later empire both the praefectus annonae and the praefectus vigilum were under the authority of the praefectus urbi who heard appeals against their decisions and from several of the provinces.

Principum placita. See CONSTITUTIONES PRINCIPUM

Proconsuls. See GOVERNORS

Proculus. A pupil of LABEO, he followed Nerva (consul before AD24) as head of the Proculian school of jurists which took his name.

Procurator. An agent entrusted with the management of property. Procurators managed the emperor's property and collected taxes, both in Rome and in the provinces. In course of time they replaced the PUBLICANI or closely supervised their work; they also came to control the mining districts and issued local rules to implement general imperial policy.

Provocatio ad populum. A PATRICIAN custom by which any citizen condemned by a magistrate to be put to death, scourged or fined had the right to appeal to the people. In 509BC the consul Valerius Publicola reduced this custom to written law and extended the right to PLEBEIANS.

Publicani. Tax gatherers or tax farmers. They entered into contracts with the CENSOR and, in return for the payment of a lump sum, acquired the right to collect taxes from the people. The SENATE could release them from their contract if they faced bankruptcy because they were unable to gather an adequate amount by way of taxes. In course of time they were replaced or closely supervised by PROCURATORS, but their position was restored by Constantine.

Quaestors. Perhaps their original function was to exercise the CONSULS' jurisdiction in criminal matters, and quaestores parricidii were appointed by the people to preside in capital cases. However, they came to assist the consuls in financial matters and were responsible for the collection of public taxes and the supervision of the AERARIUM; they also sold property (eg, slaves) which fell into the hands of the state.

At least from the early days of the republic each year two quaestors were nominated by the consuls, later elected by the COMITIA TRIBUTA. Their number increased to four (421BC), eight (267BC) and by Sulla to twenty. Caesar increased the number to forty, but it was reduced to twenty by Augustus. These magistrates were regarded as inferior to the PRAETORS and the CURULE AEDILES, although in the provinces during the empire as assistants to the governors they exercised the jurisdiction of the curule aediles, and used their edicts. In the later empire there was a quaestor sacri palatii (minister of justice) for each half of the empire.

From 421BC PLEBEIANS could hold the office of quaestor and in the later republic quaestors were entitled to be elected to the SENATE.

Quasi-contracts. Rights in personam arising by operation of law, as opposed to the consent of the parties. The following are the principal examples of quasi-contract:

i)   Negotiorum gestio, ie, where one person (the negotiorum gestor) had done something for another (the dominus negotiorum) without being asked and without being under a legal obligation so to do, eg, where a man managed the business of another in his absence. In such a case the owner of the business had an actio negotiorum gestorum directa, the manager an actio negotiorum gestorum contraria.

ii)   indebiti, ie, where money not due was paid by mistake. In such a case there was a duty upon the person to whom the payment was made to make restitution; the appropriate action was the condictio indebiti.

See also INSTITUTES, BOOK III, TITLE XXVII.

Quasi-wrongs (delicts). Justinian gave four examples of obligations which arose quasi ex delicto, viz:

i)   where a judge made a suit his own;

ii)   where a thing was thrown or spilt from an upper room so as to cause damage;

iii)   where a thing was hung or placed in a public road so that in the event of it falling it might cause damage;

iv)   where damage was caused or theft committed by the servant of a master of a ship, tavern or inn.

These quasi-delicts, which cannot logically be distinguished from delicts, were introduced by the edict of the PRAETOR. See also INSTITUTES, BOOK IV, TITLE V.

Querela inofficiosi testamenti. The plaint of the unduteous will. From the end of the republic, if a testator failed to make provision, or adequate provision, for certain near relations, the will could be challenged and upset by bringing this action in the CENTUMVIRAL COURT against an instituted heir who had entered upon the inheritance. If the action was successful the will was rescinded and the inheritance devolved as on intestacy. At first the amount that the testator was required to leave (the legitum) was not fixed, but later it was one-quarter of the amount that the complainant would have received had the testator died intestate.

JUSTINIAN provided that the action could be brought only if the person entitled had received nothing at all; if he had received something, he could maintain an action to bring the legitum up to the statutory amount (actio ad supplendam legitimam), and the will remained intact. In the case of children in AD536 Justinian increased the amount of the legitum by enacting that when the testator had four or less children, he must leave them one-third of his entire property; if they exceeded four, one-half.

The action could not succeed if it appeared that the complainant had been disinherited on just grounds. Originally the matter was left to the discretion of the court, guided by precedents and some imperial constitutions, but the grounds on which persons could be disinherited were finally settled by Justinian in AD542. It was necessary for the testator to specify the grounds in his will, and they included assaulting the parent, accusing the parent of any crime (except treason) and, in the case of a daughter, becoming a prostitute or marrying a FREEDMAN without her parent's consent. See also INSTITUTES, BOOK II, TITLE XVIII.

Quinquaginta decisiones. Fifty special decisions, resolving matters of controversy between jurists, issued immediately before work began on the DIGEST.

Quintus Mucius Scaevola. CONSUL in 95BC and PONTIFEX MAXIMUS, he wrote a digest of the civil law systematically arranged in eighteen books. This work, none of which survives, was the basis of many later works on the JUS CIVILE, and excerpts appeared in Justinian's DIGEST. It has been suggested that the Proculian school of jurists were his followers.

Quiritary right. See DOMINIUM EX JURE QUIRITIUM

Rapina. See DELICTS (WRONGS) and INSTITUTES, BOOK IV, TITLE II.

Real contracts. Contracts by acts. The essential elements of a real contract were (a) an agreement, and (b) the delivery of a res (thing) by one person to another. Real contracts included:

i)   Mutuum, ie, a loan for consumption of money or other res fungibiles, *eg*, corn. The things lent passed into the ownership of the borrower who was obliged to restore an equal amount of similar things. In the case of a loan of money the duty to restore was enforced by a condictio certae pecuniae; in the case of other res fungibiles by a condictio triticoria. An agreement to pay interest on the loan could be made by stipulation.

ii)   Commodatum, ie, a gratuitous loan for the use of moveables or, infrequently, immoveables or even res fungibiles. In this case the borrower was required to restore the actual things borrowed – they did not pass into his ownership. The borrower's duties were enforced by the actio commodati contraria.

iii) Depositum, ie, a contract whereby one person gave another a thing to be kept for him gratuitously, the other to return the thing on demand. The duties of the respective parties were enforced by the actio depositi directa and the actio depositi contraria. There were several special kinds of depositum, viz:
      a)   depositum necessarium, ie, a deposit made in an emergency, eg, civil disturbance;
      b)   depositum sequestre, ie, a deposit made pending the outcome of a certain event, eg, a judicial decision;
      c)   depositum irregulare, ie, a deposit subject to the condition that the things be returned in kind, eg, coins with a bank.

iv)   Pignus, ie, pawn or pledge. This was a means of giving security for a debt and the duties of the respective parties were enforced by the actio pigneraticia directa and actio pigneraticia contraria.

Fiducia, or pactum fiduciae, was an agreement subsidiary to a conveyance by MANCIPATIO or IN JURE CESSIO imposing a trust upon the transferee, normally to reconvey the thing in certain circumstances. It was not an independent contract and the duty to reconvey was enforced by the actio fiduciae. The transferee had a contraria actio for the recovery of his expenses. See also INSTITUTES, BOOK II, TITLE XV.

Real securities. Real rights created to secure the performance of obligations. These were created by:
i)   MANCIPATIO (or IN JURE CESSIO) cum fiducia, ie, a formal conveyance of property accompanied by an agreement as to the terms on which it was to be held, including an undertaking by the creditor to reconvey when the debt was paid. This had passed out of use by the time of JUSTINIAN.
ii)   Pignus (pledge or pawn), eg, the handing over of moveable or immoveable property by way of security.
iii) Hypotheca (mortgage), ie, security created by agreement without the transfer of possession. Hypothecs were also created by law, eg, in favour of a pupil over his tutor's estate (a general hypothec) or in favour of a person who had spent money on the repair of another's ship (a special hypothec).
See also INSTITUTES, BOOK IV, TITLE VI.

Replicatio. See FORMULA

Res communes. Things common to all men, eg, the air and the high sea.

Res corporales. Things which can be touched, eg, slaves or land.

Res fungibiles. Things dealt with by weight, number or measure, eg, money, wine or corn.

Res incorporales. Things which cannot be touched, eg, an inheritance, a usufruct or an obligation.

Res mancipi. Land subject to Roman ownership, slaves, beasts of draft and burden (including cattle) and rustic servitudes belonging to land subject to Roman ownership. Full quiritarian ownership (see DOMINIUM EX JURE QUIRITIUM) in these things could be transferred only by MANCIPATIO or IN JURE CESSIO whereas ownership of all other things (ie, res nec mancipi) could be transferred by mere delivery (TRADITIO). The distinction between res mancipi and res nec mancipi was abolished by JUSTINIAN in AD531.

Res nec mancipi. See RES MANCIPI

Res nullius. Things belonging to no one. The term included res sacrae (sacred things, eg, churches), res religiosae (religious things, eg, graveyards), res sanctae (sanctioned things, eg, city walls) and res derelictae (things which had been abandoned with the intention of relinquishing ownership). Wild animals which had not been captured were also included. See also INSTITUTES, BOOK II, TITLE I.

Res publicae. Things belonging to the state, or to private individuals, which may be used by the public, eg, rivers, harbours and river banks. See also INSTITUTES, BOOK II, TITLE I.

Res universitatis. Things belonging to corporate bodies, eg, theatres and racecourses. A corporate body existed when a number of persons were so united that the law took no notice of their separate existence, but recognised them only under a common name, which was not the name of any one of them. See also INSTITUTES, BOOK II, TITLE I.

Responsa prudentium. Under the empire 'the decisions and opinions of those to whom permission has been given to expound the law. When they are all agreed, their joint opinion has the force of law; when they differ, the judge is free to act on the opinion that commends itself the most to him' – GAIUS. Such persons were known as jurisconsulti and they were said to enjoy the jus respondendi: they were licensed by the emperor to undertake this work and to give their opinions under seal. Imperial authority was first given to their opinions by Augustus, although it was not until the reign of Hadrian (AD117–138) that opinions so authorised had the force of law and were binding on the courts if the jurists were unanimous. Other jurists could continue to give opinions, but at first they carried less weight.

In course of time, however, confusion arose because opinions expressed by jurists who lacked imperial authority were treated with equal respect. In order to clarify the position the emperors Theodosius II and Valentinian III introduced the Law of Citations (lex de responsis prudentium) in AD426 which confirmed the works of PAPINIANUS, PAUL, GAIUS, ULPIANUS and MODESTINUS and those passages from the writings of other jurists quoted by them, provided the correctness of the quotation was ascertained by a comparison of manuscripts. Where there was a divergence of opinion in the works of the five jurists mentioned above, the view of the majority was to prevail; if they were equally divided, the opinion supported by Papinianus was to be followed; if Papinianus was silent, the judge could follow whichever opinion he preferred. It is said that this enactment converted legal practitioners 'from reasoning beings into mere quoting and counting machines' (Nasmith).

In theory, at least, these rules remained in force until the time of JUSTINIAN, but after the classical period (about AD250) responsa prudentium ceased to be a living source of law and the jus respondendi was no longer given. As to the opinions of jurists of the days of the republic, see INTERPRETATIO. See also INSTITUTES, BOOK I, TITLE II.

Restitutio in integrum. A praetorian remedy given on equitable principles, after inquiry into the circumstances, to a person who had suffered prejudice. It was most frequently granted where a minor (ie, a person under 25) had, because of his inexperience, entered into an unfavourable arrangement and where a person, absent abroad in the public service, had been unable to interrupt another's possession of his land. It was also granted for force, fraud or just error, but was never available if there was an adequate remedy at law, or where one party could not be restored to his former position, or where the remedy was not claimed within one year (JUSTINIAN increased this to four years). See also INSTITUTES, BOOK IV, TITLE VI.

Rex sacrificulus (or rex sacrorum). King of sacred rites. After the overthrow of the last KING (Tarquinius Superbus) in 509BC, the king's pontifical duties were vested in this officer 'in order that the national gods might not refuse to the kingless city the protection which they gave to the royal city' (Girard).

Romulus. Founder of the city of Rome and its first king. It is said that Romulus and his brother Remus were suckled by a she-wolf and that they built the new city on the spot where they spent their early childhood.

Sabinus. The jurist from whom the Sabinian school of jurists derived its name. He was given the jus respondendi (see RESPONSA PRUDENTIUM) by Tiberius (AD14–37).

Senate. Originally a consultative or advisory body to the Roman kings, at the time of Tarquinius Priscus (616–579BC) it consisted of 300 members, all of whom were PATRICIANS; earlier its membership may have been 150, and it was not until the days of the republic that some of its members were PLEBEIANS. The early senators were chosen by the KING on account of their age and experience and they in turn probably selected the king, who held office for life. With the exception of the lex curiata, the senate confirmed the decrees of the COMITIA CURIATA.

During the republic senators (for the first hundred years of the republic the senate remained solely a patrician body) were chosen by the CONSULS, later by the CENSORS, and the senate was summoned by a magistrate (ie, by a DICTATOR, consul, PRAETOR, INTERREX or military tribune (see TRIBUNI MILITARES), but normally by a consul) or, later, by a TRIBUNE. It considered and advised the magistrates upon a wide range of public matters, eg, peace and war (treaties required formal ratification by the people) and religious affairs, and approved the enactments of the COMITIA CENTURIATA, although enactments of the popular assemblies were usually submitted to the senate for preliminary approval. However, its powers increased and from the end of the third century BC it was the state's permanent and policy-making executive. Although its resolutions (SENATUSCONSULTA) were in the form of advice or instructions to magistrates, they probably had the force of law. Proceedings in the senate were subject to veto by a tribune, but once its resolutions were passed they were committed to writing and deposited in the AERARIUM.

Sulla increased the number of senators to 600, and this number was affirmed by Augustus who also imposed a property qualification of 1,000,000 sesterces. Once elected, senators held office for life, unless they were expelled for serious misconduct. At the height of its power the senate also controlled the treasury and authorised the appointment of dictators, nominating the persons who should hold this office. It also had the right to resolve that an individual be exempt from the operation of a law, but the lex Cornelia of 67BC provided that at least 200 members of the senate must be present when such a resolution was passed.

Under the empire the senate (the 'partner in government') became a high court of justice for major offences, formally invested the emperor with his powers and assumed the right to elect magistrates and, with the decline of the popular assemblies, senatusconsulta (decrees or enactments of the senate) took the place of LEGES and PLEBISCITA as sources of law. From AD48 some provincials were admitted as members of the senate, but within a short time senatusconsulta were dictated by the emperor himself and formally approved by the senate; the magistrates were increasingly the choice of the emperor. Thus the senate lost many of its powers as those of the emperor increased, but it continued to play some part in the selection of the emperor and, at the emperor's request, would hear charges of treason. Only occasionally was it consulted with regard to legislation, and the latest recorded senatusconsultum was passed during the reign of Probus (AD276–282) in AD280. From this point in time the emperor was the sole legislative authority and his power was based upon the armed forces. The senate became little more than the city council of Rome and, although its membership was probably in excess of 2000, in AD356 it was enacted that the quorum should be 50.

In the later empire a senate for the eastern empire was founded at Constantinople, but its influence was less than that of the senate at Rome.

Senatusconsulta. Resolutions or enactments of the SENATE: they had the force of a lex (see LEGES), although at first this was not beyond doubt. Originally senatusconsulta were resolutions of the senate suspending the law in an emergency, dispensing with it in favour of an individual, or advising or instructing the magistrates on law enforcement. A PRAETOR might have included such a resolution in his edict and it would thus have become part of the JUS HONORARIUMS. It was only in the early empire that it became clear that senatusconsulta were an independent and effective source of civil law. At this period senatusconsulta were inspired by the emperor, and within a short time the senate merely confirmed his speech (oratio) embodying his legislative proposals. Later (about AD200) it was recognised that the speech itself had binding authority, and formal confirmation by the senate is last recorded during the reign of Probus (AD276–282). The emperor's speech was usually read by a QUAESTOR. See also INSTITUTES BOOK I, TITLE II.

Servi. Slaves. A person could become a slave by:
i)   Unfree birth, ie, children born of a slave mother unless she was free at the time of conception or at any time during pregnancy.
ii)   Capture in war.
iii)   Civil law. Originally, a person who evaded the census was made a slave and a father could sell his children into slavery; insolvent debtors could be sold in the same way. Under the empire a person could become a slave:
   a)   if, being a FREEMAN of more than 20 years of age, he fraudulently allowed himself to be sold with a view to sharing the price;
   b)   by judicial decree if, being a woman, she continued to cohabit with a slave after their association had been denounced by the slave's master (senatusconsultum Claudianum, AD52: JUSTINIAN abolished this method);
   c)   if he was sentenced to death or labour in the mines (servi poenae): this method was abolished by Justinian;
   d)   if, being a FREEDMAN, he showed serious ingratitude to his PATRON;
   e)   if, being the newborn child of poor parents, he was permitted to be sold into slavery with a right of redemption.
At first a master had the right of life and death over his slaves, but a lex Petronia, AD79, required him to obtain a magistrate's consent before his slaves could be sent to fight beasts in the arena, and Antoninus Pius made it a capital offence for a man to kill his slave without a just cause. As a general rule, anything acquired by a slave became his master's property, although some slaves were allowed to deal with their PECULIUM as they wished, even to purchase their freedom. Slaves could be made free by manumission: see MANUMISSIO. See also TWELVE TABLES, TABLES VIII and X, and INSTITUTES, BOOK I, TITLE III et seq, BOOK III, TITLE XXX, and BOOK IV, TITLES VII and VIII.

Servitudes. Real rights over the property of another protected by a real action. A praedial servitude was a right vested in the owner of one piece of land (the dominant estate) to do something on a neighbouring piece of land (the servient estate) or to prevent the owner of that estate from doing something which he would otherwise be at liberty to do. Praedial servitudes were either rustic servitudes (ie, for the benefit of agricultural land, such as rights of way and of drawing water) or urban servitudes (ie, for the benefit of buildings, such as rights of support and of preventing the obstruction of light). A negative servitude was one by which the servient owner could be prevented from doing something; a positive servitude was one which entitled the dominant owner to do something on or over the servient estate. No one could have a servitude over his own land.
In JUSTINIAN's time personal servitudes, ie, rights to the use of a thing, existed for the benefit of individuals without reference to the ownership of land. Personal servitudes were:
i)   USUFRUCTUS (usufruct), ie, the right to use and take the fruits of anything not consumed by use. In the early empire it was recognised that there could be a quasi-usufruct of things consumed by use: in this case the beneficiary gave security for the restoration of the equivalent when his interest was determined.
ii)   USUS (use), ie, the right to use the property of another to satisfy the personal wants of the usuary and his family.
iii)   HABITATIO (habitation), ie, the right to use the house of another, including the right to let it to others.
iv)   OPERAE SERVORUM, ie, the right to use the services of the slaves of another.
In Italy rustic servitudes were created by IN JURE CESSIO and MANCIPATIO, while urban servitudes were created only by in jure cessio. In the provinces they were created by pacts and stipulations, the method later generally adopted. Praedial servitudes could also be created by reservation on grant (deductio) and by lapse of time (USUCAPIO). Personal servitudes were created by the same

methods as praedial servitudes, but they were also created by statute (LEGE). See also INSTITUTES, BOOK II, TITLE III et seq.

Servius Tullius. KING from 578 to 535BC, he ordered a census (ie, taxed the people according to their means) and is said to have arranged them in classes according to their wealth and ability to equip the army (see COMITIA CENTURIATA). He also extended the rights and privileges of the PLEBEIANS, but was murdered by an emissary of his son-in-law and successor TARQUINIUS SUPERBUS.

Sextus Aelius. Elected consul in 198BC, he is best known for his work called Tripertita which considered the civil law under three heads, viz., the law of the TWELVE TABLES, their interpretation, and statute actions (legis actiones: see LEGIS ACTIO PROCEDURE). This work was the earliest systematic account of the civil law.

Societas. See CONSENSUAL CONTRACTS and INSTITUTES, BOOK III, TITLE XXV.

Solutio. See CONTRACTS and INSTITUTES, BOOK III, TITLE XXIX.

Specificatio. Accession of labour to moveables; the bringing into existence of a thing of a new kind out of existing material, eg, making a vessel out of gold. A natural law mode of acquisition, JUSTINIAN decided that if the new thing could not be reduced to its natural state, it belonged to its creator; if it could, there was no change of ownership. See also INSTITUTES, BOOK II, TITLE I.

Sponsio. See SURETIES

Stipulatio. See VERBAL CONTRACTS and INSTITUTES, BOOK III, TITLE XV et seq.

Sui heredes. See INTESTATE SUCCESSION

Sui juris. A person not subject to potestas (see PATRIA POTESTAS), MANUS or MANCIPIUM. It was not necessary that such a person should have arrived at any age of legal majority.

Superficies. A right to the perpetual enjoyment of anything built upon the land of another, on payment of an annual rent. See also EMPHYTEUSIS and INSTITUTES, BOOK II, TITLE I.

Sureties. A surety was a person who by contract bound himself to be answerable for the debt of another. Suretyship was created by:
i)   Verbal contract. During the classical period there were three kinds of contract of suretyship by stipulation, viz.,
        a)   sponsio (this could be made by Roman citizens only);
        b)   fidepromissio (this could be made by aliens);
        c)   fidejussio (this could be attached to any contract or obligation, whether civil or only natural).
        In JUSTINIAN's time only fidejussio was used, and it could be created by any form of words, spoken or written (see INSTITUTES, BOOK III, TITLE XX).
ii)   Mandatum, eg, when A at the request of B lent money to C, B was obliged to save A harmless from all loss sustained by the default of C to repay the money. A mandate by a surety could be enforced by an actio mandati contraria (see INSTITUTES, BOOK III, TITLE XXVI).
iii)   Pactum de constituto, ie, an informal promise to discharge an existing obligation of another on a day named, or to give security for its fulfilment. This was made actionable by the PRAETOR.
    Fidejussio created a primary liability, ie, the creditor could proceed against the surety before the principal. Indeed, before Justinian, the surety was released if the creditor sued the principal, but Justinian required the creditor first to sue the principal. If the surety paid for his principal he could recover his money from him by the actio mandati. The surety's position was improved by the benefit of cession of actions (beneficium cedendarum actionum), ie, he was given the right to sue the principal and to obtain contribution from his co-sureties. Hadrian also allowed him the benefit of division (beneficium divisionis), *ie,* he could require the creditor to divide his claim pro rata between other solvent sureties.

Tarquinius Superbus. The last of the Roman kings, he reigned from c534 to 509BC. He abolished the rights and privileges which SERVIUS TULLIUS had conferred upon the PLEBEIANS and took the entire administration into his own hands. In 509BC he was overthrown and sent into exile, and the monarchy was at an end.

Testamentary heirs. They were divided into three sorts, viz.,
i) Necessarius heres (a necessary heir), ie, a slave instituted heir with a gift of liberty, such gift being implied in later law. The slave could not refuse the inheritance, but the PRAETOR allowed him to separate his own property from the testator's estate.
ii) Sui et necessarius heres (a proper and necessary heir), ie, a descendant in the power of the testator who, on the testator's death, became SUI JURIS, eg, a son. Such a person could not decline the inheritance, but the praetor allowed him to abstain (beneficium abstinendi) if he had not intermeddled with the estate.
iii) Extraneus heres, ie, a stranger, a person not subject to the testator's power. Such a person could decline the inheritance if he wished, and the testator normally prescribed a time within which he should accept. By JUSTINIAN's time he usually applied to the praetor for time in which to make up his mind (spatium deliberandi); if he failed to decline the inheritance within the time so fixed he was deemed to have accepted the inheritance.

By a constitution of AD531 Justinian allowed an heir to accept with benefit of inventory (beneficium inventarii) and by this means the heir avoided liability beyond the value of the estate. See also INSTITUTES, BOOK II, TITLES XIV and XIX.

Testaments. At different times the following types of testament were in use:
i) Calatis comitiis (a will made before the comitia): see COMITIA CURIATA.
ii) Procinctum testamentum (a will made before the army): this passed out of use before the end of the republic.
iii) Per aes et libram (a will by bronze and balance): a mancipation (see MANCIPATIO) to another (familiae emptor: purchaser of the estate) who was given instructions by the testator as to the disposal of his property. In course of time the heir was usually named in a written instrument and the familiae emptor became a mere figurehead; later still the instrument recited that a mancipation had taken place, but in fact it had not.
iv) Praetorian testament, ie, a will executed in the presence of seven witnesses who affixed their seals: the PRAETOR gave possession of the estate (bonorum possessio).
v) Testamentum tripertitum: available in the later empire, it was called 'tripartite' because it was derived from:
a) the civil law which required the whole will to be made at the same time in the presence of witnesses;
b) the praetor's edict by which seven witnesses were required to affix their seals;
c) imperial constitutions which required the testator and the witnesses to subscribe the will.
iv) Nuncupative testament, ie, a declaration in the presence of seven witnesses: this replaced the oral mancipatory will, and JUSTINIAN accepted it as a civil law will.

Apart from these wills, Julius Caesar allowed soldiers to make wills as they could, eg, by oral declaration in the presence of comrades or by writing in blood on their shields. Justinian restricted this concession to soldiers on active service. See also INSTITUTES, BOOK II, TITLE X et seq.

Thesaurus. Treasure-trove, ie, moveables deposited in a place for so long a time that no one could tell who was their owner. This was a civil law mode of acquisition in so far as Hadrian decided that if a person found treasure on his own land, or by chance in a sacred or religious place, he could keep it; if he found it by chance on the land of another they divided it equally. See also INSTITUTES, BOOK II, TITLE I.

Traditio. Delivery: a transfer of possession whereby ownership vested in the transferee. Traditio was a natural law mode of acquisition, but the delivery had to be made with an intention to transfer the ownership. In the case of a contract of sale, delivery did not transfer the ownership until the price was paid or the seller was satisfied in some other way; when the price was paid or satisfaction given, ownership was deemed to have been transferred at the date of the contract.

An essential requirement was a physical transfer of possession of the thing (real tradition), or its legal equivalent (fictitious tradition), such as:

i) traditio brevi manu (delivery with the short hand), ie, where a person already in possession of goods was told and agreed to retain them as owner; or

ii) constitutum possessorium (agreement to possess), eg, where an owner retained possession of goods after giving them to another; or

iii) traditio longa manu (delivery with the long hand), eg, where the thing was placed in the sight of the transferee as opposed to his actual physical control; or

iv) symbolical tradition, eg, the handing over of the keys of a warehouse by which act the warehouse and its contents were deemed to pass into the possession of the transferee.

See also TWELVE TABLES, TABLE VI and INSTITUTES, BOOK II, TITLE I.

Tribes. The three ancient tribes, the Ramnenses, the Tatienses and the Luceres, comprising the Roman people in the earliest times, were each divided into ten curiae. Each curia consisted of a number of gentes (patricians) (see GENS) who shared a common name and were supposed to be connected by blood. With the increase in population SERVIUS TULLIUS rearranged the tribes and increased their number to four, and by 241BC the acquisition of new territory had made it necessary to have 35 tribes.

The tribes came to include both PATRICIANS and PLEBEIANS and eventually formed the basis of taxation and the military levy. At first only landowners could be members of a tribe, but in 312BC Appius Claudius removed this restriction and included every Roman citizen. The division into tribes was in addition to division into curiae and centuries and, although tribes were originally concerned only with local tribal affairs, it eventually gave rise to the COMITIA TRIBUTA.

Tribonian. A native of Sido in Pamphylia, Tribonian (Tribunian) was distinguished for the diversity of his mental attainments. JUSTINIAN said he was 'a most excellent personage' and he was probably the greatest scholar of his time. He became QUAESTOR and CONSUL and directed the preparation of the CODEX VETUS, the DIGEST and the INSTITUTES. Tribonian died in AD545.

Tribunes. A plebeian office created by the PLEBEIANS, probably in 494BC. At first two tribunes (tribuni) were appointed and this number was later increased to five (471BC) and ten (457BC). Their persons were declared sacred and they were immune from arrest; anyone who believed himself injured could seek refuge in their houses by day or night. The tribunes presided in the assemblies of the plebeian tribes and later acquired the right to intercede with, or veto or annul the act of, the senate or a magistrate; this right was known as intercessio.

Appointed by the CONCILIUM PLEBIS, the tribunes were the guardians of the interests of the plebeians, especially against arbitrary punishment by the PATRICIAN magistrates. They became entitled to sit in the SENATE and eventually to convoke it. They also convoked and (until Sulla deprived them of the right in 81BC) initiated legislation in the concilium plebis and were able to impeach a CONSUL.

During the empire the powers of tribunes decreased, but intercessio was still a legal possibility, although rarely used. The emperors themselves assumed the powers of tribunes.

Tribuni militares. Military tribunes. In 445BC provision was made for the appointment at the discretion of the SENATE of tribuni militares to exercise for one year the powers of the CONSULS. Normally four in number (at times as many as 20 or more were appointed), military tribunes could be either PATRICIANS or PLEBEIANS. At first the actual appointments were made by the consuls, later some were made by the COMITIA TRIBUTA. Military tribunes were elected for 50 of the 78 years following the creation of the office, but the office was abolished by the Leges Liciniae Sextiae in 367BC.

Tutela. Tutelage (tutorship): 'an authority and power given and permitted by the civil law and exercised over such independent persons who were unable, by reason of their age, to protect themselves' – Servius. With certain exceptions, at one time women who were SUI JURIS were in perpetual tutelage (see PERPETUA TUTELA MULIERUM). The ways in which tutela was created were as follows:

i)   Tutela testamentaria (by will). A PATERFAMILIAS could by his will appoint a tutor to a son who would become sui juris on his death.

ii)   Legitima tutela (by statute), eg, under the law of the TWELVE TABLES tutelage went to the nearest agnate unless a tutor was appointed by will.

iii) Tutela fiduciaria (fiduciary tutelage). Originally, this arose where a child was manumitted by the person in whose MANCIPIUM he was after the third sale and this person became the child's PATRON and, therefore, his tutor. For JUSTINIAN the term applied to the case where an emancipating parent died leaving a child under age and tutelage passed to the nearest male relatives of the child agnatically related to the deceased.

iv)   Tutela dativa (dative). If no tutor was appointed by will, and there were no agnates who could act as tutors, power was given to certain magistrates to appoint a tutor.

Unless permitted by will, a tutor required the leave of the court to dispose of agricultural and undeveloped building land (Oratio Severi, AD195), and Constantine extended this to houses and valuable moveables. The actio tutelae lay where there had been a neglect of duty by the tutor, while a tutor had an actio tutelae contraria for his expenses and an indemnity. See also TWELVE TABLES, TABLE V and INSTITUTES, BOOK I, TITLE XIII et seq.

Twelve Tables. The law of the Twelve Tables has been described as 'the foundation of all public and private law' (Livy), although Stephen said: 'The excessive curtness of these provisions implies the existence of an all but unlimited discretion in those who had to administer the law ... The laws of the Twelve Tables were of less importance in the history of the development of Roman law than the institutions by which they were carried into execution.' They were partly repealed by direct legislation and partly overruled by the equitable jurisdiction of the PRAETOR, but in theory the laws of the Twelve Tables were not superseded until the reforms of JUSTINIAN.

Written on bronze tablets fixed in the market place in the heart of the city, the law of the Twelve Tables made available to PLEBEIANS a knowledge of the law as contained in the hitherto unwritten customs or usages of the day. The law of the Twelve Tables was continually referred to in the writings of the jurists, and it formed a model on which subsequent legislation was based. Ten tables were completed in 451BC (they were drawn up by a commission of ten magistrates, the DECEMVIRS, and submitted to and approved by the SENATE and the COMITIA CENTURIATA), and two further tables were added in the following year. The later two tables were prepared by a fresh commission of ten, including some plebeians, and approved by the comitia centuriata.

The interpretation of the law of the Twelve Tables and the actions founded upon it was the prerogative of the pontiffs: see also COLLEGE OF PONTIFFS.

GAIUS was amongst those who wrote a commentary on the law of the Twelve Tables, but the full text of the 12 tables is not now available; it is said that the original bronze tablets were destroyed by the Gauls in 390BC. See TWELVE TABLES p37 et seq.

Ulpianus. Chief legal adviser to the emperor Severus, he held the office of praefectus praetorio (see PREFECTS) in AD222. His work on the edict occupied 83 volumes, and about one-third of JUSTINIAN'S DIGEST consists of extracts from his writings, a larger proportion than was taken from the works of any other jurist. Ulpianus was assassinated by the praetorian guard in AD228.

Usucapio. Acquisition by use: acquisition of ownership by possession for the length of time required by the law. A civil law mode of acquisition available only in respect of things capable of being transferred to and from Roman citizens. Lands out of Italy could be acquired by possessio longi temporis (possession for a long time, or long standing possession), otherwise known as longi temporis praescriptio (long time prescription). See also TWELVE TABLES, TABLE VI and INSTITUTES, BOOK II, TITLE VI.

Usufructus. See SERVITUDES and INSTITUTES, BOOK II, TITLE IV

Usus. See MANUS, SERVITUDES and INSTITUTES, BOOK II, TITLE V

Verbal contracts. These might have been:

i)   Dictio dotis, ie, a formal oral promise of a dos (dowry) made, *eg*, by the woman herself or by her father; or

ii)   Jusjurandum liberti, ie, an oral promise made by a slave on manumission (see MANUMISSIO) by which he undertook to render certain services to his former master; or

iii)   Stipulatio, ie, an agreement concluded by oral question and answer. This form of contract existed at the time of the law of the TWELVE TABLES. and under the empire it was a common practice to reduce the stipulation to writing. At all times the presence of the parties was essential. Stipulations were also employed in judicial proceedings, eg, as security against fraud or as security for the payment of legacies. See also INSTITUTES, BOOK III, TITLE XV et seq.

Vestal Virgins. Perpetual priestesses of the temple who received a stipend from the public treasury. They guarded the goddess Vesta's undying fire which represented the city's continuous life.

Vindicatio. An action for the restitution of property to its owner. Only the owner could bring this action; only the person in possession of the thing could be sued. See also INSTITUTES, BOOK IV, TITLE VI.

Index

Figures in bold refer to page numbers of illustrations

HOLBORN COLLEGE COURSES

SPECIALIST DIPLOMAS IN LAW & BUSINESS

Validated by the University of Oxford Delegacy of Local Examinations at degree level.

9 month course.

Diplomas in: Contract Law • Commercial Law • Company Law • Revenue Law • European Community Law • Criminal Law • Evidence • Constitutional Law • English Legal System • Land Law • Organisational Theory • Economics • Accounting and Business Finance • Computer Systems & Information Technology • Maths for Economists • Statistics

Entry: Evidence of sufficient academic or work experience to study at degree level.

FUNDAMENTALS OF BRITISH BUSINESS

Examined internally by Holborn College

To familiarise European and other overseas business studies students with UK business practice. Courses are tailor-made for groups of students on a College to College basis. Courses run for ten to seventeen weeks and permit part-time relevant work experience.

Past courses have included: Aspects of Organisational Behaviour • Marketing • Statistics • Business English & Communication Skills • Economics • International Trade • Company Law

LAW

Examined externally by the University of London.

Three year course.

LLB Law.

Entry: 2 'A' levels grade E and 3 'O' levels.

ACCOUNTING & MANAGEMENT DEGREES

Examined externally by the University of London.

Three year course.

BSc (Econ) Accounting • BSc (Econ) Management Studies • BSc (Econ) Economics & Management Studies

Entry: 2 'A' levels grade E and 3 'O' levels to include Maths and English.

DIPLOMA IN ECONOMICS.

Examined externally by the University of London.

One year full time, two year part time courses.

Completion of the Diploma gives exemption from the first year of the BSc (Econ) Degree programmes reducing them to two years.

Entry: Mathematics and English 'O' level equivalent. Minimum age 18.

THE COMMON PROFESSIONAL EXAMINATION

Examined externally by Wolverhampton Polytechnic.

9 month, 6 month and short revision courses.

Entry: Acceptance by the Professional Body.

THE BAR EXAMINATION

Examined by the Council of Legal Education for non-UK practitioners.

9 month course.

Entry: Acceptance by the Professional Body.

THE SOLICITORS' FINAL

Examined by the Law Society.

6 month re-sit and short revision courses.

Entry: Acceptance by the Professional Body.

THE INSTITUTE OF LEGAL EXECUTIVES FINAL PART 2

Examined by the Institute of Legal Executives.

9 month course and short revision courses.

Entry: Acceptance by the Professional Body.

A & AS LEVEL COURSES

Examined by various UK Boards.

9 month course and short revision courses

Subjects offered: Law • Constitutional Law • Economics • Accounting • Business Studies • Mathematics Pure and Applied • Mathematics and Statistics • Sociology • Government and Politics

Entry: 3 'O' levels.

FULL-TIME, PART-TIME, REVISION & DISTANCE LEARNING

ORDER FORM

LLB PUBLICATIONS	TEXTBOOKS Cost £	CASEBOOKS Cost £	REVISION WORKBOOKS Cost £	SUG. SOL. 1985/89 Cost £	SUG. SOL. 1990 Cost £
Administrative Law	17.95	18.95			
Commercial Law Vol I	17.95	18.95	9.95	14.95	3.00
Vol II	16.95	18.95			
Company Law	18.95	18.95	9.95	14.95	3.00
Conflict of Laws	17.95	16.95			
Constitutional Law	13.95	16.95	9.95	14.95	3.00
Contract Law	13.95	16.95	9.95	14.95	3.00
Conveyancing	16.95	16.95			
Criminal Law	13.95	16.95	9.95	14.95	3.00
Criminology	16.95				3.00
European Community Law	17.95	16.95			3.00
English Legal System	13.95	14.95		*7.95	3.00
Equity and Trusts	13.95	18.95	9.95	14.95	3.00
Evidence	17.95	17.95	9.95	14.95	3.00
Family Law	16.95	18.95	9.95	14.95	3.00
Jurisprudence	14.95				
Labour Law	15.95				
Land Law	13.95	18.95	9.95	14.95	3.00
Public International Law	18.95	16.95	9.95	14.95	3.00
Revenue Law	16.95	18.95	9.95	14.95	3.00
Roman Law	19.95				
Succession	16.95	17.95	9.95	14.95	3.00
Tort	13.95	18.95	9.95	14.95	3.00
CPE PUBLICATIONS					
Criminal Law	13.95				
Constitutional & Administrative Law	13.95				
Contract Law	13.95				
Equity and Trusts	13.95				
Land Law	13.95				
Tort	13.95				
BAR PUBLICATIONS					
Conflict of Laws	16.95	17.95		†3.95	3.95
European Community Law & Human Rights	17.95	16.95		†3.95	3.95
Evidence	17.95	17.95		14.95	3.95
Family Law	16.95	18.95		14.95	3.95
General Paper I	19.95	16.95		14.95	3.95
General Paper II	19.95	16.95		14.95	3.95
Law of International Trade	16.95	16.95		14.95	3.95
Practical Conveyancing	16.95	16.95		14.95	3.95
Procedure	19.95	16.95		14.95	3.95
Revenue Law	16.95	18.95		14.95	3.95
Sale of Goods and Credit	17.95	17.95		14.95	3.95

* 1987-1989 papers only † 1988 and 1989 papers only

SOLICITORS' FINAL	TEXTBOOKS Cost £	REVISION WORKBOOKS Cost £	SUGGESTED SOLUTIONS PACKS (a) Winter Cost £	PACKS (a) Summer Cost £	SINGLE PAPERS (b) Winter Cost £	SINGLE PAPERS (b) Summer Cost £
Accounts	14.95	9.95	14.95	14.95	2.25	2.25
Business Organisations & Insolvency	14.95		11.95	§11.95	2.25	2.25
Consumer Protection & Employment Law	14.95		11.95	§11.95	2.25	2.25
Conveyancing I & II	14.95		14.95	14.95	2.25	2.25
Family Law	14.95		14.95	14.95	2.25	2.25
Litigation	14.95		14.95	14.95	2.25	2.25
Wills, Probate & Administration	14.95	9.95	14.95	14.95	2.25	2.25
Final Exam Papers (Set) (All Papers) 1989				9.95		
Final Exam Papers (Set) (All Papers) 1990			9.95	9.95		

INSTITUTE OF LEGAL EXECUTIVES	Cost £
Company & Partnership Law	18.95
Constitutional Law	13.95
Contract Law	13.95
Criminal Law	13.95
Equity and Trusts	13.95
European Law & Practice	17.95
Evidence	17.95
Land Law	13.95
Revenue Law	16.95
Tort	13.95

'A' LEVEL	TEXTBOOKS Cost £	SINGLE PAPERS Winter Cost £
TEXTBOOKS		
Accounting	18.95	10.95
Business Studies	13.95	10.95
Economics	13.95	9.95
Applied Mathematics	13.95	9.95
Pure Mathematics		9.95
Statistics		9.95
General Principles of English Law	17.95	10.95
Constitutional Law	17.95	9.95
Government and Politics	13.95	9.95
Sociology	16.95	9.95
WORKBOOKS		
Accounting	13.95	9.95
Business Studies		9.95
Economics		9.95

§ Limited to new syllabus from Summer 1986.

(a) Packs consist of either collected Winter or Summer papers. They change in April to include the previous Summer & Winter papers respectively.

(b) Single papers are published in April & October and are the previous Winter & Summer papers respectively, together with final examination papers.

HLT PUBLICATIONS

HLT Publications are written specifically with the student in mind. Whether they are studying for A Levels, a degree or professional qualification they will find our publications clear, concise and up-to-date.

All our publications are written by specialists, the majority of whom have direct practical teaching experience. Each year all our materials are carefully reviewed and updated as appropriate.

HLT Publications is the publishing arm of Holborn College, which has experience of over twenty years as an independent college with a current student population of over 2,000. We are ideally placed to understand and respond to the needs of students. Most importantly, we are able to test our publications directly in our own lecture theatres.

Proof of the high quality of our texts is that they are widely used by students at universities, polytechnics and colleges throughout the United Kingdom and overseas, as well as by practitioners seeking an update or overview on recent changes. Given the comprehensive range of topics covered, whatever syllabus you are studying, our texts will be invaluable to you.

Textbooks provide an invaluable foundation and comprehensive introduction to the subject and aim to equip the student with a sound grasp of the basic principles involved. They include discussions of the current state of the law as well as considering practical issues.

Casebooks have been produced as companion volumes to the relevant textbooks, and aim to supplement and enhance students' understanding and interpretation of a particular area of the law, and to provide essential background reading. They contain the appropriate statutes as well as all the important cases, and include extracts from judgments together with detailed commentaries as appropriate.

Revision WorkBooks are a new series of questions and answers for students preparing for law examinations. They are arranged in the order of the topics to which they apply. This valuable revision aid is supported by key points and question analysis for each subject, recent cases and statutes, and concise notes on how to study and plan effective revision strategies.

Suggested Solutions to past examination papers are available for LLB, Bar and Solicitors' Finals examinations. They are available either as single papers covering the last examinations or in packs covering a number of preceding years' examinations. These are not intended as model answers but may be used as both a revision aid and a guide to examination techniques.

Law Update published annually in March/April gives law students at degree and professional levels, and other students with law elements in their courses, a review of the most recent developments in specific subject areas - an essential revision aid for the next examinations. Practitioners seeking a quick update will also find this a useful guide on recent changes.

The books listed overleaf can be ordered through your local bookshops or obtained direct from the publisher using this order form. Telephone, Fax, or Telex orders will also be accepted. Quote your Access or Visa card numbers for priority orders. To order direct from publisher please enter cost of titles you require, fill in despatch details and send it with your remittance to The HLT Group Ltd.

DETAILS FOR DESPATCH OF PUBLICATIONS
Please insert your full name below

Please insert below the style in which you would like the correspondence from the Publisher addressed to you
TITLE Mr. Miss etc.   INITIALS   SURNAME/FAMILY NAME

Address to which study material is to be sent (please ensure someone will be present to accept delivery of your Publications).

POSTAGE & PACKING
You are welcome to purchase study material from the Publisher at 200 Greyhound Road, London W14 9RY, during normal working hours.

If you wish to order by post this may be done direct from the Publisher. Postal charges are as follows:

UK   - Orders over £30: no charge. Orders below £30: £2.00. Single paper (last exam only): 40p
OVERSEAS - See table below

The Publisher cannot accept responsibility in respect of postal delays or losses in the postal systems. DESPATCH All cheques must be cleared before material is despatched.

SUMMARY OF ORDER   Date of order:

Cost of publications ordered:
UNITED KINGDOM: £

Add postage and packing:

	TEXTS		Suggested Solutions (last Exam only)
OVERSEAS:	One	Each Extra	
Eire	£3.00	£0.50	£1.00
European Community	£7.50	£0.50	£1.00
East Europe & North America	£8.50	£1.00	£1.50
South East Asia	£10.00	£1.50	£1.50
Australia / New Zealand	£12.00	£3.50	£1.50
Other Countries (Africa, India etc)	£11.00	£3.00	£1.50

Total cost of order: £

Please ensure that you enclose a cheque or draft payable to
The HLT Group Ltd for the above amount, or charge to ☐ ☐ ▲ ☐ VISA

Card Number

Expiry Date _____   Signature _____